D0850519

Shirt-Sleeve Diplomacy

UNDERDEVELOPED AREAS

MEXICO
• Mexico D.F.

GUATEMALA
EL SALVADOR
NICARAGUA
COSTA RICA
San José •
PANAMA

BRITISH
HONDURAS

• Tegucigalpa
HONDURAS

Havana
CUBA

ECUADOR

• Lima
PERU

Bogotá •

Cuzco •

COLOMBIA

VENEZUELA

HAITI
DOMINICAN
REPUBLIC

• Caracas

PUERTO RICO

CHILE

• La Paz

BOLIVIA

GUIANA

ARGENTINA

PARAGUAY

Asunción •

Montevideo

URUGUAY

B R A Z I L

• Rio de Janeiro

*North Polar Azimuthal
Equidistant Projection*

SYRIA

LEBANON
Beirut •

Litani R.

*Mediterranean
Sea*

Yarmuk R.

ISRAEL

Amman •
Jerusalem •

JORDAN

EGYPT

SAUDI
ARABIA

MOROCCO

AL

FRENCH WEST A

• Monrovia

LIBERIA

OF THE FREE WORLD

Shirt-Sleeve Diplomacy

POINT 4 IN ACTION

Jonathan B. Bingham

BOOKS FOR LIBRARIES PRESS
FREEPORT, NEW YORK

WILLIAM MADISON RANDALL LIBRARY UNC AT WILMINGTON

Copyright, 1953, 1954, by Jonathan B. Bingham

Reprinted 1970 by arrangement with
The John Day Company, Inc.

INTERNATIONAL STANDARD BOOK NUMBER:

0-8369-5544-7

LIBRARY OF CONGRESS CATALOG CARD NUMBER:

77-133512

PRINTED IN THE UNITED STATES OF AMERICA

HC60
.B5
1970

Dedicated to the memory of those men and women who, in the service of the ideal that their country should help its less fortunate neighbors to achieve a better life, have met violent death. In this company are

HENRY G. BENNETT
VERA C. BENNETT
ALBERT CYRIL CRILLEY
CECILE DEMOISY
WALTER S. ELTRINGHAM
BENJAMIN H. HARDY
JAMES T. MITCHELL
DAVID MONTGOMERY
ROGER ZENTS

76622

Contents

Foreword

IN MAY, 1953, the Administrator of the Technical Cooperation Administration told the Foreign Relations Committee of the United States Senate that he had been requested by his superiors not to use the term "Point 4" as much as had been customary in the past. He had not been ordered to drop the name, he said, but "in a roundabout way" the suggestion had been made that he play it down.

That the present administration should be anxious to discourage the use of the words "Point 4" is to my mind quite natural and not at all discreditable. After all, it was Harry Truman's point—the fourth major point in the foreign policy part of his inaugural address on January 20, 1949—and no administration likes to advertise the fact that it is simply carrying on a policy initiated by its predecessor.

Nevertheless, my guess is that the term "Point 4" is here to stay.

For one thing the words are a convenient shorthand for such a mouthful as, "a program of technical cooperation plus capital investment to help the underdeveloped areas of the world help themselves to develop their resources and raise their standard of living." Although many efforts have been made—even under the Truman administration—to find a good substitute for the inherently meaningless "Point 4," none has yet been suggested.

Another reason for the popularity of the expression is that it can mean all sorts of different things to different people: to the businessman it may refer primarily to the process of private investment overseas, with a little governmental technical assistance thrown in; to some Americans it means a small program under which the United Nations or the United States Government sends out experts to give technical advice to underdeveloped countries and brings some of their technicians to the United States for training; to still others, including myself, it suggests the whole concept that a country such as ours should in its own interest contribute what it can to the economic and social development of the free countries of Asia, Africa and Latin America.

But the main reason why the term "Point 4" will not disappear is that it has caught hold all over the world. In Latin America it is *"Punto Cuatro,"* in Iran it is *"Astle Charom,"* in India the sounds of the words in English are used, but they are spelled in the Hindi alphabet. Because of the vagaries of the process of translation and retranslation, the director of the program in Jordan received a letter addressed to "The Master of the Fourth Spot." To millions of people all over the world the words "Point 4" have come to stand for the idea that the American people are interested in their welfare. Because of that idea and its consequences, they have a new feeling of hope.

For all these reasons, I have used the term "Point 4" freely in this book, and without quotation marks. Indeed, Point 4 is what this book is all about. I have tried to describe what the program is like, how it operates, and what it can accomplish, and then in the latter part of the book I have sought to answer some of the questions that constantly arise whenever Point 4 is discussed, such as: how much of the job can private enterprise do? won't population increases wipe out any gains that may be made? should we funnel all our aid through the United Nations? how big should the program be? can we afford it?

I should like to emphasize that this is not a book about the underdeveloped areas or about our foreign policy as a whole in the underdeveloped areas. Consequently, I have not attempted to analyze the potentialities of those areas in terms of their resources—economic, social and physical. (Willard Espy of the *Reader's Digest* did that very well in his *Bold New Program*, Harper's and Bantam Books, 1950, and my book is in a sense a sequel to his.) Nor have I tried to cover or even to mention all the various political and psychological factors that enter into our dealings with the less developed areas of the world. Some of them have been suggested here and there, but such incidental treatment does not correspond to their importance. I can only ask the reader to bear in mind that, however important Point 4 may be as a tool with which to help build a better world, it is only one of the tools which we must use.

Because I have wished wherever possible to draw upon material with which I was personally familiar, I have inevitably devoted a disproportionate amount of attention to the work of the T.C.A. during its brief life-span and have correspondingly slighted the developmental programs carried on by the various international and private organizations, and in the Far East by the Mutual Security Agency (earlier the E.C.A.). Following the usual arbitrary definition of the "underdeveloped areas" as including no parts of Europe, I have not discussed at all the work of the M.S.A. in Italy, Yugoslavia, Greece and Turkey, although much of it was of a Point 4 character.

Now that T.C.A. and M.S.A. have been merged in the

Foreign Operations Administration, the policies which T.C.A. adopted for the conduct of the Point 4 program may be modified or discarded altogether. If that proves to be the case, my occasional use of the present tense in describing United States Government activities and policies in the developmental field may prove to have reflected undue confidence in the lasting power of sound ideas.

It is my hope that, in spite of these shortcomings, the book will provide a measure of understanding of the problems and potentialities of Point 4 in its broadest sense. While one may not agree with Mr. Truman's statement that the program constitutes the most important aspect of our foreign policy, at least it must rank very high.

I would like to express my appreciation to the many persons in and out of the United States Government who have helped me, both directly and indirectly, to produce this book. For specific editorial and research assistance I am particularly indebted to Stanley Andrews, E. Reeseman Fryer, Philip M. Glick, Haldore Hanson, Dr. Henry Van-Zile Hyde, Harold Mager, and Nancy Jo Reed. I also wish to record my thanks to Emaline Burney and Mary Flanagan for invaluable stenographic help. My indispensable editor-in-chief and keeper-of-children-quiet has been June Bingham, co-author of *The Inside Story* and also my wife.

Shirt-Sleeve Diplomacy

1. Trend to Shirt-Sleeves

A MUD VILLAGE lies baking in the punishing sun of a middle eastern summer day. Up to its walls over the stony, treeless wasteland crawls an American-made jeep. Clouds of thick white dust swirl from under its wheels and settle on its two occupants, on their clothes, on their faces, and in their noses and eyes.

Driving the jeep is a lanky, middle-aged American named Smith, a former county agent half the world away from his native Arkansas. On the seat next to him is a staff-worker from the local Ministry of Agriculture, a thin-faced man with dark skin and fine hands, his black hair whitened by the dust. Smith has on a broad-brimmed, light gray hat, but otherwise the two men are dressed about alike—heavy shoes, khaki pants, open-collar shirts.

As the jeep proceeds along a narrow lane between high mud walls, scores of ragged children appear, as if out of the ground, and follow along. Several are carrying babies on their backs, their faces speckled with flies. Stuck to the walls along the way, drying, are inch-thick discs of dung, the size of dinner plates. Hundreds more are stacked on the tops of the walls, to be used later as fuel. The smells are—varied.

In a windowless adobe house slightly larger than most, the two men sit down on the dirt floor with the local elders. First there is hospitality: a tray is passed with glasses of water, tinted slightly pink with a kind of syrup, and sweet cakes. Smith would like to refuse, but he does not wish to offend his hosts. As unobtrusively as possible he slips a halazone tablet into the water glass. Brushing off a few flies, he nibbles at the sticky cake and pronounces it delicious.

Then the talk starts. Smith and his companion ask what the village needs most. Malaria is bad, they are told, keeping men away from their work in the fields; the village well is foul, and unreliable most of the year; the sheep have been dying off; there is no school for the children, not even a schoolmaster; the wheat crop has been poor. There are ways of coping with these things, Smith says, if the villagers will cooperate. He tries to explain who he is and why he is there. He says he and his companion would like to start by seeing about the sick animals and the wheat. Other workers will come around to help on the malaria, the well and the school. The village elders are skeptical, but they have heard about what has been going on elsewhere in the province, and they are interested. They want to hear more. The children, crowded together in the doorway, continue to stare.

The American is a kind of diplomat: in seeking to help the village people solve some of their problems he is carrying out the foreign policy of the United States.

*   *   *

This is something new under the sun. Twenty years ago, or even ten, there might have been a missionary out where Smith is, or an agent of an oil company, but there would have been no official representative of the United States Government. Today, Smith is one of a small peaceful army.

In military terms, it is a tiny army—about the size of a regiment—and it is deployed all the way from Mexico City east around the world to Manila. But it is fighting a much bigger war than the war in Korea, a war that has been going on since man first rose on his two hind legs. In this year of 1953, more than two thousand Americans, from such towns as Keokuk, Elko and Bennington, are helping people to fight against suffering and want in places like Tegucigalpa, Shiraz, and Djokjakarta. Visit the dingy dining room of the Semiramis Hotel on Baghdad's beggar-ridden main street at six o'clock any weekday morning. If it is summer the temperature outside is already climbing past 95° and the big overhead fans are turning. At one table you are likely to find an agronomist from near Macon, a vocational education man from Syracuse, an office manager from Kansas City. They will be off for the day's work at 7 A.M. and will probably work a good part of the afternoon after the local people stop at two o'clock. At another table, you may find a doctor's family from Salt Lake City with two small children, stopping off in Baghdad before going down to Basra, one of the hottest places in the world. Visit other so-called hotels in other cities and towns of Asia, Africa and Latin America, and you will find the same kind of thing. Visit houses of all kinds, from adobe huts to comfortable homes; visit tent encampments in the desert or the jungle. In all sorts of queer, uncomfortable places you will find common or garden Americans putting down temporary roots.

Most of them act as if they had never lived any other way—but not all. Some of the wives cannot stand the dirt, the scarcity of wholesome food, the difficulty of communicating in a strange tongue. Some of the men are driven to distraction by frustrations, delays, and occasional sharp hostility on the part of the local people they have to deal with. Some couples are desperately lonely because they feel superior to the natives, and the latter, sensing it, leave them strictly alone. For all of these, it is best that they go back home.

Some families have to return to the United States because severe illness has struck, or because their children are not getting a proper education. Others will never return home at all: On June 25, 1951, Roger Zents, a pilot engaged in anti-locust spraying in Iran was killed in a crash. On December 22, 1951, Dr. Henry G. Bennett, first Administrator of the T.C.A., his wife, and three assistants were killed when the Egyptian plane, in which they were trying to reach Teheran, crashed in a snowstorm. Just a year later, an Iranian Airways plane crashed on almost the same spot, killing Miss Cecile DeMoisy, a Point 4 nurse. On November 21, 1952, David Montgomery, working for Point 4 in Burma with the engineering firm of Knappen, Tippetts and Abbett, was shot by insurgent natives raiding an overnight campsite on a river bank.

What are these common sensible Americans doing it for? They are not doing it because they were discontented before. Most of them left good jobs, comfortable homes, friendly communities. Nor are they doing it because they enjoy living in odd, or picturesque, or glamorous-sounding places, or because there are curious and beautiful things to buy, or because low wages make it easy to have help in the household, or even because there are new kinds of people to get to know and warm friendships to be made. They are doing it because of the satisfaction of doing a job that needs doing, of trying to build a better world, little by little.

Probably most of them had pioneer ancestors, and they

inherit a spirit of adventure and a willingness to stand hardship. But the difference is that whereas their pioneering ancestors were trying to better their own lives, these people are trying to help others better theirs. Their ancestors were planning to settle where they were; these people are planning to work themselves out of a job so they can leave where they are and come home.

*   *   *

How does it happen that these new-type diplomats are doing all this? Is the job too big for them? How do they tackle it? What can they accomplish? Is the United States taxpayer getting rooked again?

These are some of the questions Americans may well ask.

2. The Challenge and the Response

In January, 1949, the American people were worried. Although themselves enjoying a period of prosperity such as they had never known before, they were worried about losing the cold war.

The cold war, then as now, had two aspects. One was the military aspect—the possibility, and actuality in some places, of armed aggression by the communists. There was only one thing to do about that: to organize and build the free world to the maximum degree of defensive strength. A few people argued for a preventive war, but most recognized that that was a contradiction in terms.

The other aspect of the cold war was fundamentally more troublesome because no one knew just what could be done about it. This was the economic and psychological aspect. Whether we liked it or not, we were engaged in a contest for the hearts and minds of most of the people of the world.

In January, 1949, that contest was in the process of being won by the democracies in western Europe. Through one of the boldest and most imaginative programs that any nation had ever undertaken—the Marshall Plan—we had helped to set our friends in Europe back on the road to economic strength and to freedom.

But in the vast section of the world known as underdeveloped, comprising most of Asia, Africa and Latin America, where two-thirds of the world's people live, the contest was in the process of being lost. China was going under, and there was no telling what would happen next —in Indo-China, Burma, Indonesia, India, or any other country where men were hungry most of the time.

By January, 1949, America knew that we could not ignore what was going on in the rest of the world, that the welfare of the United States depended on the existence of free and friendly nations overseas. We needed their trade and their raw materials, not only for our tanks and planes, but for our cars, our television sets, our coffee, our cigarettes, and indeed for most of our comforts. Psychologically, we needed them even more. The prospect of living virtually alone in a world of Vyshinskys, Maos and Togliattis, with no truth, no humor, and no peace, was too dismal to contemplate.

Looked at from another, more positive point of view, the welfare of our neighbors in a steadily shrinking world directly affected ours. If they could make economic and social progress, our trade with them would increase, to our mutual benefit. Working together, recognizing our common interests, we could build a prosperous world which might, God willing, be a peaceful world. In short, we knew that we could not let the rest of the world stew in its own juice: we were all in the same, fiercely boiling pot.

One reason the pot was boiling so hard was that man had worked out new ways of communicating good and bad news to his fellows. From Ecuador and Paraguay to Indo-China and Formosa, people were finding out what the twentieth century could mean to them if only they were in it. Even if there had been no such thing as the Kremlin gang, there would probably have been greater discontent and restlessness than ever before. But the advent of international communism hadn't helped any.

In January, 1949, the American people were beginning to sense that our strategy in the cold war could not be entirely negative and defensive. We had to move to the offensive, psychologically. The Luce publications and John Foster Dulles had called for the United, States to embark on a great moral offensive, but nobody knew exactly how you began such a program. Propaganda obviously had its limitations. On the one hand, it was no good distributing pictures of the New York skyline and other manifestations of the "American way of life." Nor was there much point in preaching the blessings of liberty to people whose children were half-blinded by trachoma or pot-bellied with malnutrition.

Also in January, 1949, one Ben Hardy, an ex-newspaperman from Georgia working in the State Department, was sure he had a good idea. He hadn't been able to sell it within the State Department, so he had taken it to a young White House assistant named George Elsey, who promptly saw that it got to his boss. When the next draft of President Truman's inaugural address went over to the State Department for comment, Hardy's idea—the idea that came to be known as Point 4—was in it. Top State Department leaders, including Under Secretary Robert Lovett and Charles S. Bohlen, urged that it be deleted as vague and premature. But the President stuck to his guns.[1]

On January 20, 1949, Harry S. Truman announced to the world that the United States was embarking on "a bold, new program for making the benefits of our scientific advances and industrial progress available for the improvement and growth of underdeveloped areas." The enterprise was to be a cooperative one, in which all nations would work together through the United Nations and its specialized agencies as far as possible. Capital investment was to be encouraged. "Our aim," he said, "should be to help the free peoples of the world, through their own efforts, to produce more food, more clothing, more materials for housing and more mechanical power to lighten their burdens. . . . Only by helping the least fortunate of its members to help themselves can the human family achieve the decent, satisfying life that is the right of all people." *

Belittlers argued that Point 4 was neither "bold" nor "new." They said, quite rightly, that American missionaries and private business concerns had been in effect providing "technical assistance" to people of less developed areas for many decades. They pointed out that for several years the Institute of Inter-American Affairs and other United States Government agencies had been carrying out developmental projects in Latin America and Liberia, and that in 1948, the Congress had provided for the Joint Commission on Rural Reconstruction in China. What they overlooked was the restricted and specialized character of these prior activities. The work of the missionaries had been largely related to their evangelical purpose, and had been of necessity limited to scattered pilot projects, attacking only a tiny segment of the total problem. Private business operations naturally had to be closely attuned to stockholders' profits. And previous United States Government activities had been for the most part designed to serve immediate security interests connected with World War II and its aftermath.

What was both "bold" and "new" about Point 4 was

* The complete text of President Truman's Fourth Point is set forth in Appendix A.

that a whole nation should commit itself and its resources, as a fundamental part of its foreign policy, to the idea of helping all "peace-loving peoples" to help themselves. Governments had many times undertaken to assist colonies, allies or dependent nations, or had given help in return for a *quid pro quo*. And for centuries statesmen had recognized that the prosperity of friendly neighbor nations was helpful and desirable. But no government had ever thought to make that prosperity a national objective of its own, to be systematically pursued at some expense. Never before in the history of the world had a government launched a large-scale effort to help peoples to whom it was bound by no special ties other than a common interest in the world's peace and prosperity.

Like all great ideas, the Point 4 idea seems in retrospect almost to have been compelled by the circumstances in which the world found itself. People saw in it both idealism and practicality and it caught hold all over the free world.

The United Nations launched an "expanded technical assistance program" through its specialized agencies, such as the World Health Organization, and through a newly created United Nations Technical Assistance Administration. The British Commonwealth nations invited others to join them in a mutual program for the development of south and southeast Asia, an enterprise which came to be known as the Colombo Plan. France, Switzerland and Norway embarked upon modest technical assistance programs of their own.[2] Most extraordinary of all, the traditionally isolationist American people, following Harry Truman's lead, embarked on a world-wide effort.

At first, however, the United States Congress was skeptical of the Point 4 idea. Debate on the proposed Act for International Development, submitted by the State Department in September, 1949, to implement the program, was bitter and prolonged. And no wonder, for it contained among other things a declaration of policy that "The peoples of the United States and other nations have a common interest in the freedom and in the economic and social progress of all peoples."

The influential Senator Taft said, "Here we have a provision for a brand-new international program at a time when we ought to be stopping international programs and only finishing those which have already assumed a certain importance, to which we are committed." The bill, he said, "would simply be opening up a kind of wide-open distribution of all kinds of aid to all kinds of people anywhere in the world whom the President might desire to help." The American taxpayer's money would be "spread around the world in places where there is no particular demand for it." He had heard "no substantial or persuasive argument made in favor of any such program."

At one point, Senate Republicans, with the aid of a few Democrats, came within one vote of killing the measure. But it was enacted—on June 5, 1950.[3] A few months later, the Technical Cooperation Administration was set up in the State Department to coordinate the program, and Henry Garland Bennett, President of Oklahoma A. & M. College, a lovable man with a genius for inspiring people, was appointed Administrator.

From the very beginning, public interest in the program was enormous. Church groups everywhere rallied behind it, recognizing in it an expansion of their own long-cherished missionary ideals. The task of furthering international development became a favorite topic at meetings of all kinds, including labor groups, women's clubs, businessmen's luncheons, and student debates. In April, 1952, a committee of private organizations arranged in Washington a National Conference on International Economic and Social Development. Five hundred delegates were expected; twelve hundred showed up and took part in three days of discussion. One delegate tried to calculate the total membership of the organizations represented, but stopped when he had gone halfway through the list, because he had already arrived at a figure equal to the population of the United States. Many different points of view were expressed, but there was universal agreement on the basic proposition that the United States had a huge stake in the economic and social development of the underdeveloped areas, and that it could and should lend a helping hand.[4]

Naturally enough, all this public interest had its effect on the Congress. In 1951, and again in 1952, about 150 million dollars was appropriated for the United States Point 4 program (not including even larger sums for other emergency programs in the underdeveloped areas), as against 24 million dollars the first year. There was plenty of argument about amounts, and Administration requests were drastically cut, but there were hardly any voices raised against the program as such. In March, 1952, even Senator Taft, actively campaigning for the Presidency, came out in favor of it.[5]

In 1953, the newly elected Republican Administration, although substantially reducing the proposals for developmental aid contained in the final Truman budget, nevertheless asked for a Point 4 program of 140 million dollars and, in addition, for "special economic assistance" for certain critical underdeveloped areas, amounting to another 250 million dollars. After a bitter struggle, especially in the

House, the Congress appropriated over 80 per cent of the money requested.[6]

By the fall of 1953, the United States Government was carrying on developmental programs, some of them sizable, in most of the free countries of Asia, Africa and Latin America. Although the merging of T.C.A. into an overall Foreign Operations Administration and the dismissal of most of the T.C.A. top staff in Washington suggested to some that the Point 4 idea was being scrapped in favor of emergency aid with military overtones, F.O.A. chief Harold Stassen insisted that this was not so. He pointed proudly to the fact that more American technicians were in the field and more money was being spent on the Point 4 program than ever before.*

Harry S. Truman, the ex-haberdasher from Independence, Missouri, had indeed started something.

* A statistical summary of the various United States programs in the underdeveloped areas is contained in Appendix B. Appendix C contains a brief account of the shifts that have taken place in the United States organization for these programs and a discussion of some of the issues involved.

3. Learning by Doing
—in Latin America

WHAT MAKES POINT 4 different from the ordinary concept of economic aid and makes it so infinitely appealing is that it emphasizes the distribution of knowledge rather than of money. Obviously there is not money enough in the world to relieve the suffering of the peoples of the underdeveloped areas, but, as President Truman pointed out in his inaugural, there is, for the first time in history, enough knowledge to do the job.

This is indeed an exciting, even a revolutionary idea. In October, 1951, the great historian Arnold Toynbee wrote in *The New York Times Magazine* that "our age. will be remembered chiefly . . . for its having been the first age since the dawn of civilization . . . in which people dared to think it practicable to make the benefits of civilization available for the whole human race." This new ideal was born, he pointed out, because the "sudden vast enhancement of man's ability to make nonhuman nature produce what man requires from her has . . . made the idea of welfare for all a practical objective. . . ."

The trouble with this concept is that it makes the whole problem of international development sound deceptively simple. In actual fact, the process of communicating knowledge to the people in the world who need it, and of persuading them to use it, is staggeringly complex and difficult.*

One of the basic complications, too often overlooked, is that it involves two steps: the knowledge must be communicated to, and accepted by, first the governments of the underdeveloped countries, and then by their peoples. The two steps are very different, and each has its difficulties. Insofar as *governments* are concerned, the difficulties are largely psychological: pride, suspicion, inertia, and despair at the magnitude of the task of development all enter in. In seeking to communicate new skills to *people,* the difficulties are not only psychological, but physical as well. When people cannot read, have no radios, and seldom travel more than a few miles from their homes, it is a mammoth job even to reach them. And when they and their ancestors have been living the same way for centuries, and are afraid to change their ways because they cannot afford the risk that change entails, it is an even harder job to persuade them to accept something new.

By September of 1950, when the T.C.A. was set up to supervise the Point 4 program, the United States Government had already gained considerable experience in tackling this formidable problem of communication. As early as 1938, the Congress had authorized United States Government departments to detail employees for temporary duty with the governments of other American countries, the Philippines and Liberia, and in 1940, an Interdepartmental Committee on Scientific and Cultural Cooperation

---

* One of Dr. Henry Bennett's favorite sayings was that knowledge is one thing which can be given away without cost to the giver. This statement should not be taken to mean, of course, that the *process* of communicating knowledge may not be a costly one. Consider, for example, the expense of operating a school system or a radio network.

had been organized to coordinate the sending of experts overseas. Among other things, the Department of Agriculture had assisted in the development of first-rate agricultural research and experiment stations, notably at Tingo Maria in Peru. Because of the importance of developing sources of natural rubber during the war, a lot of work had been done in that field, and a disease-resistant "threestory" rubber tree had been developed, with root, midsection, and top from three different varieties. In an effort to protect the United States from communicable diseases, the United States Public Health Service had for years been working with officials of other American governments. The Bureau of Public Roads, the Census Bureau, the Civil Aeronautics Administration, the Bureau of Mines, and many others had been sending out experts on various technical assistance missions and bringing foreign technicians to the United States for training.[1]

All of this work had been valuable. Hundreds of Latin American officials were serving their people better because of it. But it had been concentrated at the governmental level, and much of it had been related directly to shortrange security interests. The task of communicating knowledge and skills to the people, so as to enable them to raise their standard of living, had for the most part not been attempted.

During the same war and postwar period, however, the United States Government had been engaged in another type of activity. Virtually by accident, a new technique of communicating new ideas and methods to governments and peoples had been developed. Among our modern school teachers, the technique is known as "learning by doing." In the field of inter-American relations, it had come to be identified by the Spanish words *servicio co-operativo* or simply *servicio.*

Originally, the *servicio* had not been devised as an educational technique, but rather as a method of joint United States-Latin American action to help win World War II. In January, 1942, the Foreign Ministers of the American Republics, meeting in Rio de Janeiro, had agreed that low health standards and food shortages were a threat to the security of the hemisphere and had resolved on a cooperative effort to do something about them. To that end the Institute of Inter-American Affairs was organized as a subsidiary of the Office of the Coordinator of Inter-American Affairs. Nelson Rockefeller, the Coordinator, became the Institute's first Board Chairman.

The I.I.A.A. was primarily interested in getting something done, and only incidentally in training Latin Americans, but it wisely decided that its work would be most effective if undertaken on a basis of cooperation with the local governments. To accomplish that end, Nelson Rockefeller and his associates drew upon the experience of the Rockefeller Foundation to create this new device for intergovernmental cooperation.

A typical example was the *Servicio Cooperativo Interamericano de Salud Publica* in Peru, which was organized in July, 1942. S.C.I.S.P., as it came to be known, was an agency of the Peruvian Government, set up within the Ministry of Health, but its Director, a North American, was "chief of field party" in the health and sanitation division of the I.I.A.A. Together, the Peruvian Minister of Health and the Director worked out a plan of action, ·covering projects in such fields as malaria control, construction of sanitary water systems, and the operation of health centers. A special fund was set up, to which both governments contributed in amounts agreed upon each year. In addition to its contribution to the servicio fund, the United States Government paid the salaries of the Director and of such other North American personnel as were needed. Most of the personnel were Peruvian. From time to time the servicio's funds were supplemented from other sources, either by the Peruvian Government voluntarily, or by a municipal council or other agency as its share of the cost of a project in its area. S.C.I.S.P.'s accounts were kept with scrupulous care, for they were subject to audit by either government.

During 1942, and over the next few years some twenty-five servicios were organized along similar lines in eighteen Latin American countries to carry out joint programs in the three basic fields of health, food supply, and education. The policy was laid down that the contributions of the United States to any servicio funds should decrease, while those of the local governments should gradually increase, so that when the servicio was terminated the local government would be prepared to go forward with its activities. Obviously that policy, sound as it was, could be carried out only if the servicios were sufficiently successful in their operations to command the support of the peoples themselves, so that the local governments would feel that the increasing financial investment was worth while.

The record speaks for itself. In the first years the United States was contributing five times as much as the local governments, taking into account the salaries of United States employees. In 1947, for the first time, the amount of local contributions surpassed the United States' outlay. By 1950, the Latin American governments were expending three times as much as the United States, and in addition many of the projects initiated by the servicios had been taken over by the local governments and were being completely supported by local funds.

Perhaps an even more extraordinary testament to the popularity of the servicios was the fact that they survived the frequent cabinet shifts. Often in Latin America, as elsewhere, new ministers coming in want to throw out everything their predecessors did, but this did not apply to the programs of cooperation with the I.I.A.A.

The servicios had become so popular because they got things done—and helped people to do things for themselves —efficiently, honestly and free from partisan politics. In effect they demonstrated to the Latin American governments and peoples what government services operated on that basis could accomplish. Although the servicios had been started as action programs, this function of "show-how"—of technical assistance in the best sense of the word —gradually became the dominant one. Through the servicio device, knowledge and skills were being effectively communicated to other governments and peoples. Yet it was being done without any offense to local sensitivity, without creating any sense of inferiority on the part of the local government. On the contrary, the servicios became a great source of pride to the Latin Americans. They looked upon them, quite correctly, as agencies of their own governments for whose accomplishments they could take a large share of the credit.

The I.I.A.A. wisely handled the dissemination of information in Latin America about its programs in such a way as to give full play to this local pride of accomplishment. Latin American nationals were hired and trained in United States information techniques so as to see that adequate information about the work of the servicios was disseminated locally, and also to help the technicians working in the servicios in the use of informational techniques for the communication of their particular skills. In this way, the United States was not in the undignified position of sending out its own press releases saying in effect: "Look what we are doing for you." Rather there was a constant flow of news from the servicios themselves about their own activities, and in these stories the basic fact of United States cooperation either appeared incidentally or was implicit.

Of course, all servicios were not equally successful. In some cases, the local governments did not live up to their commitments to contribute funds, and the programs had to be wound up, permanently or temporarily. In others, personality conflicts between individual ministers and servicio directors caused difficulties, as was to be expected from the extraordinarily intimate and delicate quality of the relationship between them. Again, there were occasional misunderstandings between Washington and the field: Washington had a tendency to look upon the servicios as projections of the United States Government to which Latin American governments contributed personnel and funds; the "field" people, more properly, regarded them as agencies of the local governments to which the United States made contributions.

But all in all, the operations of the I.I.A.A. were tremendously successful. Some of the accomplishments of the servicios in promoting economic and social development will be described in later chapters. In addition to their concrete successes, they have created immense good will for the United States, as any visitor to Latin America who took the trouble to inquire could testify.[2]

How long the I.I.A.A. would have been continued in operation after the war, if the Point 4 idea had not come along, no one can say. But the President's declaration provided new impetus, and in September, 1949, the Congress extended the charter of the I.I.A.A. for another five years. The Congress recognized that here, already in operation, was a mechanism for carrying out the Point 4 idea. The United States had itself been "learning by doing."

4. Diplomat Goes to Work
in the Middle East

THE REAL STARTING DATE of a full-scale development program was neither January 20, 1949, when Point 4 was announced, nor June 5, 1950, when its enabling act was passed, but October 30, 1951, when Congress for the first time appropriated a substantial sum for it under the Mutual Security Act of 1951. Up to that point the T.C.A. had been virtually paralyzed, not so much by the small amount of funds available from the 1950 appropriation, as by a violent bureaucratic battle being waged in Washington. The E.C.A., which was already pressing forward with sizable economic programs in the Far East, was eager to take over all overseas aid programs, and the idea that a single agency should have such total responsibility had received potent backing from the International Development Advisory Board, under the chairmanship of Nelson Rockefeller, in its "Partners in Progress" report. But Dr. Bennett, the soft-spoken man from Oklahoma who was T.C.A. Administrator, had shown extraordinary skill in arguing before the Congressional Committees that the Point 4 program should be kept separate, as a relatively small, long-range program devoted primarily to the task of communicating knowledge rather than distributing economic aid. Big private groups, especially among the church organizations, came to his aid, as did the politically powerful Department of Agriculture, and the battle was won, at least temporarily.*

Thus at the end of October, 1951, with a third of the fiscal year gone, T.C.A. found itself with almost 150 million dollars on its hands and an idea to justify. In the Latin American area, for which 18 million dollars had been appropriated, the problem was one of expanding the activities that had been going on before. The I.I.A.A. was made the regional arm of T.C.A. for the hemisphere, and was given responsibility not only for continuing to operate its own servicio-type programs, but also for coordinating the technical assistance and training activities of the Department of Agriculture and other agencies working in the Latin American area. Following the practice elsewhere in the world-wide program, a director of technical cooperation was appointed for each country where there was substantial activity, to work with the ambassador in coordinating the planning and integrating the various operations into a balanced program, designed to fit the country's most urgent needs.

Outside of Latin America, however, it was a case of starting almost from scratch. A few technicians had been dispatched here and there in 1950 and 1951, but practically no substantial work had been undertaken. Accordingly, in the late fall and winter of 1951, negotiating teams were sent to various countries of the Middle East, and to India and Pakistan, to find out what sort of programs the gov-

* In the summer of 1953, when T.C.A. was transferred from the State Department to the new Foreign Operations Administration, the danger that the Point 4 idea would be submerged in a "big-money" operation again became acute. See Appendix C.

ernments were interested in. As quickly as possible there-
after, men were recruited to go out as country directors,
and as supporting technicians, to get the programs under
way.

To give some idea of what these men were up against
at the beginning, and of how they went about their task,
the rest of this chapter is devoted to an account of a new
country director's first year in the mythical country of
Deserta, "somewhere in the Middle East." Deserta does
not correspond to any particular country, but most of the
incidents actually occurred, in one place or another.

"In November of 1951, I received a telephone call at
my home in Albuquerque, which eventually caused me
a lot of trouble. I am an engineer by profession, and had
been happily engaged for years on various types of reclamation work in the western states. I knew something about
working with American Indians and with sharecroppers.
But I was totally unprepared for this call.

"It was an old colleague of mine, calling from Washington. He asked me if I had ever heard of the Point 4
program, and I replied that I had, in a vague sort of way.
What I had heard about it sounded pretty good, and I said
so. My friend said that he was in T.C.A., which was running the program, and that they had decided I was the
perfect man to take over the program in Deserta. I put
up an argument on that one, saying that I had had no foreign experience, except in the Navy Supply Corps in the
Pacific during the war, and that I knew nothing about the
Middle East, and less than nothing about Point 4. 'Who
does?' he said. 'The whole thing is so new that we're all
groping. You like people, and you know a lot about the
desert. You're elected.' He went on to give me a long spiel

about the importance of the work, and actually began to make me feel like a heel if I didn't go.

"To make a long story short, after a trip to Washington and a lot of palaver, I agreed to go. My wife even admitted she was kind of excited by the prospect. Our two older children were grown, and we would only have to take Ann, who was sixteen, and Bill, who was ten years old. Neither of them of course wanted to go one little bit. We decided that I should go on ahead to find a place to live, and that the others would come over in the summer.

"I filled out all the papers, and signed the one saying I had never been a member of any of the organizations on the Attorney General's list, thinking how lucky I was that I had not sent two dollars or so to one or two that had been familiar names in the thirties. Then I settled down to wait for the clearance to come through, and began reading all the books about Deserta that I could lay my hands on. My clearance took six weeks, and by the end of that time I was sick of people asking why I was still around. My friend in Washington said, though, that six weeks was almost a record and that all kinds of pressure had been brought to bear to get it done so fast. Other cases took three months and often five or six.

"So in January I went to Washington for my 'indoctrination.' This was supposed to include a course at the Foreign Service Institute and some language training, but I hardly got any of it. It seemed that a United States negotiating team had visited Deserta, that the government there was vitally interested in a broad program, and that it was imperative that I get right out there. I was whirled about for a week by the T.C.A. 'desk man' for Deserta, saw my friend once or twice in the corridor, had fifteen minutes with the young Acting Administrator, during

which neither of us seemed to know what to say, got un-
intelligible 'briefings' from experts on Deserta and specialists in procurement, accounts, etc., met a lot of people at
the Department of Agriculture and other agencies who
said they would give me all the "technical back-stopping"
I needed, received a passport and an intensive course of
shots, and was put on a plane with a nice young man
named Brown, who had been whirled around with me,
and who was to be my executive officer.

"During the long flight Brown and I read over some of
the mass of reading matter we had been given. Most of it
had to do with procedures, but there was very little to tell
me what I was actually supposed to do. The material on
the programs in Latin America was interesting, and there
was one paper which seemed to contain some policy statements, such as:

'1. *First things first.* The basic problems of the underdeveloped areas are hunger, disease, and ignorance. Point 4
must concentrate on them first.
'2. *Teach and show.* Point 4 is basically an educational
program, involving teaching, training, demonstrating. It
must not be a "big giveaway" program.
'3. *A grass roots program.* To be successful Point 4 must
get to the people, and start where they are, helping them
to do the things *they* want to do, one step at a time.
'4. *Cooperation essential.* Point 4 is not charity, and
cannot be just a United States program. It must be a joint
enterprise, in which the host government takes pride. For
this reason it is best to operate through a joint fund or else
a "servicio" (i.e. cooperative service) arrangement.
'5. *Act only on request.* Point 4 never gives any assistance
unless requested to do so. It is our aim to do what the host
government wants to do, not what *we* want. The host government's requests should be formalized in a program
agreement, signed by the Foreign Minister, and project

agreements signed by the Ministers of Agriculture, Health, etc.

'6. *Cooperation with the United Nations.* Competition with the United Nations technical assistance activities is to be avoided, as well as duplication. There should be a complete exchange of information, and thorough cooperation.' [1]

"All of this sounded like good sense to me then, and still does, but I found out that these principles were not so easy to carry out in practice, and that sometimes they seemed to conflict with each other. Moreover, they still didn't give me much of an idea as to what to do *first,* or even second.

"After a short stopover in Rome to meet some of the people in the F.A.O., I stepped down from a rickety DC-3 at Suqs, the capital of Deserta, at 3 A.M. on a chilly February morning. The ambassador was at the airport to meet us, which I thoroughly appreciated. On the drive in, he explained that he would squeeze us into the embassy for the time being, but that the space there was already inadequate and that I should try and find an office for the Point 4 staff first thing. At last I had found out what ought to be done *first!*

"Rooms had been reserved at the best hotel, the Palace, which proved to be comfortable enough but quickly productive of the Suqs shudders, the local variety of violent stomach upset which hits most visitors to the Middle East sooner or later. Brown came down with it within twenty-four hours, and I was laid low two days later. Thanks to the sulfa drugs and other remedies, it can usually be cleared up pretty fast, but it keeps coming back. Anyway the shudders and other local ailments were a major problem to me and my staff for the first several months. Our doctor had to spend entirely too much time treating our own people, including himself. On a day when half the staff was laid up, I was likely to think: 'How in the world can we tackle the health problems of this country, if we can't solve our own?'

"The second day after our arrival, the ambassador took me to call on the Prime Minister. He was exceedingly polite, said he was glad to welcome me to Deserta, asked me if I was being made comfortable, told me that he was very much interested in the development of his country and was sure that the United States could be very helpful, and recommended that I not miss the local museum of antiquities. He spoke in his native tongue through an interpreter, and I answered him the same way, finding it odd but perfectly easy. I asked him if he had any requests for technical assistance to make of the United States. He replied that the United Nations was doing some good work and suggested that I talk to the Foreign Minister. The entire conversation lasted about twenty minutes, several of which were occupied with the passing of tea and cakes.

"The next day we called on the Foreign Minister. This conversation was almost an exact replica of the one with the Prime Minister, except that the Foreign Minister spoke English. He also added that there was some dissatisfaction in his country over the fact that the Point 4 General Agreement had been signed six months before but nothing had yet happened.[2] I reminded him that we had an expert already at work in the Ministry of Agriculture on cotton breeding, and a railroad man making a survey of the transportation system, but he brushed those aside.

" 'We have had plenty of surveys,' he said, 'we should like to see some action.' When I pressed him for concrete suggestions, he was as vague as the Prime Minister. We had tea and cakes again.

"I went back to the Palace Hotel that evening, very

blue, and thinking, 'Is it really true, what the economy bloc is saying back home, that we are foisting our help on these people?' It turned out that (a) it was not true, and (b) I was coming down with the shudders.

"Our cotton-breeding man, Dexter, came up to my room, bringing a bottle of pills. 'Don't get discouraged,' he said. 'Wait till you get to my ministry and some of the others. You'll find they want plenty of help.'

"He was right. The Minister of Agriculture and especially his director general were full of ideas. It seemed that X division needed a soil scientist and Y division a livestock man; there were several vacancies in Z section which the F.A.O. had not been able to fill; and so on; quite a long list. This was technical assistance all right, but it didn't sound quite right somehow. Were we just supposed to fill in the gaps in their own staffs? I took down the items gravely, and was reassured by a wink from Dexter.

"At the Health Ministry it was yet another story. I called on the minister, accompanied by a United States Public Health Service doctor, who had been loaned to me from a neighboring country for five weeks. The minister greeted us effusively, offered us tea and cakes, said he knew all about the Point 4 program, praised the United States for being so far-sighted, and handed us a three-page typewritten list of requests. I took a quick look at the first few items:

> 'Tuberculosis hospital in Sand Province, two hundred beds; equipment for same.
> 'Operating room and other equipment for projected medical school at Strand.
> 'Four maternity and child health centers, with appropriate equipment.
> 'Five thousand tons of D.D.T. for malaria control.'

"The P.H.S. doctor ran his eye down the list and handed me a note, reading 'Roughly 40 million dollars worth.' I said that we would give the list careful consideration, but explained that Point 4 was primarily a technical assistance program, a program of teaching and training. The minister nodded brightly: 'but we would need to have people trained for the medical school and the tuberculosis hospital and so forth.' I gulped, and shortly bowed myself out.

"As we drove back to the embassy in our jeep, which had somehow miraculously arrived from the States and for which Brown had hired a local driver, the P.H.S. doctor was very reassuring. 'It's always like this,' he said, 'either they don't know what to ask for, or they ask for all sorts of absurd things. The main thing to remember is that the need is there: look at those children with sore eyes. That's trachoma. Look at the flies all over that peddler's basket of bread. Look at that woman dipping water out of the gutter; that gutter acts as a sewer for all the people up the street. If you think that's bad, wait until you get out into some of the villages. We can find some things on that list that will be OK as a starter. Your problem is going to be to find the right kind of personnel from the States. I have to leave in two weeks.'

"I felt better until I got back to the embassy, and found Brown, white-faced, holding a long telegram. It was from Washington, apparently a circular which had been sent to other T.C.A. missions as well. It began something like this:

'For Congressional hearings on MSP starting March 15, need (a) detailed description TA program your area this fiscal year, including description of going activities, summary of project agreements signed, sums obligated and sums expended, and (b) outline program for FY53, including amounts needed under each activity classification and justification for same. Telegraphic summary of material must reach TCA/W not later than March 1, detailed documentation by March 7.'

"The telegram then went on with a careful outline for the 'documentation,' specifying all the factors that should be taken into account, and ending with a bland request for a 'rough projection of amounts expected to be needed in each of next five years.' [3]

"Livid with rage, I stormed into the ambassador's office. To my surprise he was quite calm, although he had a copy of the telegram in his hand. 'But this is absurd,' I shouted. 'They can't expect me to do this. They know I've only just arrived. They must have sent it here by mistake, or else they've gone nuts.'

"The ambassador let me blow on for a while, and then he cut in. 'Take it easy,' he said. 'This kind of thing happens all the time. It can't be helped. The point is that the Congressional Committees will want this information. If we don't do it here, as best we can, the boys in Washington will have to dream something up themselves. Would that be any better? You know more than you did a week ago. I'll put my two economic people on it with you.'

"I calmed down, and we set to work, pretty much night and day. We got some sort of a telegram off by March 3, two days late, and put the whole job in the air pouch on March 6. It looked pretty good to me. If we could carry out a program such as we had projected, we would have accomplished something.

"The next day, the 7th, a telegram arrived from Washington, changing the outline all around but not changing the deadline. It had been delayed in transit, but even so it had left Washington only on the 4th. The Foreign

Service people accepted this much more philosophically than I did. 'Probably had trouble getting it cleared,' they suggested. Again we buckled down, hoping that what we sent in would suit their royal highnesses.

"At this point I began to appreciate the difficulty of doing business over a long cable wire. It was reminiscent of communicating with Sears Roebuck about a mail order. You know, like the man who ordered a case of red raspberries c.o.d.; after he had refused a case of black raspberries three separate times, he wrote and gave them hell; they sent him an apology and a refund check for three cases of red raspberries. The State Department isn't quite that bad, but almost, and of course they think the same of us. Answers to urgent questions come in late and garbled, or they give irrelevant information, or they don't come at all, week after week. It isn't anybody's fault. Everybody has too much to do. It's just that the world isn't as small as we sometimes say it is.

"My next shock came early in April, when at 11 P.M. on a Saturday night the Prime Minister sent word that he would like to see me right away. I hurried over, not knowing what to expect. The Prime Minister introduced the Minister of Commerce and Industry, whom I had met once at a reception but had not yet had a chance to call on. The Prime Minister seemed nervous, and I suddenly remembered someone telling me that the Minister of Commerce and Industry was a political power. But he said nothing during this entire interview, except 'Good evening' and 'Good-bye.'

"The Prime Minister had in his hand the draft of a general program agreement which I had been discussing with the Foreign Minister. 'This document,' he said through his interpreter, 'is very interesting. I see that you propose to do something in agriculture and education, and to undertake some projects with the Ministry of Health, but there is nothing here about industry. This is going to be very difficult for me. The people of my country are very much interested in industry. If this paper is published, they will say the United States does not want to help us industrialize. I have been thinking over this Point 4 very carefully, and I have come to the conclusion that it would be better if you concentrated on one big project that the people could see. One thing we need very badly in this country is a steel mill. We have to import all our steel. I wish to propose to your government that you provide us with such a mill as evidence of your good will.'

"I tried to ask a few questions. Where did they propose to get their iron ore, since there was none in the country? What about coal? Had they looked into the possibility of interesting one of the European or American steel companies in the venture? If the venture was a sound one, I was sure private capital could be found. I would be glad to help on that score.

"The Prime Minister replied to all of these questions that he was not interested in the details, which would be handled by his Minister of Commerce and Industry. He finally told me that he had another appointment and that he would anxiously await my government's response to his proposition.

"Of course, our negotiations on the program agreement had to stop until the matter was settled. Obviously the steel mill was an absurdity, but I had a political problem on my hands. The ambassador strongly advised that I work out some sort of project in the industrial field to pacify the Minister of Commerce and Industry. After several talks, I finally persuaded the minister that his pet project was impractical and, if carried out, would not make him a popular hero but rather the contrary. We then agreed that Point 4 would help in the development of a new fertilizer process which was desperately needed, and would bring over a team of experts to survey other possibilities.

"After that our program agreement went through without further trouble, and along about the middle of May I began to see some real progress. We had an office and a couple of secretaries. My top agricultural and health experts had arrived, along with three or four other technicians, and others were being recruited (at least so I was assured by Washington; the process was dishearteningly slow). We had hired some excellent local people, including a young assistant for me who seemed to know everybody important in the country, and several of the ministries had provided 'counterpart' personnel to work with our people. In the health field we had set up a cooperative service arrangement, and some good projects were getting under way. Our agricultural chief had persuaded the Ministry of Agriculture that its biggest trouble was a failure to reach the farmers of the country with the scientific knowledge already in hand, and an extension service was projected. We had arranged for several dozen people in various fields to go to the United States for training. It looked as if we had a show on the road.

"Then in June, along with appalling heat, came political trouble. The cabinet fell, and there were some nasty riots in Suqs and elsewhere. All our work came to a halt. A stray shot hit a window in our office, and one of the girls had hysterics. When the new cabinet was appointed, the ministers did not know what Point 4 was all about, and were hostile to it, because the old government had been in favor of it. They declared that the overall program agreement we had signed was invalid, along with all the other acts of the old government.

"The local communists profited by the confusion to step up their attacks on our program. The press, which had never been too friendly, took up the idea that we were foreign imperialists. On the one hand, they accused us of doing nothing; on the other, they said we were interfering with Deserta's sovereignty.

"At the beginning of July, just as it began to look as if we would get thrown out of the country, my wife and two children arrived. I had a house ready for them, but was unprepared for the host of new problems. Within a few days, all three were down with the shudders and wanted to go home. The thermometer hovered around 115° and the dust in the air was terrific. The locally built air cooler brought the heat in the living room down to about 95°, but increased the humidity.

"Our furniture had arrived, but, after my wife had burned out the washing machine, we discovered that the current was wrong for all the gadgets. We had to buy a transformer at a black market price.

"As the children recovered, the problem of keeping them busy became acute. After the riots stopped so that he could roam around a little, Bill began to find some friends, but Ann's problem was more difficult. She occasionally met nice boys her age, but I was advised against letting her go out with them even in the daytime, since the custom of dating was unknown in Deserta, and she would be considered a 'loose woman' and treated accordingly.

"All these problems straightened themselves around in the end, and the family actually grew to like the place, but it took time. In September, the American parents banded together to organize a little school on the Calvert system, and that kept a lot of people busy.

"Meanwhile, we had made friends with the government. One of the new Prime Minister's first requests was that I dismiss my useful young assistant, as an enemy of the state and a spy. I knew it was pure politics, but couldn't very well ignore the request. With the government's consent, we sent the young man off to the States on a training grant in public administration.

"The new government embarked on some promising programs of its own, especially an ambitious land distribution scheme. They knew very little about the problems involved, however, and soon found themselves in a jam. The new landowners, with no source of cheap credit for seeds, tools, etc., and with no experience in farm management, were running into trouble right and left, and delegations began arriving in town asking to have the landlords back. At this point the government, which had earlier said it needed no help on this program, thank you, turned to us in desperation. We rushed a team of experts out from the States, contributed some funds to get a farm credit system going, and set up a jointly operated school to train rural officials in methods of providing guidance to the new landowners.

"In August we had urged the government to set up a Cabinet Committee for Development, which would coordinate all development activities and could lay out a program and some priorities, instead of having each ministry scrambling for its own pet projects. We suggested that the Resident Representative of the United Nations and I might be asked to attend meetings of the committee so as to assure the best possible coordination between the United Nations and the United States programs. The idea was turned down. But a month later the Foreign Minister announced the formation of such a committee, and gravely asked me the next day if I didn't think it was a good idea. He invited me to attend the meetings, along with the United Nations representative.

"The government asked us if we could finance a 50-million-dollar dam at one end of a big valley, where the water rushed down in great quantities for a few weeks a year. We said we couldn't finance it, but that we might help find the capital, either from public or private sources or both. In any case it would be necessary first to make test drillings at the dam site, to see if the dam would hold water. We sent for a team of experts from the United States Bureau of Reclamation for that purpose. They duly arrived, full of ginger, talking a blue streak about the project, but not knowing who I was or what I had to do with it. They never did get the idea that the Government of Deserta or T.C.A., or anyone but the Bureau, might have something to say about the dam, but they knew their stuff and the test drilling got under way fast. If the site proved out, and if we could locate the capital, it would mean thousands of acres of new land irrigated, and a source of power for industry.

"I want to say here that, except for an occasional prima donna, our Point 4 people worked together wonderfully. Although most of them were technically employees of the Department of Agriculture, or some other department, or were employees of some private outfit working under contract with T.C.A., for the most part it was all one team. I gather that in Washington there were plenty of inter-agency fights, but somehow when you get out into a country like Deserta, where there's such a terrible lot to be done, the bureaucratic arguments look pretty silly.

"In November, 1952, I took my third trip out into the hinterland. By this time things were beginning to happen all over, and the word of Point 4 had really got around. Every village we came to, the whole population would be out on the road to welcome us, waving banners and shouting. The village council usually had a list of things they wanted help on—a new well, a schoolhouse, a health center. They would supply the labor, if we could give them a start with some materials. It was touching, but it was also frightening. We couldn't be everywhere at once. There were only a handful of us. And neither the Government of Deserta nor T.C.A. had much money to work with. But each time I promised that we would try to get some one thing started soon.

"One day in January, 1953, I got to the office as usual about 7 A.M. An assorted fleet of jeeps, cars and carryalls was leaving for the countryside, each with a local driver, a Point 4 technician, and a local counterpart official. I knew that the same thing was happening in other parts of the country where we had outposts. A block away from the office, the walls of the country's first public health laboratory were beginning to rise, under the watchful gaze of local sidewalk superintendents. A group of young men was waiting in the office for me to give them a send-off speech before their departure for the States to study agricultural extension work. I suddenly remembered that I had arrived in Suqs just a year before. Somehow or other, in the meantime, Point 4 had come to Deserta."

5. The Free World Marches on Its Stomach

"Whoever could make two ears of corn, or two blades of grass, to grow upon a spot of ground where only one grew before, would deserve better of mankind than the whole race of politicians put together."
—JONATHAN SWIFT.

IF YOU VISIT the Middle East or India, you will see a lot of children everywhere. Although many of them look sick and undernourished, the majority do not. But after you have been there about a week, you will suddenly realize with something of a shock that you have not seen any children roughhousing or playing games or even shouting. The sad fact is that they don't have the energy.

Most of the people of the less developed areas are suffering from undernourishment in one form or another. Many millions of them do not get enough food of any kind—the daily intake of calories per capita in India is estimated at about 1700, as against a minimum requirement of 2250 and a United States figure of 3130—but a more widespread trouble is that they eat almost nothing but carbohydrates. In many areas, cereal grains, starchy roots and sugar account for three-quarters or more of the calories consumed (as compared with 43 per cent in the United States). In some countries, such as Indo-China and Indonesia, the average consumption of animal protein is only about an ounce a week, as against roughly a pound in the United States. The average American gets about twenty-five times as much milk and milk products as, say, the average Filipino. Green vegetables are almost unknown to the rural people of many countries.

As a result of such deficiencies, people cannot do a hard day's work. They are apathetic and highly susceptible to disease. They are in fact suffering a long-drawn-out kind of starvation.

And the over-all food situation has been getting worse rather than better. The terrible truth is that in some countries—India is an outstanding example—people have less to eat today than they did fifty years ago. On a world-wide basis, mankind is losing the race between population and food. Over the last fifteen years, the world's population has increased distinctly faster than the world's food supply. Moreover, the cruel discrepancy between per capita food production in the developed and in the underdeveloped countries has widened instead of narrowed. Whereas in Europe the prewar level in per capita food production has been regained, and in the United States and Canada it has been exceeded, in the Far East (the figures include India and Pakistan, but not Communist China) it has dropped off almost 15 per cent.[1]

All this means that the problem of food supply is the number one problem of the underdeveloped areas. If it could be solved, we would not need to worry quite so much about the cold war. On the other hand, as long as people are hungry most of the time, they are almost bound, sooner or later, to turn in their desperation to some extreme solution.

In its first three years, the T.C.A. devoted more than half its funds to the problem of helping people to produce more food. Virtually all the efforts of the Food and Agriculture Organization of the United Nations, and a high proportion of the developmental programs of the E.C.A. (later the M.S.A.) in the Far East were devoted to the same end.

The job is not only huge, but complex. It cannot be done in any one single way. Much can be accomplished through better seeds, and better methods of cultivating the land. But often the soil, depleted through centuries of single-crop cultivation, has to be replenished and enriched with natural and chemical fertilizers. More land is needed, and what land there is has to be prevented from being washed away to the ocean. Pests of all kinds have to be fought. Sometimes, there is too much water; more often, even where the land is waterlogged, the greatest need is for water. New sources of food have to be tapped—in the ocean, in the jungle, and in the desert. Livestock has to be made more productive and kept free from disease. The food that is produced has to be better stored and processed. Last but not least, farmers have to be given an incentive, and the credit they need, to produce more food.

Not all of this can be accomplished merely through the communication of knowledge and skills. But much of it can, especially if there is money enough to use the technique of learning by doing.

Considering the magnitude of the task, it is fair to say that the work has only just begun. Only in one or two countries can overall statistical progress be recorded. But the beginning is nonetheless propitious. Exciting things have happened, and more are happening every day.

The Etawah Story

Point 4's classic story is that of the pilot project at Etawah, in India, but the project's beginnings actually date back to 1948.

In the spring of that year, the U.P. (Uttar Pradesh, formerly United Provinces) State Government was anxious to find ways and means of raising food production in its section of the Ganges Plain. An imaginative American architect from New York named Albert Meyer, who was serving as an adviser to the U.P. Government, suggested that much might be accomplished through the use of agricultural extension techniques developed in the United States. On his recommendation, a former county agent from Tennessee named Horace Holmes, who had been working with U.N.R.R.A. in China, was hired as consultant for a pilot project in an area of about 100 square miles near Etawah, 170 miles southeast of Delhi. Holmes went to work with a small team of Indians; he contributed his knowledge of American extension methods, while they furnished an essential understanding of Indian ways.

The principal crop of the district was wheat, but yields were pathetically low, considering the intensive character of the cultivation, averaging thirteen bushels per acre. The first thing Holmes and his team tried to do was persuade the local farmers to use better seed, but the farmers were suspicious. Like any people living close to the edge of starvation, they were afraid of change, because change meant risk, and they could not afford to take risks. Eventually, a small group of farmers was found in the village of Mahewa who agreed to try out the new seed, called Punjab 591, on small strips of their land. When the crop was ready, a committee was appointed to see that the results were fairly measured. The new variety was harvested separately, threshed and carefully weighed: it was found to have produced 26 per cent more than the usual seed. A bulletin board was erected in the village, proclaiming the results with appropriate pictures, and attested by the participating farmers. The next year whole fields were planted with Punjab 591.

From then on, Holmes' suggestions were accepted more readily. The traditional method of plowing was to scratch the fields back and forth with a wooden plow; the farmers found out that the job could be done quicker and better with a steel pointed plowshare which cost only one dollar and seventy-five cents. They learned the value of insecticides and fungicides, and of homemade compost fertilizers.

Building up the fertility of the soil presented a variety of problems. The usual legumes (plants such as alfalfa which enrich rather than deplete the soil) were virtually useless because the ever-present cows always got into the fields sooner or later and ruined the crop. Holmes found that a native weed distasteful to the cattle made a good legume, which could be plowed under while still green to provide green manure. But here some of the farmers objected that taking the life of a plant before it had matured was forbidden by their religion. This difficulty was finally overcome when research revealed that the book of Vedic Laws stated that the *first* obligation of a farmer was to feed himself, his bullocks, and his family. Finally, an eight-inch steel turning plow, which had been developed at the Allahabad Agricultural Institute (originally a Presbyterian mission) was shown to be capable of turning under the sturdy legume when pulled by two bullocks. This technique involved a greater investment of time, effort and money than the other innovations and so was the slowest to be adopted, but it proved to be the most important of all in raising the production of wheat.

In 1950, Horace Holmes returned to the United States, only to be promptly hired by the United States Government and sent back to India to carry on his work. In August of 1951, three years after the start of the Etawah project, he told the Senate Foreign Relations Committee that the farmers who had cooperated in the work had succeeded in raising their per acre wheat production from thirteen to twenty-six bushels. One not-so-young farmer by the name of Neghu Ram had followed all the expert's suggestions so conscientiously that he had pushed the yields on his three-acre plot up to sixty-three bushels per acre. Extraordinary increases had been recorded in the production of potatoes as well.

Altogether, the estimate was that food production in the Etawah area had gone up almost 50 per cent. And the people of the area, finding themselves on an upward trail in the field of agriculture, began to want to improve their living conditions and to secure an education. What started out as agricultural extension turned into community development on several fronts. The work is going forward today, carried on entirely by Indian personnel and the community leaders themselves, with no foreigners in sight. For a time they were harassed by too many visitors from America and elsewhere, who wanted to witness the miracle of Etawah, but now, as other centers of extension work have been put into operation, even that problem has been solved. The people of Etawah are well on their way to a better life.[2]

But this is just a tiny corner of India, and there is no automatic way in which what is happening at Etawah can be made to happen elsewhere. Holmes estimated that it would take sixty thousand Indians, carefully trained, to carry on the work all over India, and in addition there is need for more steel for the new plows, for more fertilizer, and above all for more water so that the people can put their new-found skills to use. In 1952 and 1953, Point 4 has been helping along all these lines, but the core of the program is still the communication of knowledge and skills, not necessarily from Americans to Indians, but from Indians to Indians.

Nothing is more thrilling about the results of successful self-help measures than the pride of accomplishment it gives to those who have cooperated, and the sense of confidence that yet better things can be done. One day in the summer of 1952, I visited an extension project near Patiala, in P.E.P.S.U. state north of Delhi. The local extension agent nearly ran me off my feet, he had so many things he wanted to show me. Until recently his conception of his job had been to work three or four hours a day, at his desk; a Point 4 man named Perry Jameson had shown him what hard work with the farmers could mean, and he had definitely "got religion." Even prouder than the agent was the particular farmer whose fields we were inspecting—an aging Sikh, with his long hair covered by a turban. I took a picture of him and the agent, in amongst the tall, shiny green cotton plants. Just as we were climbing into the car to leave, three young boys in their late teens began hammering on the car windows. They also had been working with the agent and they insisted that I must come and take a picture of *their* cotton. "It is much higher than the old man's," they shouted.

A Modern Johnny Appleseed

In 1944, Frank Pinder, a graduate of the Florida Agricultural School for Negroes, went to Liberia as part of a United States Economic Mission. He found a country with no paved roads, no beasts of burden, and a Bureau of Agriculture with a budget of a few hundred dollars a year.

Refusing to travel in the usual manner of important people in Liberia—in a hammock slung between four bearers—Pinder explored the back country of Liberia on foot. On arrival in a village, he would present himself to the chief, and that evening there would be a long talk with the village elders in the "palaver house." There might be tales of hunting expeditions and boundary disputes, but Pinder always brought the conversation back to the problem of food. The dry season was known as the hungry season, when rice would not grow on the uplands. Protein foods—meat, fish and eggs—were virtually nonexistent. Although an agricultural country, Liberia did not grow enough food for its population of about a million, and the bush people had hardly any means of earning the cash to buy the few things they needed.

Pinder attacked the dry hungry season by showing the villagers how they could grow rice in the inland swamps. At first the chiefs and elders protested that the swamps could not be cleared, because the growth was too dense. Pinder finally persuaded one village to make the attempt, and he helped them to do the job himself, showing them how to use the steel tools he had brought along. At the time of the harvest, Pinder arranged for the chiefs and elders from nearby villages to come and see with their own eyes the miracle of a rice crop in the dry season. The next year, other hungry farms, as they were called, began to appear in the swamps.

In an effort to get the inland people started growing some cash crops, Pinder launched what he called his "two-cent program." Wherever he went, he carried seeds—for cacao, coffee and Nigerian oil palm. He was always ready to show people what to do with the seeds, but he did not give the seeds away. Instead, recognizing that the farmers would take far greater care of their new crops if they had invested even a small amount of money in the project, he sold the seeds for a nominal price. A cocoa pod, containing twenty-four seeds, he sold for two cents—hence the program's name. Pinder also encouraged vegetable production by the same method, especially in the vicinity of Monrovia, the capital city. One village chief reported with pride that in a few years the annual cash income of each family in his village had increased from less than five to about twenty-five dollars a year.

In all of this activity, Frank Pinder has been training Liberians to carry on the work; and stimulating the government to develop its own services. By 1952, Liberia not only had a real Department of Agriculture, but was devoting 20 per cent of its total budget, or about 1 million dollars, to the cooperative developmental programs in agriculture, health and other fields. Although Firestone and other private companies have doubtless been primarily responsible for the fact that United States exports to Liberia have increased twenty-nine times since 1938, Point 4 can take some credit too.

Other Americans have contributed mightily to the work, but in January, 1952, Secretary of State Dean Acheson paid special tribute in a major speech to "Frank Pinder, of Florida, who has walked through most of Liberia like a modern Johnny Appleseed, leaving a trail of growing things where he has been." [3]

Fighting the Scourges

No one who has ever seen a swarm of locusts on the rampage will ever forget it. They darken the sky, they fill the air with a deafening rustle, they are so thick on the ground that locomotive wheels slip helplessly. Often people are violently nauseated at the sight and sound, especially if they have to walk out of doors and scrunch the big yellow grasshoppers under foot at every step. The result of such an invasion is utter devastation. After Egypt's eighth plague, "there remained not any green thing in the trees, or in the herbs of the field, through all the land of Egypt."

When a swarm really gets going, man cannot stop it even today. But the locusts can nevertheless be controlled if they are located and attacked early enough, before they can fly. In the summer of 1951, T.C.A. received an urgent message from Iran that the locusts were beginning to swarm. Within a matter of days a contract had been made with a private concern to carry on spraying operations, and six Piper Cub planes were on their way by air freight. The spraying operation is hazardous, since the planes have to fly at an altitude of about ten feet, and one of the pilots was killed. But the locust invasion was stopped in its tracks. Since then, Point 4 spray planes have operated in Iraq, India and Pakistan also, using the United States-developed "aldrin," which is so powerful that two ounces in a gallon of water or diesel oil will kill an acre of young locusts. In each country, local nationals have been trained, not only to serve as flag men on the ground, but also as spray pilots. Breeding in different seasons in different areas, the locusts migrate backwards and forwards over a huge area from Kenya north and east to India, but with every year more is learned about their mysterious habits. If a concerted attack on the problem can be sustained for a few years, with local government agencies, F.A.O., the British-operated Desert Locust Control Service, and the United States Government all cooperating (not an easy task), it will be possible to keep this age-old enemy of mankind under strict control.[4]

Another of the plagues the Lord brought upon Pharaoh's Egypt was the grievous "murrain of beasts," which killed all the cattle. Nobody can be sure, but as like as not the "murrain" was the terribly infectious rinderpest, which has taken a fearful toll of cattle and sheep from time to time throughout the centuries. Today this disease can be controlled through vaccination, and F.A.O. has taken the lead in a world-wide campaign to that end.

With vaccination of human beings against smallpox, now a fairly familiar practice even in remote areas, the immunization of cattle is more readily accepted by the rural people than might be supposed. In a primitive Indian village near Nehru's home city of Allahabad, I saw a team of young Indian workers vaccinating the village cattle one after another under a clump of trees. The local people were eagerly helping and were engrossed in trying to control the kicking cows. No one paid any attention to a frail old woman who was quietly vomiting nearby. Perhaps she was sick, but it may also be that she was just horrified at what was being done to the sacred cattle.

Probably the only reason the plagues of Egypt did not

include a blight upon the crops is that, after the hail and the locusts, there were no crops left for the aphids or the fungi or the worms to attack. Until the advent of modern chemistry, there was no scourge against which mankind was more helpless than that of plant disease. By the same token, well-trained extension agents today can make a quicker impression on potential clients in this field than in any other. If a poor man's crop is dying before his eyes, he is no longer conservative and afraid of change. He is desperate and will try anything. If a man comes along with some spray that can save his crop, that man is his friend for life.

A couple of years ago, the potato farmers of Ecuador were about ready to give up. For several years, their crops had been 75 per cent destroyed by a blight which they did not know how to control. United States experts were able to identify the disease and to demonstrate the effectiveness of a relatively inexpensive chemical pesticide. Today, Ecuadoran farmers who have cooperated with the servicio's extension workers have been able to increase their potato crop six-fold. Similarly, the production of cacao in Ecuador, which had been paralyzed by the disastrous pod rot and "witches' broom" blight, has been effectively revived through the introduction of strains naturally resistant to these diseases.

The success of Peruvian extension agents operating under the United States-Peruvian agricultural servicio, S.C.I.P.A., in introducing the use of chemical pesticides in Peru has had two startling effects: it has, of course, greatly increased agricultural production, but it has also led to the establishment of a new industry to meet the farmers' demands. A few years ago chemical methods of controlling plant disease were virtually unknown in Peru, and at first

S.C.I.P.A. had to act as distributor of the chemicals, as well as of the information. But as the demand among the farmers grew, private industry stepped in to meet it, and S.C.I.P.A. was able to step out. In March of 1953, the Dupont Company's manager in Lima showed me through a new mixing plant for pesticides and was frank to admit that S.C.I.P.A.'s operations were responsible for its construction. Moreover, Dupont was competing with three other new plants.[5]

Uncle Jackass

In November, 1951, a live American dynamo named William Warne resigned as Assistant Secretary of Interior to take over the job of T.C.A. director in Iran, which was then already suffering from the effects of the oil dispute. Within a few weeks Warne had launched, in cooperation with the Iranian Ministry of Agriculture, a project which made Point 4 known across the face of Iran. He arranged to have seventy-five thousand sturdy baby chicks flown from the United States, some to be distributed to farmers and some to be kept in brood flocks, to strengthen and improve the stunted local breeds. In addition, superior goats and sheep, Brown Swiss bulls, and big Cyprus jackasses were brought in for breeding purposes. At this point Iran's communists and extreme nationalists, who had been attacking Point 4 as an imperialist plot from the start, switched their line: no longer able to say that the United States was doing nothing constructive, they seized upon the chickens and the jackasses as a way of ridiculing the program. For example, one newspaper said editorially: "Why does the United States Government that plans to incite the Middle

East against the Soviets send us chickens? They had better keep their jackasses and chickens and leave us alone."

This sort of propaganda backfired; it only advertised the program. Typically, one farmer rode 250 miles to the livestock station at Hyderabad to trade some scrub hens for the new American stock. (The trade-in procedure was followed in order to avoid any implications of charity; the old chickens received were sold in the market.) From a remote province, a tribal chief sent a courier with the message: "I offer you the salutations of my people and beg you to assign two of these fine donkeys to Firooz Abad."

Ironically enough, a sizable section of the American press, always inclined to be hostile to Point 4, played up the jackass story as an example of bureaucratic bungling. Cartoons appeared showing Uncle Sam in the guise of a donkey, an object of ridicule. The real significance of the story was missed completely.

The livestock improvement program is going ahead full blast, at very little cost to the United States. Contrary to the fears of some, Iranian farmers receiving chicks have not eaten them, but have recognized their value for breed-ing purposes and have taken excellent care of them. About half of the chicks were set aside for brood flocks to be maintained at various livestock stations around the country, so that in 1953, and subsequent years, hundreds of thousands could be distributed. The idea of making maxi-mum use of the bulls through artificial insemination has caught on, and several stations for that purpose have been set up. On a visit to one provincial city in August, 1952, Warne and I were proudly shown the livestock *bungah* with its new chicks, bulls and sheep. In typical Persian fashion, before we could see the animals, we had first to sit around a long table and listen to speeches, and make speeches in return. One of the guests on that occasion, characteristically dressed in a western suit, tieless shirt, fedora and suede shoes, was a powerful Bakhtiari tribal chief. Another was the mayor of a distant town who was urging that Point 4 establish a branch there.

In Egypt, with the enthusiastic cooperation of General Naguib's government, a similar livestock improvement program is under way. Seventy thousand baby chicks (mostly Rhode Island Reds, so that the eggs would be identifiable by their brown color) were purchased by an interdenominational American church group known as the Heifer Project Committee and shipped to Egypt by T.C.A. Upon arrival, the chicks were housed temporarily in one of ex-King Farouk's palaces, where there were suitable accommodations. Instead of the trade-in procedure followed in Iran, farmers had to promise to bring in one hatched chick or two fertile eggs for each chick received. The fellaheen have responded to the program with such enthusiasm that a difficult rationing problem has arisen. The project is popular not only because the egg production of the new chickens is four times as great as of the old, but also because the fellah's chickens are his own, and he does not have to share the produce with his landlord.

Water from Heaven

Of course all fresh water comes from the sky originally, but on some occasions more than others it seems to come like manna. Point 4 has not tried to teach rain-making, but it has sought to introduce better methods of conserving and using what rain there is. To the people involved, some of these methods seem almost magical.

Take the case of the water-spreading program in Jordan,

for example. Most of Jordan is desertlike, but rain occasionally does fall. The trouble is that, when it does, it runs off the sun-baked earth, taking some of the scanty soil with it, and roars down rocky stream beds called wadies, doing nobody any good. Using techniques developed in our western grazing states, the Point 4 team in Jordan has shown what can be done by building a series of low walls across shallow gullies and on nearby slopes. These dikes, consisting of earth and rock, can be built by hand and animal labor. They act as baffles to the occasional freshets and slow down the flow of water so as to permit the sediment to settle and the water to soak into the ground. Even without seeding, the result is green vegetation in one season, where before was only sand and rock. And of course the process is helped along by sowing a hardy variety of range grass in the areas above the dikes.

The nomadic Bedouins have marveled at the results of the water-spreading demonstrations in Jordan. With a little help in the design of the structures, they should be able to make use of the technique far and wide.[6]

Another skill that has been brought to Jordan—the use of rain-catching reservoirs—was known and practiced by the Romans two thousand years ago but had since been lost. The Romans had constructed a series of reservoirs along their desert routes, square cisterns 190 feet on a side, sunk into the ground and lined with masonry and then concrete. They were located in depressions where the winter rains would flow in from the surrounding slopes and fill them up, providing water for the caravans and roving flocks all through the blistering summer. So much of the idea was simple enough. But something else was needed to make it work: a small tank, just above the big one, to catch the silt in the water before it flowed into the big tank. Every year, after the rains, the small tank had to be cleaned out. What happened was that, when the Romans left, the desert people let the small tank silt up, and when it was full the big tank began to silt up also, year by year. After a century or so, there was no more reservoir.

When the Point 4 team arrived in Jordan late in 1951, one of the first things they did was to buy a secondhand dragline and dig out one of the old cisterns about forty miles east of Amman, and of course they dug out the silt-trap too. The first season brought disappointment. The water collected, all right, but the tank leaked because most of the old Roman cement lining was gone, and by mid-summer it was dry. The next fall the Bedouins in the area were organized into a cement-laying brigade, and the cistern was once again lined. Now there is water all summer long for the Bedouins and their camels, donkeys, goats and sheep. What is even more important, several other villages in the vicinity have caught hold of the idea and cleaned out similar cisterns on their own initiative.

On rising ground not far from the cistern there is a cluster of low, black goats' hair tents belonging to the local Bedouin sheik. In the summer of 1952, I paid a call on him, along with Tracy Welling of Utah, the able and energetic Point 4 director for Jordan. We sat in a circle on some beautiful Persian rugs and drank coffee out of a single small cup which was filled and handed to each person in turn. Sheik Aly apologized that he had not had sufficient warning of our visit to have a feast prepared, but we were grateful for this, as a feast would have involved quantities of lamb, cooked four different ways, all greasy, and served in great platters for everyone to dip into with his fingers. The Sheik's four wives—he had the full quota allowed by the Koran—stayed modestly behind a goats' hair partition in another part of the big tent, but he proudly trotted out some of his grandsons for us to admire. I felt a little nervous when Welling in his breezy western manner taxed the Sheik with having charmed Mrs. Welling on an earlier occasion, but the Sheik roared with laughter. Welling's handling of the proud and sensitive old man was perfect, and they' have since become fast friends. To the detriment of his stomach, Welling has many times been able to confirm the traditional hospitality of the desert.

A third, and the most ambitious, attack on Jordan's water problem involves the development of the Yarmuk River, a sizable stream which flows westward between Syria and Jordan and empties into the Jordan River just south of Lake Tiberias (Galilee). Until recently the Yarmuk had been thought to be unsuitable for damming, because of its sharp rate of fall, but early in 1952, Welling's chief engineer, Mills Bunger, spotted a promising dam site at the confluence of five wadies, while on a flight from Beirut to Amman, and work has since been started on the engineering of the project. The dam, which would be the highest rock-filled earth dam in the world, would not only provide power for industry in both Jordan and Syria, but would store enough water to irrigate a large section of the Jordan Valley and permit tens of thousands of refugees from Palestine to be resettled there. The project would of course be an expensive one, and capital would have to be obtained from the International Bank and also from the United Nations organization for the relief and rehabilitation of the refugees from Palestine. In addition, like all questions disposing of international water rights, it is an explosive one politically, even though Israel would not be deprived of any water that Israeli farmers at the lower end of the Yarmuk had been using. But if the dam should materialize, it would be a striking example of how Point 4 can act as a spark, or catalytic agent, for capital development. In a case such as this, it is often hard for the T.C.A. experts to infuse an adequate amount of caution into local government representatives, once they have seized upon the idea. Because of its insistence on exploring the feasibility of the project in every respect, including not only the geológy of the Yarmuk canyon, but the types of soils to be irrigated and the pattern of land ownership in the area to be resettled, and because of its desire to see the potentially dangerous political questions settled before work is actually started, the United States has been accused of dragging its feet.*

In the light of this kind of behavior, it is ironic to read of a blast by Dorothy Thompson in a speech in Omaha in the fall of 1952. She accused Point 4 of moving "into a country like an Abercrombie and Fitch safari with enough grandiose schemes to last a hundred years." If she had bothered to check her facts, she would have discovered that one of Point 4's greatest difficulties is talking local officials out of impracticable grandiose schemes of their own.

Even though it has nothing to do with water, another story about the program in Jordan deserves telling here parenthetically, because of the light it throws on the pitfalls that lie in wait for the administrator of an aid program. In the late fall of 1951, Jordan was reported to be in the clutches of a near famine. The United States re-

---

* The so-called T.V.A. plan for developing the Jordan Valley, which involves using Lake Tiberias for storage, would be more economical than the Yarmuk project, would be preferable for Israel and would perhaps serve Jordan just as well (except in terms of electric power). But, in spite of Eric Johnston's optimistic reports after his special mission to sell the plan in the fall of 1953, it seems most unlikely that the Arab states will ever accept the idea so long as they remain at war with Israel.

ceived an urgent request for about a million dollars worth of wheat, backed in the strongest terms by our diplomatic representatives in the area. Reluctantly, Dr. Bennett agreed to the use of T.C.A. funds for the purpose, feeling that the proceeds from the sale of wheat could be used as local currency to support the Point 4 program proper. The wheat was rushed to Beirut and laboriously hauled overland by way of Damascus. By the time it arrived in Amman, the famine scare was all over. Grain had appeared on the market from hoarded stocks in great quantities, the price had dropped, and the American wheat could not be sold! It was eventually sold to the United Nations at a substantial loss. Yet the painful fact is that, if the American wheat had not been forthcoming, there would have been a real famine, with the speculators letting their wheat go in dribs and drabs at fantastic prices.*

Getting back to the question of water, of course the science of irrigation is nothing new under the sun. Flying over the flat plains of Mesopotamia, between the Euphrates and the Tigris, one can see the remnants of canals dating back thousands of years and long since silted up. But the science of irrigation is a highly technical one, and the methods used by untrained people are often wasteful. At the agricultural experiment station of Abu Ghraib near Baghdad, T.C.A. experts have demonstrated that by introducing canal water to larger rectangles of land than are customary in Iraq, a great deal of labor and water can be

* The wheat shipped to India under the 1951 loan was also very slow to be absorbed by the market, which indicated that hoarders and speculators had contributed to the shortage. This fact, and the Jordan incident, prompted the not-so-absurd suggestion that the United States should keep two or three freighters loaded up with wheat and cruising around the world, ready to move toward any area where a famine was reported imminent, but never having to unload!

saved. Moreover, in many areas improper irrigation can literally destroy the fertility of the land. What happens is that the water table is raised almost to the surface, and the water, evaporating rapidly under the hot sun, leaves a deposit of salt. If this process is allowed to continue, within a few years nothing will grow. Pakistan, for example, is losing thousands of acres of land each year through waterlogging or excessive salinity. In 1952, the West Punjab's Chief Minister told me that this was his number one problem. Nor is it an easy problem to attack, as many western American farmers have discovered. Drainage canals are essential, and it may also be necessary to put in deep wells equipped with diesel pumps, to lower the water table and at the same time to provide additional water so as to rinse or leach the salt out of the soil. F.A.O. and T.C.A. engineers are collaborating on a major trial of this method in Pakistan. The method is expensive, and there is no guarantee that it will work, but the alternative is to do nothing.

One of the most thrilling Point 4 stories is being written today by a group of small farmers near Chincha, 100 miles south of Lima. The coastal plain of Peru is a true desert, but water can make it flower. Under a law similar to our Homestead Act, Peruvian farmers can acquire title to government land if they will irrigate it. In 1952, a Peruvian engineer working with the agricultural servicio encouraged the Chincha farmers to undertake the construction of an irrigation canal several miles long to bring water from a nearby river to a ten-thousand-acre tract called Pampa de Ñoco. All the engineer did was to survey and design the system for them and to give them advice as they went along. The farmers used their fiesta money to buy equipment and to hire two experts to do the dynamite work on a one-thousand-foot tunnel through a ridge. Most of the back-breaking work they have contributed themselves, taking turns away from their fields. When I saw the project in March of 1953, the tunnel was less than half completed and much of the canal remained to be dug, but by the end of 1954 the water should have started to flow. Later on, they will line the ditch with concrete to save water. Eventually, these mestizos will have more than doubled their income. They will have done it through their own energy and sacrifice. Point 4 will have provided the spark of hope that it could be done.

Save the Soil

Erosion is a long-range problem. That is why it is difficult to persuade farmers to do anything about it. Their preoccupation is to make a crop for this season, and soil conservation measures don't contribute much to that objective.

Here is a perfect illustration of the difficulty of bridging the gap between the laboratory or the experiment station and the workshop or the farm. Every Ministry of Agriculture in the underdeveloped countries knows perfectly well what sheet and gully erosion can do to a country, but there are very few that have been able to translate that knowledge into action on the land.

Today, Costa Rica is an exception. On a visit there in early 1953, I scarcely saw a field that was not plowed on the contour. I saw huge areas striped with lateral ditches. Five years earlier, I was told, conservation practices were virtually unknown. How was it done? The answer is that, with the help of the United States, Costa Rica has developed within a few years one of the best agricultural extension services in the world.

In 1942, the I.I.A.A. launched a food production program of its own in Costa Rica, designed to provide more food for war-busy Panama and the Canal Zone. Three agencies were set up, in San José, Cartago, and Alajuela, to promote increased production among the farmers of the surrounding districts. The work was so successful that in 1948 a servicio was organized, known as S.T.I.C.A., to carry on and extend it on a joint basis. Five years later, thirty extension offices had been set up, which, in a country half the size of Kentucky with only a third the population, is good coverage. The extension agents, who are all Costa Rican, have increased their farmer contacts every year and most of them are now overloaded with work because so many farmers come to them with their technical problems. The farmers know, incidentally, that if they are working with a S.T.I.C.A. agent they can get a loan from Costa Rica's excellent farm credit system almost automatically.

As in Peru extension offices at first sold fertilizer and pesticides to the farmers, but stopped doing so when the demand was sufficiently established to attract private distributors. The role of the few United States technicians has been to provide guidance, especially in any new ventures, and occasionally to help get difficult things done. For example, one expert from Texas went back to the States to buy up a lot of old horse-drawn equipment which was not being used or produced any more, but was just right for Costa Rica's stage of technology.

As a part of the extension work, great progress has been made in the development of the 4-H Club idea, known as 4-S in Costa Rica. Scores of clubs have been formed among both boys and girls—and also, occasionally, adults, at their own request—and fairs, exhibits, and competitions to display the project accomplishments have attracted intense interest. In the Palmares area the 4-S boys expanded a home-grown vegetable project into a tomato export business, and ended up with a twenty-eight-thousand-dollar profit.[7]

The net effect of all this is that Costa Rica has turned from a food importing country to an exporter. The young Minister of Agriculture told me that now his biggest problem was to know what to do with the constantly increasing production.

Within a year or two, according to Howard Gabbert, S.T.I.C.A.'s director and Point 4 chief, the United States should be able to withdraw its support from the S.T.I.C.A. extension service and let the Ministry of Agriculture take it over. It is so popular that the people of Costa Rica will insist that it be carried on. The measure of that popularity is suggested by the action of the farmers of the town of Grecia, who came into the San José headquarters of S.T.I.C.A. and asked that an extension office be set up in their town. When told that the budget for that year would not permit it, they asked and found out how much it would cost. Within a week they were back with the money, which they had scraped together through voluntary contributions and a loan.

Flying over the lovely rolling uplands of Costa Rica, with the lines of contour plowing looking like huge fingerprints everywhere, one cannot help thinking with horror of all the good soil that is being dumped in the sea every year by rivers like the Nile, the Indus, the Irrawaddy, and the Amazon. At the same time, one gets a glimmering of hope that some day it can be stopped.

Fish Stories

The sea, which covers most of the world's surface, is full of living things, but so far we have only just begun to tap this vast supply of food. One reason is that the fruit of the sea is usually hard to pluck.

The people of Indonesia have always known how to fish, both in the sea surrounding their islands and in inland ponds. But in 1950, when an E.C.A. mission first arrived in Indonesia to assist in its development, the offshore fishing industry was almost at a standstill. The boats used by the local fishermen had no power, other than oars and sails. They were not only slow and inefficient, but they had to limit their operations to the space of a few miles. If they ventured further out, their catch would spoil before they could bring it in. And the inshore waters were yielding less and less.

An American fisheries expert attached to the E.C.A. mission discussed the problem with the Indonesian Sea Fisheries Service, and as a result E.C.A. purchased in Japan sixty diesel-powered *majang* fishing boats to serve as the nucleus of a deep-sea fleet. Cooperatives of sixteen fishermen each were organized and trained to operate and maintain the boats. Before long, they were busy proving that the deeper waters were indeed full of fish. Fifteen per cent of each catch was set aside to pay for the boats.

The next step for E.C.A. was to bring in a hundred diesel engines, and later two hundred and forty more, and to encourage the construction of the majang boats locally. In spite of primitive tools and methods, scores of the fifty-foot boats began to take shape in the local yards.

By 1953, the Indonesian Government was so enthusiastic about the possibilities of motorized fishing, not only to make the most of the waters around Java, but to exploit the relatively untapped waters of the other islands, that it wanted to invest 10 million dollars in more boats of various types. Obviously, the demonstration stage was over. The role of T.C.A., which had taken over the program on July 1, 1952, was now to help the Indonesians plan the expansion and obtain financing from some other source for it.

At the same time that Indonesia's salt-water fisheries were being helped, Indonesia's highly developed methods of inland fish farming were being carried to still other countries. Over the centuries the Indonesian rice farmers have learned how to grow fish and rice together. When the rice paddies are flooded, fingerling carp are brought in from nurseries, and allowed to feed while the rice grows and matures. When the terraces are drained for the ripening of the rice, the fish are the size of large sardines. In addition to such fresh-water fish culture, thousands of Indonesians are engaged in the breeding and domestication of salt-water fish. Coastal marshes are put to good use by enclosing them with sea walls and keeping them flooded with tidal waters.

Among other countries in the underdeveloped areas, Israel and Haiti are seeking to increase their supply of protein food by promoting fish-farming. Knowing that they could learn much from Indonesian methods, the F.A.O. has provided fellowships for two Israelis and a Haitian to study those methods on the spot.

Thailand has a different kind of problem. Finding that they can earn more from full-size carp than from rice, many Thai farmers have stopped draining their fields at all. Worried about the loss of rice, Thai experts are trying to find a way in which rice can be raised and at the same time the carp can be allowed to grow to full size, such as through use of a sump in the middle of the field. Again, the F.A.O. has provided funds for Thai fish specialists to study the various methods used in other countries. [8]

In just such ways as this, special skills and knowledge flow back and forth under the Point 4 concept.

Don't Let It Go to Waste

In times of emergency, the United States goes in heavily for anti-waste campaigns. (I can remember as a small boy in 1918 trying to get Mr. Hoover on the telephone to tell him that Nellie was using too much Dutch Cleanser.) But most of the time, we throw away mountains of food a day, down our dispose-alls or into our garbage cans.

Strange as it may seem, the waste in the hungry, under-developed countries, although much less casual, is probably just as great, perhaps even greater. Our transportation and refrigeration systems get food to us before it rots, and our grain storage elevators and warehouses keep the rats out. But in many countries, these elements of a highly developed economy do not exist.

Consider Ethiopia, for example. No one knows how many people there are in Ethiopia—the figure of ten million given in the almanacs is just a guess—but to the traveler it looks as if there are as many cattle as people. Countless numbers of those cattle die every year, and their meat is often allowed to rot, because there is no way to preserve it or transport it to a market. There is no meat-packing industry to speak of, only one railroad, and few roads. Faced with this situation, T.C.A. and the United States Department of Commerce have tried to interest private capital in investing in a meat-packing plant, to be located southeast of Addis Ababa on the railroad line to the coast.

A similar surplus of perishable foods has been dealt with successfully in the Shan States of northern Burma. With technical help from Americans, first under E.C.A. and then under T.C.A., a small canning factory was constructed by a group of Burmese. By 1953 its production had been doubled and it was aiming at a rate of two thousand cans a day. The plant had all the orders it could fill, mainly from the Burmese Army, and an assured source of supply from the surrounding area.

Many countries have inadequate storage facilities for wheat and other grains, and the losses from vermin or moisture are tremendous. One expert on Point 4, consultant to both F.A.O. and T.C.A., has estimated that 10 per cent of the world's cereal production is destroyed each year by rodents and insects.[9] Typical of the attack on this problem is one project in Jordan, where T.C.A. has helped the government to construct 10 semi-spherical grain storage bins of a new type, inexpensive and suited to desert conditions. If the demonstration is successful, Jordan plans to build enough storage bins to carry over about 300,000 tons of grain from the good years to the lean years, in the manner of Joseph, and all without fear of loss from pests.

Improper handling and packing of food, especially fruit, is another source of waste. One of T.C.A.'s first successes in Lebanon was the work of an expert in orange handling, who went along from Beirut to Trieste with a cargo of Lebanese oranges and was able to find out why such a large proportion were decaying en route. In Israel also, where citrus fruit is the chief export, packing techniques have been improved under the guidance of an American expert and two Israelis who spent three months on Point 4 training grants studying methods used in Florida, Texas and California.

Still another form of waste occurs even after food reaches the consumer. In many countries tapeworms and other denizens of the intestinal tract are so prevalent that a frighteningly high proportion of the food consumed goes to feed the parasites, rather than the human hosts. But this is really a public health problem and belongs in the next chapter.

It is both discouraging and encouraging that, for a few decades at least, the world's food problems could be largely solved without any increase in production, if all the food that is grown could be put to good use.

One-Fifth to the Cultivator

Most of the obstacles to increasing the food production of the underdeveloped areas are nature's, but one of the most maddening of all is man-made. It is the economic and cultural pattern which in some countries deprives the cultivator of most of the fruits of his labors and therefore leaves him with no incentive to try to grow more.

Consider the case of Khalil Hoda, a farmer of Iran. He is trying to support a family of five on the produce from two acres which he does not own. Four-fifths of what he can grow he has to turn over to somebody else, one-fifth for seed, one-fifth for water, one-fifth for the loan of oxen, and one-fifth for rent to the landlord himself. Khalil does not even have any security on the land. Next year, on the landlord's whim or because a cultivator comes along who is willing to pay an even higher rent, he may be booted out. Why should Khalil Hoda make any special effort to enrich the land with manure or to adopt some newfangled method of cultivation?

No problem in the field of international development is more difficult than this one, and it is a problem which occurs in one form or another from Chile around the world to Formosa. In a few places, such as Lebanon and Costa Rica, the majority of farmers own their land, but most countries face the necessity of land reform of one sort or another if they are ever to realize their potential in terms of agricultural production. Moreover, nothing plays into the hands of the communist agitators so much as an inequitable system of land tenure. "Come with us," they say, "and we will get rid of your landlord." In parts of southern India the communists have been able to frighten some landlords into making "voluntary" rent reductions and have spread word of these achievements far and wide. In the Philippines, the strength of the communist-led Hukbalahaps has been directly attributable to the miserable condition of the tenant farmers and landless peasants of central Luzon. A communist type of land distribution scheme in Guatemala has caused unrest elsewhere in Latin America.

Yet the problem of land tenure in the underdeveloped areas is not one that is within the United States' capacity to solve, unless of course it be in the position of an occupying power as it was after the war in Japan. Fundamentally, the countries must solve the problem themselves, for it goes to the very roots of their social structures. All the United States can do is to help the process along, in a variety of ways.

The most obvious, and least controversial method of helping along the process of land reform is to provide technical guidance on the subject to those who want it. In the fall of 1951, for example, T.C.A. and E.C.A. together financed a conference on land tenure at the University of Wisconsin. The sessions lasted several weeks and were attended by representatives of thirty-six countries, including a number with important responsibilities in the field.

One of the outstanding United States efforts in support of an indigenous land reform program has been through our participation in, and financial contributions to, the Joint Commission on Rural Reconstruction in China. The J.C.R.R., established in 1948 under the China Aid Act of that year, consists of three Chinese members, including the Chairman, and two American members. Except for one year of operations on the mainland—surprisingly successful operations considering the circumstances—the Commission has necessarily had to limit its efforts at rural reconstruction to Formosa. Probably the greatest emphasis in the program of the J.C.R.R. has been on problems of land tenure. Recognizing that land reform did not necessarily mean enforced redistribution, the Commission first encouraged the adoption of measures reducing farm rentals to 37.5 per cent of the main crops and requiring lease contracts that would give the tenants greater security of tenure, and then helped to make the measures successful. Obviously there was a great need for trained local personnel to administer the program, and the J.C.R.R. has provided funds for the training of these workers and for the printing of necessary instructional materials.[10] Most observers have agreed that the reforms have worked out well.

Whenever and wherever indigenous efforts at land reform are being made, the United States Government has stood ready to provide expert advice and assistance. The details of General Naguib's land reform decree issued in the summer of 1952, reflected to a considerable extent the suggestions of Paul V. Maris, one of America's leading authorities on the subject. In Iran, Maris had earlier devised a system for providing new landowners under the Shah's land distribution scheme with necessary credit and guidance. When Premier Mossadegh announced his own reform scheme in 1952, consisting of a tax on landlords' income, to be used for local improvements under the direction of village committees, T.C.A. Director William Warne was ready with a plan to provide the village committees not only with advice but with some initial funds, so that the scheme would not appear to be a failure because of delays in collecting the money from the landlords. A sizable segment of the Point 4 team in Iraq is working exclusively on various aspects of the Iraqi Government's ambitious *miri sirf* program of settling farmers on government lands.

This kind of help is invaluable to countries that are making efforts at land reform, because the administrative and social problems encountered are enormous, and if the efforts fail because of mistakes, the cause of land reform may be set back for generations. One of the most difficult problems to solve is the farmers' complete lack of experience in managing their land. As tenants they have always been wholly dependent on their landlords and have never had to exercise responsibility. In one Arab country, for example, amounts of money advanced to a group of settlers for tools and seed were promptly spent on items of greater prestige value: guns and additional wives.

In the Veramin Plains area east of Teheran, the Near East Foundation operating under a contract with Point 4 has started a vegetable garden program, partly to give the villagers a better-balanced diet, but also to give them experience in farm management. The Foundation's representatives succeeded in persuading local landlords, some of whom have a considerable sense of responsibility toward their tenants, to make available plots of ground for the purpose, without exacting any rent, and the villagers have shown tremendous interest and competitive spirit in these, their first farms.

But, with the partial exception of the J.C.R.R. program, these various American activities have all been directed at making spontaneous efforts at land reform more successful. The question of what to do about hastening the process is much more difficult and controversial. A few attempts have been made. In the Philippines in 1950, the E.C.A., in return for a virtual promise of 250 million dollars of aid over a five-year period, extracted a commitment from the Quirino government that fiscal and land reforms would be pressed. The fiscal measures were adopted, but steps to remedy the land tenure situation have bogged down. In Nepal, Ambassador Chester Bowles was apparently able to persuade the government to make a start on a reform program, and in India he persistently urged the Centre Government to see to it that the state governments effectively carried through the land reform measures they had put on their books, but he felt that progress was painfully slow. Aside from such scattered efforts, and from supporting pious resolutions in the United Nations, the United States has not done much to push the cause of land reform.[11]

This is not to suggest that Point 4 aid should be withheld from any country that is not taking sufficiently vigorous steps to solve its land tenure problems. The impracticability of such a course, and the irresponsibility of those who have advocated it, will be discussed in a later chapter. But it is nevertheless true that powerful elements in the United States State Department and Foreign Service have been too much afraid of antagonizing the big landlord elements in many of the governments of the underdeveloped countries. In consequence, the United States has often failed to encourage the taking of steps toward land reform where it could have done so, either behind the scenes or publicly in such a way as to avoid the charge of interference. In other words, it has tended to leave to the communists as their exclusive preserve the fertile field of unrest among the landless.

The Importance of Credit

Closely related to the problem of land reform, in fact a part of it, is that of farm credit. In many areas of the world the farmer's only source of credit is the bazaar moneylender, who may extract an interest rate of anywhere from 40 to 300 per cent. Often the landlords and the moneylenders are the same, but even where they are not, the effect of the high interest rates is to deprive the tenant of any reasonable opportunity to strike out on his own. Moreover, aside from its tendency to perpetuate an inequitable land tenure system, the absence of fair credit has a harmful effect on food production. Even the individual farm owner will make every effort to avoid borrowing money if he knows that, once he starts, he will probably be in the moneylender's clutches for good, and may well end up by losing his land. Faced with this unwillingness to borrow money, even the best agricultural extension agent cannot persuade his clients to invest in better tools or fertilizer.

It is not enough, however, for a country to set up a land bank authorized to make loans at reasonable rates. Where farmers are illiterate and unused to handling money, the making of loans must be coupled with careful supervision to see that the proceeds are fruitfully used. Just as agricultural extension work usually depends for its success on the availability of credit on reasonable terms, as for example in Costa Rica, so a farm credit system is likely to go bust unless the farmers are getting sound guidance along with their loans.

How the two operations can be successfully combined has been demonstrated in Paraguay by the Servicio Tecnico Interamericano de Cooperación Agricola. In 1943, a system of supervised credit was set up with funds provided through the Bank of Paraguay, modeled after the United States Farm Security Administration which had been so successful in helping sharecroppers during the depression.

At first the idea was slow to catch on among the farmers. They were afraid of going into debt and suspicious of what seemed like getting something for nothing. Even Albion Patterson, the Yankee schoolteacher who was rapidly earning the love of Paraguayans at all levels and who later became Point 4 Country Director, had trouble persuading the farmers that the scheme was on the level. Finally, a few venturesome souls applied for loans, but they still could not believe that life really would change for them. Patterson quotes one of them as saying: "Of course, I take the loan. Who, being poor, will dare refuse so nice a help? Pablo, my brother, says the same. But we are not so foolish. If tomorrow we don't pay, maybe we will be slaves to the *Nortes*. Maybe all my country must be sold one day to *Nortes* to pay for this nice help."

When a year's experience showed that the idea worked, it spread like wildfire. Supervised credit meant that a farmer who applied for and received a loan was given a plan by a farm credit supervisor for improving his farm so as to make enough money to pay back the loan. Paraguayans, both men and women, were trained to act as supervisors by a small team of Americans. They would help the farmers choose their purchases—possibly a new pair of oxen, a steel plow, and a knapsack sprayer—and they would explain, and insist on, crop rotation and the use of legumes. Family incomes doubled and trebled, even after paying the annual installment on the loan. Stimulated also by other activities of the servicio, the demand for agricultural equipment so increased that by 1948, the Government of Paraguay ordered $2,500,000 worth from the International Harvester Company, and in 1952 with the servicio's help prepared an application to the World Bank for a $5,000,000 loan, largely for farm equipment, which came through in record time. Characteristically, the system of supervised credit has been turned over entirely to the Paraguayan Government, and the servicio continues to act merely in an advisory capacity.[12]

In the summer of 1952, Paraguay's experience and those of many other nations were discussed at an International Conference on Agricultural and Cooperative Credit, conducted by the University of California at Berkeley, with financial assistance from the United States Government. The conference, patterned on the Land Tenure Conference of the previous year, was attended by seventy delegates from thirty-four nations and lasted six weeks, covering every phase of the subject. Although an unfortunately high proportion of those present were students already in the United States, the delegates did include a member of the supervisory council of Iran's Agricultural Bank, a Branch Manager of Japan's Central Cooperative Bank for Agriculture and Forestry, the Indian state of

Orissa's Minister of Development, and a number of other influential officials.

In the underdeveloped areas, as elsewhere, one of the most effective ways of attacking the farm credit problem is through the formation of cooperative purchasing associations and other types of farm organizations. The possibilities of building such institutions, and the obstacles in the way, are discussed in Chapter 9.

Tractors or Hoes?

"Send me a hoe" was the laconic wording of a telegram sent to his headquarters by an F.A.O. cotton expert soon after his arrival in Afghanistan. He had found that the Afghan farmers had never seen a long-handled hoe and had always used instead a short implement with a broad head, known in some places as a "back-breaker." When sample hoes did arrive, the response of the Afghan farmers was immediately enthusiastic. Use of the hoes, combined with row-planting of the cotton (instead of broadcasting the seed), meant greater production. Similarly, F.A.O. has introduced rakes, forks and scythes into Afghanistan, all of which the local blacksmiths can make. The scythe, for instance, takes the place of a primitive little sickle, which the farmer uses sitting on the ground and grasping the grain in his left hand. With the scythe, a crop can be harvested five times as fast.

Stories like this one, which are sometimes said to be "the essence of Point 4," almost always appeal to people. They make the whole process of agricultural development sound so easy, somehow so charming. Unfortunately, the same thing is not true when you start to talk about introducing tractors.

For one reason or another, the mere suggestion that tractors should be included in a technical cooperation program makes some people see red, especially on Capitol Hill in Washington. Even such a highly intelligent supporter of Point 4 as Senator Fulbright of Arkansas scolded the State Department in the summer of 1951, because it was proposing to send some tractors to Iran. "I think an equivalent number of steel plows would probably be much more useful," he said.[13] The truth is that steel plows might or might not be more useful, depending on the circumstances.

Senator Fulbright would, of course, not deny that in the economic development of the United States, mechanization of agriculture has played a vital role. Tractors and combines and all the other complicated items of farm machinery have made it possible for less than 15 per cent of America's workers to produce more food than the country can consume, leaving the remaining 85 per cent to produce all the other goods and perform all the services that our standard of living requires. In the long run, most of the underdeveloped countries will have to reduce the high proportion of their people engaged in agriculture, through at least partial mechanization, if they are ever to achieve real progress. For some, that goal is decades away; but for others, it is time at least to make a start.

Up to now Point 4 has concentrated far more on introducing hoes and steel plows than tractors and diesel engines, but here and there steps toward mechanization have been encouraged with striking success. The demonstration of diesel-powered fishing boats in Indonesia was one. The establishment of machinery pools in Peru has been another.

Much of Peru's irrigated coastal farm land is highly suited to mechanized agriculture. Some years ago, the director of the agricultural servicio S.C.I.P.A., a former county agent from Wyoming named John R. Neale, devised a way of meeting the need. Knowing that most of Peru's farmers could not afford to buy expensive machinery, he established through S.C.I.P.A. a series of depots from which the farmers could rent tractors and other equipment. Peruvians were trained not only to operate the machinery, but to keep it in repair. The response has been so great that some of the machines, especially bulldozers used for land clearing and leveling, have had to be equipped with headlights for night operations. At one outlying S.C.I.P.A. office in March, 1953, I saw the logbook which showed that some of the machines had been working as much as twenty-two hours a day. But this fact alone does not demonstrate that the introduction of tractors was sound economically. What does demonstrate it is that in those sections of Peru where the machinery pools were first started, the need for them has now virtually disappeared, because sizable landowners and groups of small farmers have taken to buying their own equipment. United States exports of farm equipment to Peru have multiplied several times in the eleven years of S.C.I.P.A.'s operations.[14]

Obviously, there are areas where no purely labor-saving device will contribute much to the development of the country, because labor is plentiful and all available land is already intensively cultivated. (This is just as true of a scythe as it is of a tractor, but the inexpensive scythe may be worth introducing just to make life a little easier for the farmer.) For example, in the delta area of Egypt and the Ganges plain of India, extensive use of tractors for plowing and cultivating makes no sense, and will not for a long time. But even in such areas, certain types of mechanization are badly needed. For example, in Egypt the precious Nile water can often be more efficiently used if it is pumped and piped onto the land, instead of just being sluiced in from ditches. In India, the necessity of securing more water for irrigation calls for hundreds of deep tube wells, to be drilled and operated by diesel power, as well as gasoline-driven pumps to lift the water out of small ponds onto the fields, and T.C.A. has given India substantial help along these lines. In addition, huge caterpillar-type tractors are required to restore to cultivation thousands of acres in India which have been ruined by the deep-rooted "Kans grass," and one of India's loans from the International Bank has been for that purpose.

In other parts of the underdeveloped areas, extensive cultivation of sparsely populated land is definitely in order. The big tractors proposed for Iran—but not sent because of Senatorial objections—were in fact needed to develop the great plains areas of northern Iran, and Iranians could have been trained to maintain them. In many parts of Iran, small farm tractors are already in use, either on a rental or cooperative basis. From the Veramin Plains the Near East Foundation's representative reported early in 1953: "Plowing and discing on a custom basis continues in great demand. Our equipment is kept busy and we are unable to meet the requests for help. Plots were plowed in four villages last month. They will serve as demonstrations of the value of modern tillage."

One of Dr. Henry Bennett's great dreams was that the deep black soil of Ethiopia, which is no more densely populated than Texas, could someday be made to grow enough food to meet the food deficits of the whole Middle East. If his dream is ever to come true, Ethiopia will need not only a better transportation system, but a great deal of mechanized farming. That day is a long way off—in many parts of Ethiopia, even the wheel is still virtually unknown—but Point 4 can hasten its arrival. No tractors are being sent to Ethiopia yet, but young men of the country are being trained in modern methods of farming. Under a Point 4 contract, Dr. Bennett's old college, Oklahoma A. & M., has sent out some of its best people to help Ethiopia get agricultural secondary schools and a college under way.

All of this adds up to the fact that you cannot generalize about what is needed to help the free world grow more food. Hoes and scythes may be the best thing in one place but not in another. A fungicide that works here may not work there. Some farmers may be ready to mechanize, others are not. The job requires ingenuity and flexibility, as well as determination.

6. Sick People Also Eat

LIKE SPECIALISTS EVERYWHERE, Point 4 experts can often be found arguing about whose field is the most important. Norris E. Dodd, the successful Oregon rancher who became Director General of the United Nations Food and Agriculture Organization, once told me that the World Health Organization was F.A.O.'s greatest enemy. Of course, he was being facetious, but there was an undercurrent of seriousness in his remark. The people who are concentrating on trying to help the underdeveloped areas grow more food tend to look with suspicion on those who are trying to keep human beings alive. On the other hand, the public health physicians, nurses and sanitary engineers who are working as shirt-sleeve diplomats are convinced that nothing is more important to international development than what they are doing.

"How much can you accomplish in any country," they will ask, "if most of the inhabitants are sick most of the time? The sick ones still eat, but they have no energy to work."

Of one thing we can be sure. If, as Point 4 experts often say, our approach must be to help people meet their "felt needs," i.e. to help them improve their lives in ways that *they* are interested in, work in the health field must rank near the top. Sometimes, indeed, the only way to win the

confidence of proud and suspicious country folk is to profit
by the helplessness and desperation they feel in the face of
serious illness.

A few years ago in a village near Damascus, the Near
East Foundation found its efforts to help the people frustrated by a hostile mayor. Late one night, however, the
mayor unexpectedly sent a messenger to ask the Foundation's young public health nurse to come to his house
immediately. When she got there, the mayor met her at
the door, his face twisted with terror and grief, and told
her that his daughter-in-law had been in labor three days
and that the midwife said she was dying. Was there anything the nurse could do? The young American was in a
quandary. If she tried to help, and the girl died—and the
poor thing was probably beyond saving by this time—the
Foundation would be blamed. But one look at the almost
unconscious girl made her forget questions of policy. She
went to work, and was lucky enough not only to save the
young mother, but to deliver a son—the mayor's first grand-
son. A couple of years later, when I visited the village, the
same mayor proudly showed me the spick-and-span adobe
house that had been turned into a health and domestic
science training center for the village girls; later he made
a little speech, extolling the Foundation and its works, at a
gathering of the newly established farmers' association in
a building they had erected to serve as their headquarters.

Of course, treating the sick, while it may be the first
step, cannot be the objective of an international development program. For one thing, it can never be more than
a drop in the bucket. For another, and more importantly,
it can have no permanent effects, because it is not attacking
the root of the problem. That is why the emphasis must
be on prevention, that is, on public health, rather than on

cure. The furnishing of medical care for the sick is to the health side of Point 4 what shipping in wheat is to the food supply side.

Even within the area of preventive medicine, there are some activities which contribute more than others to the economic development of the countries concerned, in that they concentrate on keeping people well enough to pull their weight in the economy, rather than on adding to the number of mouths that must be fed. An outstanding example is malaria control.

War Against the Anopheles

Perhaps a quarter of all the people in the underdeveloped areas have malaria each year. In many places the incidence goes up to 90 per cent. Sometimes malaria sufferers are so sick they cannot get up from their earthen beds or their charpoy cots. For weeks and months they may be weak and apathetic, capable of working only an hour or two a day. Yet malaria is unnecessary in the modern world. With the training of control teams, and with D.D.T. and a minimum of equipment, the job of wiping it out can be, and in a number of places has been, done.

The elimination of malaria used to involve trying to prevent the Anopheles mosquito from breeding by spreading oil on ponds and swamps or else by draining away all standing water, either of which was a tremendous task. In recent years, the development of the technique of residual spraying with D.D.T. has made the job much more manageable. With knapsack-type hand pumps, a solution of D.D.T. is simply sprayed on the interior surfaces of all the houses of a village, and presto! no new cases of malaria appear. The technique is based on the fundamental fact that it takes two bites—about ten days or more apart—for the female Anopheles mosquito to transmit malaria. (Contrary to popular impression, she does not bring it with her from the swamps.) And the technique works because of two peculiar habits the Anopheles has: she tends to fly around and bite only at night, when people are in their houses, and once she has bitten, she likes to sit down on the nearest surface and digest her meal. If the surface has been sprayed with D.D.T. within four months, that is the end of Mrs. Anopheles. Thus, even though the person bitten may have malaria, the disease goes no further.

Results with this method have been spectacular. In parts of Iran, where three-quarters of the babies contracted malaria within the first year of their lives, that proportion has been reduced in two seasons almost to zero. Even those people who already had malaria have experienced great relief, because they have not been reinfected and the attacks of the disease have become less frequent and less acute.

In many of these communities, grown men and women had had malaria since before they could remember. They literally could not conceive how they would feel without it. With release from the disease, they experience *joie de vivre* for the first time. Life takes on a wholly new meaning.

It was such a feeling of ecstasy, I believe, that prompted an Iranian farmer in a village east of Teheran to make a moving little speech to me in the summer of 1952. Various kinds of activities were going on in his village, with the assistance of the Near East Foundation working under a T.C.A. contract. A new well had been dug; vegetable gardens were being grown; adult literacy classes were under way. But, best of all, malaria had been brought under control. As the American visitor was being shown through the vegetable garden, the farmer rushed up, pulled off his hat, and said, in Farsi: "We were dead, and now we are alive."

Probably nothing that Point 4 has done in Iran has had a greater impact on the people of that country than the malaria control program, carried on in cooperation with the local Health Ministry officials and with experts from W.H.O. In 1952 over 20 per cent of the country's population was given protection from malaria through residual spraying. The village people caught on quickly and, when the teams arrived with equipment and D.D.T., went to work themselves, after a brief demonstration, to do the actual spraying. After the job was completed, big blue stencil marks were prominently applied on the outer walls of the village, bearing the Point 4 insignia in Farsi and giving the date when the spraying was carried out. All over Iran one saw those symbols of progress and of international cooperation.

Successful malaria control demonstrations have also been carried out, for example, in Peru, Brazil, Indo-China and Indonesia. In India, a project carried out under W.H.O. leadership has shown that whole areas which had been virtually abandoned because of malaria could be re-settled and restored to productive use through the modern method of control. Centuries ago the *terai*, a broad plain along the edge of the Himalayas, was a populated and fertile country, but through faulty methods of irrigation it became waterlogged and intensely malarial. Most of the people were driven out and the terai became jungle land largely inhabited by tigers and other wild animals. It was referred to as having a deadly climate. In May, 1949, the Indian Government, recognizing the potentialities of the terai as a food-growing area, asked for help from the

United Nations. A team consisting of a Greek malariologist trained at Johns Hopkins and an English public health nurse went to work, assisted by Indian personnel, and with necessary supplies and equipment furnished by the United Nations International Children's Fund (U.N.I.C.E.F.). In this area, the people were suspicious and were afraid the spray would poison them and their animals. Their confidence had first to be won by providing curative treatment to sick children here and there. And then there was an unexpected difficulty created by the villagers' custom of replastering their houses every so often, which meant that they had to be resprayed. Nevertheless, within two years the incidence of malaria had dropped sharply, and by 1951, F.A.O. was invited in to lead the work of building up food production in the area. As of 1953, resettlement of the terai was proceeding apace.[1]

In 1953, also, T.C.A.'s program for India included a big chunk for a country-wide malaria control program that was aimed to wipe out the disease in that huge country by 1956. In addition to supplying large quantities of D.D.T., the United States would be helping the Indian Government to organize and administer such a vast undertaking. The chances that the tricky problems of Centre-State relationships in such a program could be solved were enhanced by the fact that in 1953, for the first time, Dr. Estella Ford Warner of the United States Public Health Service had managed to bring health officials of the Centre and the States together in a joint conference to discuss their mutual problems instead of operating as if separated from each other by an insurmountable wall.

If this one problem of malaria could be licked in India, it would provide tens of millions of country people with a feeling that they were making progress under a free government.

Followers of Chic Sale

Most of us, being somewhat coprologically minded, tend to grin at any mention of privies. Even those shirt-sleeve diplomats who are engaged in promoting the use of sanitary privies in underdeveloped countries are no exception.

In Costa Rica, the health servicio, under the direction of a solid-citizen American named Paul Fox, is running an efficient "privy plant" for the manufacture of wood and concrete latrine covers. The two-seater manufactured at the privy plant is an intriguing two-level job known as the "mother-daughter model." It is painted battleship gray, is equipped with hinged seat tops and wire-mesh-covered ventilators, and fits neatly on top of the standard square concrete slab which in turn fits over the latrine hole. Offered at an attractive price, this model is selling like hot cakes in Costa Rica, and the plant can't keep up with the demand. The privies so equipped are known far and wide as "fox-holes," and Mr. Fox doesn't seem to mind.[2]

Whether privies are funny or not, the fact is that the usual methods of sewage disposal in the underdeveloped areas are a constant menace to the health of the people, and the use of sanitary latrines represents a big step in the right direction. In the Middle East, where toilet-seats are unknown even in all but the fanciest hotels, Point 4 does not go in for anything as elaborate as Mr. Fox's "mother-daughter models." But it is important that people be taught to dig their latrine pits deep enough and not too close to a well, and also to keep them covered against flies. The simplest type of latrine top, which can be made in quantity very cheaply, is a concrete slab about four feet square, with a hole in the center which itself can be readily covered. In some of the villages of Iran where the Near East Foundation has been working, such sanitary privies have been installed in the outer courtyard of every house.

Point 4 has embarked on its most extensive privy program in Egypt, where hundreds of hand-operated augers have been brought in to stimulate the drilling of deep latrine pits. To be successful the project will require an intensive educational effort, and some of the public health experts are frankly skeptical, for the fellaheen are often capricious and sometimes seemingly perverse. In several villages of the Nile Delta area, for example, $30,000 steel-tower water tanks stand virtually unused by the villagers, because the Egyptian Government which built them failed to provide piping to bring the water nearer to the village homes. Although the fellaheen understand vaguely about the value of using sanitary water, they prefer to use the canal water which is convenient rather than to carry water a half-mile or so from the tank.

Health Education Is Basic

Any one who has traveled in the Middle East or Asia can testify to the prevalence of intestinal bugs of one sort or another. In Cairo it is "Gyppy tummy," in Amman it is the "Jordan jumps," in Iraq it is "Baghdad belly," in China it used to be the "Yangtze rapids." Usually, these pet names cover a variety of troubles, most of them related to one form or another of dysentery, but almost without exception they are transmitted through human excreta. Partly, unsanitary water supplies are to blame (sometimes the effect of a filtration plant is nullified by seepage from open sewers into the pipe line). The practice of using night-soil for fertilizer contributes, not because the bacteria get into the vegetables, or other crops—indeed the Allahabad Agricultural Institute in India uses untreated sewage to irrigate its own experimental gardens and orchards—but because the contaminated outer surfaces of the vegetables, etc., are not properly washed or peeled. Perhaps most serious of all is the complete absence of toilet paper or any substitute: the left hand is commonly used instead, and the fact that only the right hand is supposed to be used for eating does not wholly solve the problem.

Although these intestinal diseases are most unpleasant, they are not generally dangerous for visitors who can afford the modern drugs, but they are seriously debilitating for the local people who suffer from them almost constantly, in one form or another. The attack upon them must be two-pronged: certain essential, if rudimentary, improvements must be made in sanitary facilities, and a few basic principles of health education must be effectively communicated to the people.

The Point 4 team in Iran, for example, is moving vigorously ahead on both fronts. On the physical side, deep tube wells have been dug and equipped with diesel pumps in a number of villages. Typically, the pump is operated for an hour or two a day by a village cooperative, allowing the people to fill their vessels, and supplying water for the all-important community center: the village bath. In most of these villages, even polluted water was so scarce that the bath, a large square tub set in the floor of a super-heated underground room, could be filled only once or twice a year. As the villagers themselves said with a wry grin, they would change the water when they could shovel it out. With the water from tube wells, it is possible to persuade the villagers to change over to a shower-type bath, and a number have been built, with the villagers themselves providing the labor.

In addition, Point 4 in Iran has materially assisted the city of Teheran to install a water treatment plant. As late as 1953, Teheran, although a beautiful city with broad streets and fine white buildings, was still using open gutters, called jubes, as a water supply system; by the time the water reached the lower end of the city, it was brown and foul with refuse and sewage, yet one could see women filling their pots with it for household use. By 1953, an underground piping system was almost complete, but the city had no money for a filtration plant. T.C.A. provided the needed funds. In smaller towns also, T.C.A. sanitary engineers have helped local officials to construct simple water supply systems, through providing them with designs and supervising the work.[3]

Far more important fundamentally than any physical improvements has been the effort to teach Iranians basic principles of public health. In this field, the training techniques of learning by doing and physical demonstration are often not practicable, and the technicians must turn to the various audio-visual training aids, such as films, film strips, posters, cartoon books, etc. A film-making team from Syracuse University has been in Iran since early 1952, making a series of movies with local people as actors and, of course, with Farsi sound track. In the summer of 1952, I witnessed a typical showing in a village about 40 miles from Isfahan, the ancient Persian capital. A gasoline-driven generator provided power for the portable projector, and the image was cast on a screen set up against the outside of the village wall. Some five hundred people sat on the hard-packed ground, the women all together at one side, and paid rapt attention to films on locust control and on the dangers of contaminated water. Doubtless many of the villagers had never seen a moving picture before, and the showing was obviously a great event. The two members of the projector team, both Iranian, explained the films before and after and, at the end of the evening, promised to be back in a few weeks with another pair of films. In the meantime, they said, they would be visiting other villages in the area.

Early in 1953, the T.C.A. health team in the region north of the Elburz Mountains along the Caspian Sea reported a tremendous interest in such showings, and asked Teheran headquarters for eleven projector units, and twenty-two film strip units, capable of being operated from a jeep battery. As an example of how even the most difficult ideas are conveyed by films and then passed on, the chief of the team cited the case of a village woman near Babolsar who had indicated to a group of Point 4 trained midwives that she had learned about microbes from her husband after he had seen the film "Care and Maintenance of a Village Home" in another village.

Public health nurses being almost entirely lacking in Iran, an effort has been made to train promising young girls to serve as health visitors. They can provide some care and assistance, for example, to young mothers, but more importantly they act as conduits of knowledge to the village people. One horrible practice which they can discourage, for example, is that of applying an ointment called *khakastar* to a newborn baby's umbilicus. The ointment is commonly a mixture of kerosene, flour and ashes. Since the usual household fuel is dried animal dung, as often as not the imperfectly consumed ashes contain the germ of tetanus.

Other methods of health education are through the schools—the teacher training program in Iran is touched on in the next chapter—and through the establishment of health centers, which can communicate ideas at the same time that they provide treatment, inoculations, etc. In the village of Dastgerd, not far from Isfahan, I attended the opening of such a center, which had been built by the local people, along with a new school, and furnished with basic equipment by Point 4. The center contained a simple house and office for a *behtar,* a man with medical training but not quite a doctor, and would serve as headquarters for the local health visitors. Several hundred men and boys crowded into the courtyard for the ceremony, and as it proceeded a number of women and girls appeared also, jammed together on a little porch, pulling their shawls tightly around their heads, and generally trying to be inconspicuous. The villagers had set out a row of chairs for the dignitaries and a big table laden with fruit and cakes, which the beautiful black eyes of the children scarcely left. There were several speeches by Point 4 people, as was expected, and then a man rose to speak for the village, a teacher in Teheran who had come home for the ceremony. He expressed first the wonder of the villagers that Americans should come such a long way to help them, and then gave his own version of what the Point 4 program was and why the United States was carrying it on, not as charity but as a neighborly helping hand. Finally, he spoke of the pride of the village in what had been accomplished, and of the love they felt for their new friends. It was a moving and a humbling experience to hear him.

To supplement the health centers which can only be launched slowly, the Point 4 team in Iran has also been using three specially equipped buses as mobile health units. Some Point 4 health experts question the long-range usefulness of such mobile units because, of necessity, they can do little to encourage the growth of indigenous local institutions, but there is no question that they are preventing disease and building good will for the United States. In one of his reports Bill Warne, T.C.A.'s Country Director in Iran, described as follows a visit he had made to inspect the operations of a mobile health unit in a remote part of the country:

"We approached the village of Khoshkrood after night had fallen, at the end of a four-hour ride from Teheran. We were met on the road more than a kilometer from the village by several hundred men led by mayors. In the biting cold, lighted only by the stars and a few lanterns, the men and boys were drawn up in ranks on either side of the road. We were escorted between the lines to resounding cheers, and despite our ardent protests two sheep were sacrificed and their blood spread across our paths to expiate the evil eye. We walked into town with the mayors—the Kadkhodas —with the villagers following.

"As we approached the village, we came upon the women and children, and additional sacrifices were made, again against our protests. The cheer, now familiar to us was *Astle Charom*—Point 4! The only illumination in the scattered cluster of mud huts was the lanterns in our procession and, deep in the center of the village, a half-dozen electric bulbs powered by the generator of our mobile health unit. It seemed that virtually every living soul who was not bedridden was out in the bitter night to greet us.

"We met with the regional health team and the seven Iranians who manage the mobile unit. They reported that the impoverished village had been suffering from a typhoid epidemic since early December. Apparently an ancient subterranean umbar, the only water source, is contaminated. The young Iranian doctor, Akbar Roboobi, said that more than six hundred of the thousand inhabitants had been vaccinated against typhoid, three hundred persons against smallpox, and three hundred children against diphtheria. More than two hundred ill persons had been brought from sixty-one other villages, some as far as sixty kilometers, for there is no other health facility in the area."

Warne ended his account with the statement: "Again I had the feeling that I gained in the trip to the Bakhtiari country, that Point 4 is the hope of rural Iran. If they could share such experiences as this trip, the American people would surely feel that their bread, cast upon the troubled waters of Iran, is being returned tenfold."

The health problem of Iran is enough to discourage anyone but the hardy Iranians, Americans and others who are working at it. In addition to malaria and the various dysenteries, there is widespread trachoma and tuberculosis, neither of which can be prevented or cured by any simple method. Respiratory troubles caused by the excessive dust, and infectious hepatitis are common and have afflicted several members of the Point 4 staff. In some sections, there is a dreadful disease called dracunculosis, caused by a parasite that first inhabits a tiny crustacean called cyclops, which itself lives in rain-water cisterns. In the human body the parasite becomes a worm, sometimes as much as a yard long, which feeds on the flesh and finally breaks through the skin. It must be treated very carefully because if it dies, it contaminates the body of its human host. Whenever the protruding worm contacts water, it emits germs which are eaten by the cyclops to renew the cycle. An Iranian doctor working with T.C.A., who contracted the disease, recovered only after six weeks of special care and several operations. The only way to wipe out dracunculosis is to destroy the cyclops by substituting sanitary wells for the usual rain-water cisterns or umbars. Add to these plagues occasional epidemics of typhoid, diphtheria, typhus, and others, and you have indeed a grim picture. And it is a picture, which with variations, can be duplicated in most of the underdeveloped areas.

Point 4 teams can make a start. They can demonstrate the value of clean water and of sanitary sewage disposal, and they can give a few people the rudiments of health education. But more is required. Not only must general levels of living be raised through activities in other fields of development, but indigenous health services have to be developed and maintained by the countries themselves.

The Record of S.E.S.P. in Brazil

The development of such local services has been, at least in the postwar years, the main objective of the I.I.A.A. in its health programs in eighteen countries of Latin America. Although outstanding successes were scored in Bolivia, Chile, Ecuador and Haiti, among others, perhaps the finest example of institutional development was in Brazil.

Shortly after the American Foreign Ministers, meeting in Rio in January, 1942, had recommended a cooperative attack on the hemisphere's health problems, the governments of the United States and Brazil agreed to form the *Servicio Especial de Saúde Pública,* known as S.E.S.P. One of the first projects launched was an effort to protect the health of laborers in work camps along the Vitoria-Minas Railroad in the Rio Doce valley. The railroad was badly needed to transport iron ore and other strategic materials to the coast, and health conditions in the camps and in the towns and villages of the valley were appalling. From 84

per cent to 98 per cent of the people examined were in-
fested with worms of one type or another, while leprosy,
schistosomiasis (Bilharzia), dysentery, tuberculosis, tropical
ulcer, yaws and malnutrition were all taking a toll. In
some areas the incidence of malaria was over 50 per cent.

Starting with the camps and then carrying on in the
towns and villages, S.E.S.P. launched a broad-scale offensive, concentrating on three types of activities: the development of safe water supplies, the construction of sewage
disposal facilities, and the establishment of health centers
staffed with public health physicians, nurses, sanitary engineers, and sanitary inspectors. The result was a speedy
and dramatic drop in the death rate and in the incidence
of disease. After the war, the program was continued and
expanded to include the completion of one hospital and
the construction of another, to be operated in conjunction
with two of the health centers.

S.E.S.P. undertook a similar program in the Amazon
region, with headquarters at Belém. Doctors, nurses, and
nurses' aids traveled by launch, serving forty-one of the one
hundred-odd towns in the Amazon Valley. Health centers
were constructed and manned, as well as a number of
auxiliary posts, and in isolated communities a few hospitals have been built. Over a period of ten years, death
rates dropped as much as 50 per cent. In the town of
Cametá, for example, the death rate as of 1942 was an
appalling two hundred out of every thousand (including
infants, of course). By 1949, it was down to seventy per
thousand. Even though this is still seven times the highest
death rate of any of our states, it is the trend that counts.

The nurses' aides, or *visitadores,* play a key role in all of
this, giving pre- and post-partem advice and help to
mothers, organizing health clubs along 4-H lines, and in-

sisting that sick people visit the health center clinic. In 1951, a visitor to Cametá reported on the day's work of a tiny eighty-nine-pound *visitadora* named Maria José Ribeiro as follows:

> "By noon, Maria José had checked the health of sixteen people; collected samples of urine, blood and spittle for laboratory analysis; checked the feeding of four infants and the pulse and temperature of their mothers; and given helpful information to a young wife pregnant for the first time. Nor was this a cue to call it a day. In the afternoon, Maria José, acting as clinic receptionist, helped examine eighteen patients and wrote out the doctor's instructions for them, promising to explain them on her next visit for those who could not read. When I left, she was planning, for the next day, her weekly class for midwives, and, for the day after that, her talk to the juvenile health club."

Since the beginning, S.E.S.P.'s personnel has been mostly Brazilian. Over the years, the degree of United States supervision has steadily lessened, while a total of 2,800 Brazilian doctors, engineers, nurses and other health workers have received training in Brazil and 250 in the United States. As of 1953, the Amazon operation was exclusively Brazilian, and there were only 20 North Americans in all of S.E.S.P., as against some 1,500 Brazilians. Even the Superintendent of the servicio is a Brazilian, operating under the joint direction of the Minister of Health and Dr. Eugene Campbell, I.I.A.A.'s able chief of field party. S.E.S.P. personnel are rightly proud of the fact that a former Superintendent, Dr. Marcolino G. Candau, is now Director General of the World Health Organization.

Even more striking is the trend in the rate of contributions by the two governments. Under the initial agreement, the United States contributed $5 million to Brazil's $450,000. By 1952, the proportions were more than reversed. Brazil was putting up about $5 million a year, as against a United States contribution of $300,000. And this does not even take account of the cost of maintaining the many water supply and other projects which have been turned over to federal, state or local authorities to operate on their own.

This has become the Brazilians' own program. The United States' help is almost incidental. Yet on every structure that S.E.S.P. puts up goes a bronze plaque, reading: "This building—the symbol of a Good Neighbor Health Policy—was constructed by the United States of Brazil and the United States of America."

The question might well be asked: "Why should Brazil want to continue S.E.S.P. on this basis? If the United States contribution is so inconsequential, why shouldn't they take over the whole operation themselves?" The answer is twofold: they realize that the American personnel in key positions can still contribute a great deal, and they also realize that, as long as S.E.S.P. is operated on a joint United States-Brazilian basis, it can be kept free from the interference of local politicians.[4]

The Temptation of Do-Goodism

Shirt-sleeve diplomats never like being called "do-gooders," and usually they don't deserve the name. But sometimes they do, for sometimes they succumb to the temptation of doing things for people instead of helping them to do things for themselves.

Take the case of a doctor, imbued with the spirit of Hippocrates, who has stimulated the establishment of a health center clinic in a remote Latin American town. Day after day he sees the pathetic lines of people, many of them from distant villages, waiting for badly needed medical care. His native assistants are willing enough, but they are not fully trained, and they are overloaded with work. The doctor knows that, if he leaves, the clinic's work will not be done as well, and it may even suffer from political interference. In principle, the doctor recognizes perfectly well that Point 4's emphasis must be on training and demonstration, rather than on operations. But in practice, he finds it awfully hard to live up to that principle.

This natural humanitarian tendency is one that the administrators of a Point 4 program have to fight against constantly. Because most of the Latin American programs were started to get a job done, rather than as training and demonstration programs, the problem in that area has been particularly acute. The process of handing over activities to the local governments, and the stimulating of new projects, has not been as rapid in all cases as it should have been. But the Washington headquarters, spurred on by the propinquity of Congress, has been pressing, and the trend has been in the right direction.

Another type of temptation which has to be constantly resisted—particularly, but not only, in the health field—is that of promoting the establishment of institutions which are beyond the capacity of a country to maintain. Some of the hospitals built in Latin America in the early years of the Institute's programs have never been fully utilized, either because trained personnel were not available or because the country could not afford to operate them.

Over-enthusiasm can also lead to mistakes of a different kind, if planning is not sufficiently foresighted and does not take into account all the relevant factors in a given situation. A story from Puerto Rico illustrates the point. At one stage in the program of rural electrification, the country people were encouraged to buy small electric refrigerators as a hygienic measure against food spoilage. An epidemic of undulant fever was the surprising result. It turned out that the rural people had been used to boiling their milk to keep it from going sour, but had assumed that it was unnecessary to continue doing so once they had a refrigerator. Of course, the milk had been contaminated, and chilling it preserved the germs as well as the milk.[5]

There is a third type of temptation to be "do-gooders" which affects the doctors and nurses engaged in international development work. Because of their training and their natural instincts, they are inclined to believe that all types of public health work are beneficial. A joint T.C.A.-W.H.O. conference held in Geneva in February, 1953, attended by technicians from all parts of the underdeveloped areas, resolved as follows:

> "*All* health work, whatever its nature, contributes to a greater or lesser degree to social and economic development. The effect may be promptly apparent and readily measurable in terms of economic development, or it may not be apparent except after the passage of a considerable length of time and even then difficult to relate directly to social and economic progress. Nevertheless a favorable effect always is produced by any well planned and successfully implemented project in the field of public health."

Such a statement is, to say the least, controversial. While it accurately reflects the point of view of W.H.O., there have been those in the United States Government agencies who would not agree with all of it. They would argue that, in a country where food supply is a big problem, and especially where serious overpopulation exists, health programs which add to the population are not necessarily helpful to the country's development, even long-range. While work in the maternity and child health field is tremendously appealing on humanitarian grounds and may contribute greatly to overall progress because of its morale-boosting effect, it would seem that programs which concentrate on building up the health and stamina of productive adults ought to be given first priority.

The scarcity of trained personnel, especially public health physicians, is particularly acute in the health field. Most of the personnel of the right sort are already at work doing vital jobs for the United States or state health services. While an arrangement for borrowing personnel from certain state services has been worked out, that arrangement is susceptible of misunderstanding locally, because it tends to suggest that the people are not so badly needed in the states if they can be spared even temporarily. No matter what devices may be tried, it will always be true that there will not be enough United States doctors, nurses, or sanitary engineers to carry out even a minimum Point 4 program in the health field. That being the case, it seems obvious that a scale of priorities should be agreed upon and observed.

According to the constitution of W.H.O., "Health is a state of complete physical, mental and social well-being and not merely the absence of disease and infirmity." In that sense, all of the various phases of the Point 4 program contribute to raising the health standards of the peoples of the underdeveloped areas not only because they help these people achieve better living conditions, but also because they give them that priceless ingredient of health: hope. The Iranian farmer who made the moving little speech about being alive instead of dead was still living under conditions of hardship almost inconceivable to Americans. But for the first time in his life he had hope that, by his own efforts, and with some help from outside, he could go on improving his lot bit by bit.

7. Education for Life and Work

IN ISRAEL they will tell you that a Yemenite Jew, if he can read at all, often prefers to read upside-down or sideways. The reason is that, during the long centuries of the Yemenites' isolation in the southern tip of the Arabian peninsula, their copies of the scriptures became very scarce. The few children who learned to read had to sit in a circle around the book, each one always at the same point of the compass. Thus they became accustomed to reading at all sorts of unusual angles.

Considering the slavery and other terrible hardships the Yemenite Jews had to live through, it is remarkable that they were able to preserve their spiritual heritage at all. Had they not clung to it and kept their identity as Jews, they would not have been brought to Israel by an airborne trip surely no less miraculous to them than the Exodus from Egypt was to the followers of Moses. At the same time, one might argue that the Yemenite Jews would have been better off if, in their educational methods and in other ways, they had paid more attention to matters practical. For the Yemenites when they were rescued were a very primitive people indeed. Although learning of a sort had been infinitely precious to them, they were by present-day standards almost wholly uneducated.

Like the Yemenite Jews, most peoples of the underdeveloped areas have a cherished cultural tradition, which has been preserved and passed on from generation to generation by the elite few who learned to read and write. As was the case in the industrialized West not so long ago, education was not intended to meet the practical, day-to-day needs of ordinary mortals, but was designed to train scholars. The function of the scholars was to pass on their learning. They were not expected to soil their hands with menial work.

While the notion that education was something for the elite has passed out of the picture almost everywhere, it has left a painful heritage. Most of the underdeveloped countries do not have enough schools or teachers. The teachers they do have were trained in the old authoritarian methods, in which the heart of the educational process was learning by rote a lot of more or less incomprehensible material. Perhaps most harmful of all, the idea that an educated person should not do physical labor has persisted. To become a white collar man sitting at a desk is a dazzling objective. Even in the field of agriculture, if a college graduate has to leave the capital city at all, which is rare, he is likely to have an assistant with him who will do whatever touching of the soil, the plants, or the animals may be required.

Patterns like this are not easy to change. A country's educational system lies perilously close to the heart of its culture, and criticism of it by outsiders is not always welcome.[1] Yet the fact remains that ignorance is the nub of the whole problem facing Point 4. In some countries illiteracy is appallingly high, ranging up to 90 per cent or more; for the underdeveloped areas as a whole the rate is estimated at from 50 per cent to 70 per cent. Even more widespread is the lack of any familiarity whatever with the most rudimentary principles of science as applied to everyday life.

Moving slowly, with a high degree of caution and tact, it is possible to attack some of these problems.

Basic Education in the Andes

Of the pure- or nearly pure-blood descendants of the American continents' aboriginal inhabitants, probably more than two-thirds live on the high Andean plateaus of Bolivia, Peru and Ecuador. It is in this area, where the Indians have lost their ancestors' skills but modern civilization has not yet arrived, that the I.I.A.A. has concentrated a large part of its activity in the field of primary education.

When a highly trained educator from the United States starts to work in the Andes, he finds that his approach toward the problems of education requires a lot of readjustment. Dr. Willfred Mauck, former director of I.I.A.A.'s education division, described the first visit of such a technician to a rural school in a remote area, accompanied by a representative of the local Ministry of Education, in these words:

> "In the middle of a stony field stands a small adobe, tile-roofed building. Our specialist is led to a low doorway, and peers inside, searching the darkness, for his body is shutting off most of the only source of light. 'But where are the windows?'
>
> " 'There are none. We have been waiting for you to suggest where and how they should be cut through.'
>
> " 'But someone has taken out all the furniture except that rude desk. I suppose that is because they have not yet laid the floor?'

" 'No, sir. There is no other furniture, and the bare earth is the only floor used hereabouts. The children sit on that.'

" 'Just on the floor? But, aside from their health, how can they see the blackboard from there?'

" 'There is no blackboard, sir.'

" 'No blackboard! Then we must buy one at once.'

" 'There is no money for blackboards. You must show us how to make one out of local materials.'

" 'Oh! And how can children, sitting on the floor, in this semi-darkness, read their books?'

" 'The teacher reads the book, sir. All the children have to do is to copy in their notebooks what the teacher tells them to.'

"And so it goes. And on the return journey a bewildered 'specialist' in modern classroom instruction begins to adjust his ideas. From now on, he is a specialist in school construction, furniture making, textbook writing, curriculum construction, and sanitation, as well as in teaching methods."

Obviously a handful of United States technicians cannot themselves begin to work directly in the thousands of villages where such schools are the only source of education. The I.I.A.A.'s educational servicios have emphasized teacher-training as the key to the problem, and have sought to improve both the quality of the training and the quantity, by assisting in the construction of new normal schools. In the rural areas themselves, they have used the nuclear school system, concentrating their efforts on a few selected schools so as to make them centers of educational improvement for the surrounding regions. The rural teachers are shown how to use simple teaching aids, such as alphabet blocks and pictures, and how to conduct classroom discussions. They are taught the elements of gardening, home economics and personal hygiene—enough to pass on this new practical learning to their pupils. In addition, the adults of each community are encouraged to take an interest in their school, to improve its facilities and buildings, and to participate actively in its life.

Dr. Mauck tells of an unannounced visit to a nuclear school in an Indian village near Lake Titicaca on the *altiplano* of Bolivia. A few months before the visit the school had been a sorry affair, poorly attended both because of crowding and because of the parents' feeling that "since the youngsters were learning little that could be useful to them in later life, they might better be at home learning the tasks of farming and homemaking."

"My first impression," says Dr. Mauck, "was that the whole community had gathered at the school." In addition to the dozens of children, there were adults standing by the doors and windows, listening to a discussion on nutrition. The teacher described how parents and children had pitched in to install windows, paint walls, build adobe benches and desks, and make a blackboard by covering a smooth adobe surface with lampblack and eggwhite. In addition, there were new buildings, a row of sanitary latrines, a school garden, and a kitchen for hot lunches. Some of the food was purchased by the servicio, but most of it was grown in the garden or brought in by the children.

Besides the work at the school itself, teams of children had been organized under the leadership of a Parents' Auxiliary to help people in the community improve their homes in simple ways. Cooking fires had been moved from main rooms, which had no outlet for smoke, to sheds built against outside walls; pigs and chickens likewise had been moved outside; niches had been cut in adobe walls for food storage off the floor; latrines had been dug.

The *alcalde* of the village told Dr. Mauck that at first he had been suspicious of the work "because it seemed dangerous to meddle with the ancient ways of doing things," but that now he was most enthusiastic and "wished to be considered a colleague in the program." At the end of the visit, the dignified old Indian said in Quechua, with a twinkle in his eye, "I was born in an evil time, as you can see. When I was young, I had to be silent and listen to my elders, and I longed for the day when I should be grown and able to speak with all authority. Now I am old, and lo! I must be silent and listen to my children." [2]

There is no question about the eagerness of the Indian children for learning—the new way. In the old mountain city of Cuzco, Peru, in March, 1953, I visited a demonstration school being held during the summer vacation period as a part of a training course for rural schoolteachers and supervisors of the high Sierra district. The pupils of the demonstration school, bright, appealing kids with flashing black eyes, were usually brought into Cuzco from the villages of the surrounding area by bus or truck. One youngster of about seven, I was told, had been picked up by the truck a few days before, several miles from his home, trudging down the mountain road toward Cuzco. When asked why he was walking, he replied that he had dreamed the truck was not coming, so he had started out before dawn to be sure not to miss a day of school.

Uses of a Volley Ball

In the Middle East, Point 4's most extensive program in elementary education is in Iran. An incident that occurred in its early days is the subject of one of Point 4's classic stories. Stanley Andrews, the lanky ex-farm editor from Arkansas who made a worthy successor to Dr. Bennett as Administrator of T.C.A., likes to tell it, about like this:

A gentleman from the T.C.A. staff in Iran went down to one of these villages one day and began to talk to the village seniors about the possibility of a school. The senior said: we have no buildings, we have no money, we have no teachers—there's no hope of a school here. The T.C.A. fellow said: "Well, if we cannot have a school, then let's play volley ball." He went to his jeep and pulled a volley ball out of the back, and the net, and set up the volley ball court and got the little boys out in that village to play around with that ball a little bit. And remember this: in most of the villages out there, little boys don't play. This fellow said: "I'm going to leave this volley ball here and this net, and I'm coming back next week to visit you." And he came back the next week, and they had quite a bit of excitement with the volley ball game, and the seniors had come out to watch the kids play. It didn't take too long before the seniors said, "Well, maybe we can find something. We can do something about a school." They found an old barn. The United States taxpayers bought them lime and cement and some wire glass windows and a door and some chalk and a blackboard, and got one of the teachers that had been trained to come down and take over that school. Well, to make a long story short, there are thirty-five little Iranian boys going to school and even four little girls—and remember, girls don't go to school in the Middle East. They've added a room onto this barn—which is now a school—so the little girls can go to school.

In the Middle East, everything is behind a wall. The teacher said: "Here is whitewash. Here is a nice proud building. Let's let the world see it. Let's tear down the wall." That was a real revolution in that particular village. And they tore that wall down; and today if you go down to that particular village, you will see a whitewashed building—the only building in the village that has glass in it. You'll see a teacher going about teaching the people a little about their own country, about their own environment, and about themselves.

As Stanley Andrews goes on to say, this was merely "one

little drop in a great sea of illiteracy," but the drops have been accumulating in Iran, thanks to the extraordinary efforts of a soft-spoken Georgian named Hoyt Turner and his team of educators.

In each of the eight (out of Iran's ten) *ostans* where T.C.A. has regional teams at work, a demonstration school is being established, and efforts are being made to help communities get new schools started and to improve those that already exist. For the first time an in-service teacher training program has been launched. In April of 1952, a group of bright Iranian teachers were brought together at the demonstration school in Teheran for an intensive course in modern educational methods; then these men and women in turn gave the six weeks' course to a total of twelve hundred selected teachers in seven provincial centers. Trouble was predicted, because of the large proportion of teachers supposed to be pro-communist—indeed at the last moment the Ministry of Education got cold feet and wanted to call off the summer schools—but no serious difficulties arose. The enthusiasm of the teachers, most of whom had had only a few years of education themselves, and none of whom had had any later training, was tremendous. They were each given some simple teaching materials, and were taught how to make others; they learned the value of activity lessons, field trips, and organized games. One student-teacher wrote in later:

"The simple practical new method of teaching adopted by you together with your own devotion and the way you explain the lessons in the Summer Short Course classes have revealed to me the moral of a real education. . . . If I say that what I have learned in this short period surpasses everything I had learned in the past years, I am not exaggerating. For the lessons are on the subjects which concern my daily life and it is necessary that everybody should know them."

In February, 1953, a week-long conference was held in Teheran to bring together the Point 4 educators and forty Iranian Ostan Chiefs of Education and chiefs of independent school systems. At a dinner concluding the conference, Iran's Minister of Education, Dr. Azad, called on the Iranian personnel to cooperate fully with Point 4 and requested T.C.A. in turn "to give all the assistance possible to the Ministry in the development of a modern educational system." This at a time when, to read some of the more sensational news reports from Iran, one would have supposed that the Iranian people were hostile to America and to Point 4.

Training Craftsmen and Technicians

Whereas the relationship of primary education to economic development is long-range and not always apparent, in the case of vocational and technical training the connection is immediate and obvious. Moreover, the suspicion of foreign "interference" does not raise its ugly head as often, and the tricky problems of intercultural differences are less troublesome. So it is not surprising that practically all the underdeveloped countries have asked for help along these lines, in one form or another.

The type of program differs from country to country, of course, in accordance with needs. In Brazil, which is industrializing rapidly, there is a shortage of welders, machinists, electricians, and the like. A servicio was organized in 1946 to promote industrial education and has established twenty-three vocational schools.[3]

In Ethiopia, which is at a much earlier stage of development, T.C.A. has provided equipment and technical guidance for a handicrafts school and a trades school, both in Addis Ababa. As mentioned earlier, a team from Oklahoma A. & M. has successfully launched an agricultural secondary school at Jimma, 175 miles southwest of Addis. The school is thriving, in spite of such minor difficulties as two knife fights among the students, and the fact that the school yard could not be crossed safely for a while because the Ethiopian honey bees housed in a cluster of demonstration hives turned out to be far more ferocious than the Oklahoma variety.

Libya, a newly independent country with staggering economic problems and only a handful of native college graduates among its entire population, needs people trained in virtually every kind of skill, including stenography and bookkeeping. Accordingly, in 1950, U.N.E.S.C.O. established a Clerical and Technical Training Centre in Tripoli, to which T.C.A. has contributed such humble but essential supplies as ruled paper, erasers and typewriters.

And so on, literally around the world. Boys and girls are being trained to become carpenters, metalworkers, automobile mechanics, radio technicians, plumbers, and all the other skilled artisans that developing economies need. For the most part the American technicians are not doing the teaching themselves. They are training new teachers and helping those already at work to plan their courses and to make them more effective. And the United States, jointly with the host governments, is providing equipment of all kinds, with which teachers and students can work.

So far as higher education is concerned, the emphasis in the United States programs has again been almost entirely on the practical side—training technicians in those fields which are closely related to Point 4's principal activities.

Substantial assistance has been given to Burma, for example, in the development of a new medical school to help meet a critical shortage of doctors. Nursing schools have been established in Brazil, Panama and elsewhere. Part of the Oklahoma A. & M. project in Ethiopia is to build up a College of Agricultural and Mechanical Arts similar to our own land grant colleges, and in several other countries established agricultural colleges are receiving assistance.

Since local facilities for technical training at the college and post-graduate levels are still inadequate in virtually every underdeveloped country, the United States Government has awarded thousands of grants to individuals for training in the United States or at institutions such as the American University of Beirut and the University of Puerto Rico. In the winter of 1952-53, for example, T.C.A. was paying some or all the expenses of over nine hundred trainees in the United States, most of whom were given a short period of instruction at an American college or university and also an opportunity to observe at first hand private or governmental activities in their special fields.[4]

The program of providing training in the United States has many disadvantages, as American officials have been well aware. Some of the trainees become so captivated by America that they want desperately to remain, and return to their own countries unhappy. Others, because their dark skins have exposed them to insulting treatment or for other reasons not always ascertainable, acquire a real hatred for this country. Another group, overwhelmed by the industrial might of the United States and its fantastically high standard of living, go home in deep despair, feeling that their countries can never hope to catch up. Finally, there are those who, having returned to their jobs full of enthusiasm about what they have seen in the United States and determined to put it all into effect immediately, get frustrated and discouraged, and turn cynical.

The United States Government has tried to minimize these risks by sending most of the college-age trainees to local or regional institutions, and by bringing to the United States only reasonably mature people, who have had a considerable amount of experience and "on-the-job" training already. The periods of training have been kept short, and most of the grants have been made in connection with going Point 4 projects, on the clear understanding that the trainees would return to work on those projects. In consequence, it is probably fair to say that the great majority of the men and women who have received training in the United States have not only carried home a friendly feeling and a better understanding of America, but have been enabled to put their newly acquired technical knowledge and practical know-how to good use in the development of their own countries. Nevertheless, the United States and United Nations experts are agreed that, as far as possible and to a steadily increasing extent, technical training should be provided not in the United States, but in areas where the conditions more nearly approximate those with which the trainees will be faced in their work.*

In addition to formal courses in local or nearby universities, there is another type of regional training which has

* This conclusion does not apply to the various exchange scholarship and fellowship programs, both governmental and private, under which foreign students and teachers are awarded grants for general courses at American colleges and universities, and vice versa. Here the primary question is not, how best to train technicians to help in the social and economic development of their countries, but rather how to bring about the maximum of international contacts and understanding. The risks of doing more harm than good in individual cases are still substantial—thanks mainly to American provincialism and color prejudice—but they are risks which must be run if the barriers of international suspicion and distrust are ever to be broken down.

great possibilities, so far largely unexplored. As developmental programs achieve success in various countries, they can be used as ideal training grounds for potential technicians from neighboring countries. To a very limited extent, this has already been done. While I was in Costa Rica in February, 1953, six Panamanian agriculturists were in the country, each working with a S.T.I.C.A. regional office, helping out and at the same time learning how Costa Rica's successful extension service was being run. One of the Panamanians was so enthusiastic that he asked if he could come back and spend his vacation in Costa Rica, learning more. Similarly, after a community development program was under way in India, arrangements were made for a group of Pakistani officials who would be working on the same sort of program to visit India and see what the obstacles were and how they were being tackled. The United Nations agencies and the regional international organizations, such as the Organization of American States, are in a peculiarly good position to provide for this sort of cross-fertilization, and have done a considerable amount of it, but more could yet be done.

Are We Stirring Up Trouble?

In the spring of 1953, a Point 4 educational expert on a routine visit to a Middle Eastern school inquired about a particularly noisy group of children on the playground. He was told: "Oh, they are practising at demonstrating."

This little incident points up what is actually a very serious question: how can we be sure that teaching people to read and write, so that they can learn more about the world, is not going to make for greater unrest in the underdeveloped areas, rather than less? During the hearings on the Point 4 program before the House Foreign Affairs Committee in 1952, Representatives Judd of Minnesota and Ribicoff of Connecticut did some sharp probing along these lines which was most uncomfortable for the Executive Branch witnesses. The question will doubtless be raised again, and the advocates of Point 4 cannot simply brush it aside; they must face up to it.

At some future hearing, a colloquy between a Congressman and a bureaucrat on this subject might go like this:

Congressman: You say that one reason for growing restlessness in the underdeveloped areas is that people are beginning to realize how badly off they are compared to people elsewhere?

Bureaucrat: That is correct.

C.: How do the people in the rural areas become aware of those things if they cannot read newspapers and have no radios?

B.: By word of mouth mainly, sir. The restlessness is perhaps more acute in the towns and cities where the means of communication are better.

C.: Now, in your program aren't you trying to improve methods of communication, and to decrease the number of illiterates?

B.: (beginning to squirm) Yes, sir.

C.: Well, then, the more people can read and the more they can learn about the outside world, the more restless and discontented they are going to be. Isn't that true?

B.: I can't deny it, sir, as far as the short run is concerned. But remember that Point 4 isn't purely an anti-illiteracy program. And even if it were, I don't see how we in America could follow a policy of trying to keep people in a state of ignorance everywhere. How could we show so little confidence in the merits of our case—of freedom's case, if I may say so?

C.: Who's asking the questions here, you or me?

B.: You are, Mr. Congressman. I beg your pardon.

C.: All right then. Now, why don't you just cut out this

educational stuff and go on with the agricultural work and the rest?

B.: Because it can't be done that way, sir. The job of Point 4 is basically one of trying to communicate new ideas and new skills to people, and as long as most of them can't read and write, that job is practically impossible. The remedy for the unrest you speak of is not less education, but more economic progress. If through Point 4 we can give people a sense of confidence in their own power to build better lives for themselves, they won't pay much attention to the communist agitators.

C.: According to my information, in the Indian elections of 1952, the communists got the biggest votes in Mysore and Travancore-Cochin, two of the states with the highest literacy rate. What have you got to say about that?

B.: Your information is correct, Mr. Congressman. But it happens those were two of the states with the greatest food shortages also. Moreover, in the winter of 1951-52, virtually no developmental projects had been carried on there. The despair of the people was all the deeper because they had expected that independence would solve all their problems and it hadn't. Recently, things have been improving, and the communists have lost out in a number of local elections. By 1956 the situation should be entirely different —God and the Congress willing.

C.: Young man, Congress may be powerful, but it is not omnipotent.

B.: May I say, sir, that sometimes we in the Executive Branch are not so sure.

8. The Community Development Idea

THERE IS A KIND of peaceful revolution going on in India today and Point 4 had something to do with getting it started.

The philosophy of this revolution is expressed in a little creed which the trainees at a school for "Village Level Workers" near Allahabad worked out for themselves in the summer of 1952. Here is the creed, slightly condensed:

> I believe in village life, that it can be rich, full and wholesome—in village families founded on mutual affection and respect—in village youth in their longings for opportunity and in the fulfillment of their right for trained minds, healthy bodies and clean hearts—in village people in their ability to solve their own problems and in their power to develop their lives—in my own work in the opportunity it affords to be of service to others.
>
> For all men need self-respect, friendship, recognition, opportunity—and therefore in all my work I shall seek at all times to be friendly, honest, sincere, and humble.
>
> I shall with sincerity of purpose work with village men, women and children for better family living, by helping them to make their fields and livestock more productive, their homes more comfortable and beautiful and their community more satisfying.
>
> And because I believe in all these things, and shall to the

best of my ability fulfill them, I am a *Gaon-Sathi* ("Village Companion").

Perhaps of all the less developed countries, India was until very recently the most imbued with the concept that work with the hands was degrading. Their whole caste system was originally based on work specialization, and "the sweepers" were at the bottom of the heap. Moreover, most Indians, like most Asians, Africans, and even Latin Americans, were almost devoid of any feeling of responsibility for the welfare of their fellow human beings outside the family circle. The Hindu teachings, unlike the Judeo-Christian, tended to make people accept life as it was, and not try to improve it. Social consciousness was a rarity.

Mahatma Gandhi stood for something different, and many of his followers have sought to live a life of service. But all during Gandhi's lifetime, except for his last six months, the overriding struggle was to achieve independence. Any effort to better the lives of the masses was secondary and would have to wait.

By the time Chester Bowles got to India as Ambassador in October, 1951, India's independence was four years old and new forces were stirring. The Etawah experiment and other pilot projects had demonstrated that village people could and would change their ways if guided and helped by trained instructors, that they were eager to grow more food, to be free from disease, to educate themselves. The Government of Jawaharlal Nehru was in the process of working out a Five-Year Plan for India's development, a very important objective of which was to increase India's food grain production by 15 per cent or seven million tons a year. The Government had already spent substantial sums on a much publicized Grow More Food Campaign, and as a result there had been a great many memoranda flowing back and forth between the Centre's handsome red sandstone buildings in New Delhi and the various ministries of the twenty-eight state governments. Nothing much had been happening in the fields and villages, however; so far as anyone could tell, the per capita production of food, which had been declining for decades, was still going down, and the prognosis for India's economic ailments was negative. Last but not least, the United States Government had waked up to the fact that India was (a) in trouble, (b) important, and (c) trying to help itself, and therefore T.C.A. was prepared to spend 54 million dollars —over a third of its 1951-52 budget—in the next 8 months to help out.

As Bowles considered these facts, he remembered what Dr. Y. C. James Yen had told him of his work in North China in the twenties and thirties. Starting with the idea of a literacy program, Yen had found that the problems of the Asian farmer were manifold and had to be attacked, not just through adult education, or in any other single way, but by a combination of efforts involving agricultural extension work, public health measures, and local government improvement.[1] Bowles also concluded that whatever was to be done in India had to be done on a vast scale. The time for pilot projects, such as those which the missionary groups in India had been concentrating on for years, was past; if any real impact was to be made on India's problems by the next elections in 1956, not hundreds or thousands, but tens of millions of people had to be affected.

Within a few weeks of Bowles' arrival in India, and after intensive discussions with Prime Minister Nehru and other government leaders, a plan was evolved. Essentially, it was that the Etawah project be duplicated across the face of India. With American help, India would embark on a huge Point 4 program amongst her own village people, communicating to them the knowledge and skills that would enable them to better their own lives.

There followed months of conferences, during which the plan went through a number of variations. An ambitious proposal for building the rural development projects around self-sustaining industrial centers was abandoned as too expensive.[2] Goals and budgets were set up and knocked down by the dozen. But the essential idea remained intact.

Finally, in June of 1952, the governments of India and the United States entered into a formal agreement providing for the launching of what was by far the largest Point 4 undertaking. The agreement contemplated that 55 community development projects—at least one in each of India's 28 states—would be started the first year, each to consist of three "blocks" and to include about 300 villages, 200,000 people and 150,000 acres of land. The United States agreed to put up some 25 million dollars, about 40 per cent of which would go for salaries of United States advisers and for project supplies and equipment, and the rest for related purposes, such as drilled tube wells in the project areas, imports of fertilizer, and imports of steel needed for plows and other agricultural implements. India undertook to pay the equivalent of 72 million dollars in rupees, most of which was needed to pay the salaries and expenses of Indian personnel. The administration of the program was to be entirely in Indian hands, with United States experts acting only as advisers.

Obviously the success or failure of the whole scheme would depend on the quality of the Indian personnel. Since it was impossible to have specialists in the various activities working with all the villages (16,500 the first year), thousands of multi-purpose workers would have to be trained in the essential principles of agriculture, health and education, and in the technique of passing on their knowledge. In each block there would be specially trained supervisors whom the village workers could come to for help and guidance, and at the top, block and project directors.

The Indian Government, T.C.A. and the Ford Foundation all pitched in together on the training job, the Foundation agreeing to pay a substantial share of the rupee costs of the first training centers. In August of 1952, I visited three of the schools, one for village level workers near Allahabad, one for specialists at Bakshi-ka-Talab near Lucknow, and one for the project directors themselves at Nilokheri, north of Delhi. In all three, the spirit of the trainees, and their devotion to the ideal of community improvement through self-help, was inspiring. Many of them had never done a day's manual labor in their lives, but they had quickly adopted the principle that constructive physical work, no matter how unpleasant, was honorable. This was particularly noteworthy among the future project directors, for many of them were members of the elite I.C.S. (Indian Civil Service) with considerable seniority. Yet every morning from six to eight, they were out in the villages, cleaning out wells, putting drains in muddy village lanes, building roads, and rapidly putting blisters on their soft hands.

Indeed, this group criticized their instructors, both Indian and American, for giving them too many lectures and too little practical work in the villages. They recognized the enormity of the gap that separated them from the humble country people, and they were at a loss as to how to bridge it. In some villages we visited, the future directors had been unable to get the local people to participate in what they were doing. The farmers would simply stand by and watch, apparently thinking: "if these strangers from the cities want to break their backs fixing up our village, they can go right ahead, but the whole performance is definitely very odd and we'll have no part of it." The dark eyes of the onlookers would merely widen a trifle when my wife and I ostentatiously carried a few basketfuls of dirt or took turns with a shovel.

It was at the village level workers' school at the Allahabad Agricultural Institute that the students had composed the "Gaon-Sathi's creed." These young people, selected from a large number who had responded to a small newspaper advertisement, were relatively close to the village people in background and had been able rapidly to acquire their friendship and trust. As an experiment, seven married couples were being trained, in addition to the single men. In one village we saw, the couple was living in a house donated by the villagers. It was one of the typical adobe structures, but was spotlessly clean and brightened up so as to make an attractive little dwelling. The man did not specialize in agriculture and the woman in home economics, as one might have supposed; rather, he worked with the village men and she with the women, but they concentrated on the same subjects at the same time.

In all three training centers, the Indian and American instructors stressed over and over again the importance of not trying to push the villagers too fast, of working within the framework of their cultural patterns, of finding out who the leaders were in each case and winning their confidence first. The village workers, being Indian, would not have as difficult a time as foreign missionaries had had, but in view of the intricacy of the village social structure and the strength of family and village solidarity against all outsiders, their job would be hard enough.[3] There was some difference of opinion as to whether the initial emphasis should be on agricultural improvements, literacy, home improvements, or felt needs (i.e. whatever each village itself felt was most needed). And the Allahabad Institute, in connection with the school work, was trying out the four different approaches in four sets of villages.

The first fifty-five projects were launched on October 2, 1952, with Prime Minister Nehru officiating at a ceremony in a village near New Delhi. Some observers felt that the opening was premature, since only a small fraction of the needed village level workers had been trained, but at the end of eight weeks a survey conducted by *The Times of India* indicated fairly good progress on the whole. Hundreds of miles of roads had already been built (important because the villages are often physically inaccessible, especially during the monsoon season, and crops cannot be marketed); thousands of compost pits had been dug; wells had been disinfected and repaired; cattle had been inoculated; fertilizer and good wheat seed had been distributed, some of the seed going to certified growers for multiplication purposes; and schools were going up. From the Punjab, for example, a *Times* reporter wrote: "Caste Hindus and Harijans [untouchables] are working together to build village drains and some badly needed culverts. Swamps are being filled. The villagers' enthusiasm for building schools for their children was heartening." In Hyderabad state, the villagers had "enthusiastically taken to town planning in the shape of widening the old narrow, winding roads and leveling thoroughfares; for this purpose they are demolishing the old unsanitary mud houses and constructing houses of stone and flat tiles according to a plan they have themselves evolved."

On the other hand, there were areas where progress was slow. In Bihar it was "reported from almost all project areas that there is no popular enthusiasm" and in Bengal the villagers were said to be either "apathetic toward the general development scheme or ignorant of it."

In the succeeding months the press of India continued to be full of stories about the progress of the community projects. At the turn of the year, the *Hindustan Times* commented:

> "From the point of view of general rural development, the fifty-five community projects initiated this year form a landmark in the country's history. . . . As the object of these community projects is to raise the standard of village life, which is the backbone of the country's economy, public opinion has enthusiastically welcomed the initiation of these projects. . . ."

As of the summer of 1953, there were still many problems to be ironed out. The delicate questions of federal-state relationships had not been solved satisfactorily (the states not only had the primary operating responsibility for the projects, but also were expected to put up an increasing percentage of the funds the first three years, and 100 per cent after that). The large advisory committees, which had been set up in each project area to bring the local leaders into the administration of the program, were proving to be a serious obstacle to speedy and efficient operations, especially since they had authority to approve and veto all project expenses. There were rumors of corruption here and there. The training program was not proceeding as fast as had been hoped, and it was quite possible that all the projects would not achieve the food production increases that were hoped for (10-15 per cent in 1953-54, 20-25 per cent the next year, 30-40 per cent after that).

The Indian Government, however, confident that these difficulties would be overcome, was going ahead with plans for extending the community development work. On April 1, 1953, the second blocks of all of the first fifty-five projects were opened, and the remaining blocks, as well as the second fifty-five projects, were scheduled to be in operation by October. On November 14, 1953, Nehru's sixty-fourth birthday, the Indian Government's Community Projects Administration announced that one out of every eight of India's villages was already benefiting from the program in one way or another. As a birthday present to the Prime Minister, villagers in all states sent word to him of promises to build 820 schools and to contribute to hundreds of other projects. If the resources for financing such a gigantic endeavor could be found, there seemed to be no reason why the goal of bringing one-third of India's population within the program by 1955-56 could not be met.[4]

The idea of concentrating on specific areas with a multi-purpose program has caught on in other countries as well as India. Just such an approach was followed by the J.C.R.R. in its year of operations on the Chinese mainland, and its program on Formosa, while island-wide, aims at across-the-board rural development. In Pakistan, a sizable segment of the Point 4 program is devoted to concentrated projects of Village Agricultural and Industrial Development (known as the V-AID plan). In Egypt an ambitious joint project was launched in early 1953, with the United States and Egypt each pledging 10 million dollars for intensive reclamation, resettlement and village development activities in the Nile Delta province of Baheira and in the province of Fayum upstream from Cairo. In Lebanon, a combination irrigation and multi-purpose rural development program is under way in the Kasmie area along the Mediterranean, south of Beirut. In Haiti and Afghanistan, where Export-Import Bank loans have made possible the construction of dams on the Artibonite and Helmand rivers, Point 4 is assisting the local governments in turn to help the people settling in those valleys make the most of their opportunities.

It may well be that, as the years go by, there will be fewer and fewer Point 4 projects in which the sole concern will be agriculture or health or education. Progress in any one of these basic fields is so dependent on progress in the others that a multi-purpose approach, which tends to promote *balanced* development, may prove to be the best answer.

9. Strengthening Democratic Institutions and Industry

OF ALL THE KINDS of know-how that are needed for a country's development, probably none is more important than the know-how of organization. In America we tend to take for granted our thousands of federal, state, county and town bureaus and boards, our business and credit institutions, trade associations, labor unions, farm organizations, P.T.A.'s, citizens' committees, church groups, women's clubs, fraternal organizations, veterans' groups, 4-H and Future Farmers clubs, charities, colleges and universities, cooperatives, political organizations, and all their various ramifications, offshoots, affiliates and subcommittees. Although each one of us has our pet dislikes among these institutions, collectively they make up the fabric of our democratic society. Our habit of organizing to do something is as much the secret of our standard of living as any other one thing.

In contrast, many of the countries of Asia, Africa and Latin America are as underdeveloped institutionally as they are economically. Their government agencies are inadequately equipped and trained for the complex tasks that confront them, and private organizations that might supplement the work of the public institutions are virtually unknown. Thus, in huge areas where democracy is on trial before the people, its muscles, nerves and tendons are still immature and weak. If they cannot somehow be strengthened, nothing Point 4 can do in the realm of communicating knowledge and skills will be of much permanent value. Even if improvements are achieved in physical living standards, the objective of Point 4 will not be reached if there is not also a parallel strengthening of the people's desire for freedom and self-government. And this does not follow automatically. As has been often said, "development does not necessarily make nice people." [1]

Improving Government Services

In the basic fields of agriculture, health and education, the Point 4 process is, as we have seen, a complicated, two-step affair, because first the government and then the people must be reached. For the purpose of developing indigenous institutions in these fields, the most effective device is probably the cooperative service (or servicio) which permits American technicians to exercise a considerable degree of responsibility. Where local officials retain all operating responsibility—as in India, for example —the American advisers have little or no leverage to get things done. On the other hand, where the United States retains complete authority over a developmental operation —as in most of the Iran program—the institution being built up is American, rather than indigenous, even though many local nationals are hired and trained. (This, by the way, is the pattern of much American private agency activity.) While the functions of the organization may eventually be transferred to the host government, if the latter is willing to assume them, the vitality of the new institution cannot readily be transferred.

In Latin America, as we have seen, the servicio device has been widely and successfully used. In the Middle East and Asia, where Point 4 is newer and where the fear of foreign interference is even more acute, the servicio has not yet been widely accepted. Hopefully, however, the cooperative services that do exist—as of the summer of 1953, there were five in Jordan and one in Iran, in addition to the somewhat similar J.C.R.R. in Formosa—will in time provide a convincing demonstration of the merits of the idea from the local governments' point of view.

The process of building and strengthening local government services is not nearly so difficult when only a one-step operation is involved, that is, where the purpose of the activity is not ultimately to convey knowledge and skills to the people, but merely to *serve* the people in one way or another. It is here that pure technical assistance, as it is commonly understood, is most appropriate. Local technicians can be trained on the job by American experts or they can be given specialized training in the United States in a wide variety of fields, ranging from civil aviation and natural resource development to vital statistics and social security. In April, 1953, a single graduating class from the four-week orientation course given to all outgoing shirt-sleeve diplomats by the State Department's Foreign Service Institute included the following (in addition to the usual agriculturists, health specialists, and educators): a railway train dispatcher from Bakersfield, California, going to Ecuador to help modernize railroad methods in use there; a mining engineer from Denver, going to Nepal to serve as a consultant to the government on mining and minerals, a meteorologist from Lincoln

Park, Pennsylvania, going to Liberia to help set up a weather station network; a bridge engineer from Berkeley, California, going also to Liberia as a consultant on highways and bridges; a housing specialist from Fort Collins, Colorado, going to Colombia to advise the local authorities in his field; a labor analyst from Nashville, Tennessee, going to Peru to assist in establishing a public employment service.

In addition to the experts in various specialized government activities, there is a growing corps of advisers on methods of public administration. At one time, it was thought that this field was too delicate for United States experts to operate in, because they would necessarily seem to be interfering with the internal operations of the local government, and that consequently it would be better if all such experts came from the international agencies. But many of the local governments have not wanted it that way. Especially in Latin America, there has been a growing demand for United States technicians trained to analyze government organization and procedures and make suggestions for their improvement.

In Costa Rica, the first job that the I.I.A.A. was asked to do along these lines was to study the garbage collection and disposal system in use in San José and recommend needed changes. The result was so spectacular, in terms of better service for less money, that the Costa Rican Government began asking for all kinds of help along similar lines, including recommendations for the establishment of a civil service system. Studies of the entire government set-up, along the lines of the Hoover Commission in the United States, have been requested in Chile, Uruguay, and Panama, and similar studies of particular parts of the government are in progress in Brazil, Colombia, and

Mexico. Paraguay has asked for help in establishing a new budget and fiscal system. The degree of confidence in the good faith and objectivity of American experts which these requests represent is truly an extraordinary phenomenon in international relationships. But the importance of the activity lies in the fact that by this means free and friendly governments will be enabled to serve the needs of their peoples better than before.

Outside of Latin America, the speed with which the work in public administration has gone forward in any country has to some degree reflected the host government's attitude toward the United States. In Liberia, for example, which has a traditionally close relationship with America, United States experts have helped to codify the country's laws for the first time and to set up a new budgetary system for the government. In Saudi Arabia a new monetary system, complete with Central Bank, has been set up as a result of one of the earliest Point 4 projects. An over-all technical assistance program in public administration is in the process of development in Israel. In the Philippines, a public administration expert has established a close relationship with a number of ministries by showing them first how to set up an efficient filing system (he likes to say that one of mankind's great advances was made when papers were first filed upright). Both there and in Formosa, more United States experts will be at work in 1954 in public administration than in any other field.

One of the characteristic governmental weaknesses which the international agencies, as well as the United States, have tried to correct is a lack of machinery for planning and coordinating the economic development work itself. A few countries, such as India, have their own highly competent planning bodies, but in many more the big policy questions—for example, as to whether industry or agriculture should be emphasized, or as to how much present sacrifice for long-range benefit the people should be asked to accept—are simply not answered. Individual ministries tend to compete for technical and other assistance from all possible sources, and no overall priorities are laid down.

In a number of countries, a good start toward the solution of these difficulties has been made by setting up an inter-ministerial committee for the coordination of aid requests. In others, joint United States and local committees or commissions have been organized to make the major decisions on development. In Brazil, for example, a Joint Development Commission was set up in 1951, with the head of the T.C.A. mission as the United States member. While the Commission did some good work in determining relative priorities among Brazil's capital needs, it might have been more successful if the United States member had been a private citizen, rather than an official representative of the American government.[2] This has been the set-up in the case of Iraq's Development Board, which has authority over the disposition of Iraq's multi-million-dollar oil royalties, 70 per cent of which are allocated to development. Wesley Nelson, a former Assistant Commissioner of Reclamation, is a member of that Board in his own right and has so won the confidence of his colleagues that he is probably the Board's most influential member. The Board is nevertheless purely an Iraqi institution, and the United States Government has no responsibility for its decisions, good or bad.

"We Must Industrialize!"

When the imaginary Prime Minister of Deserta asked the United States for a steel mill, he was expressing the feeling of his people that, in order to develop, they must industrialize. To him, as to his people, the physical presence of a steel mill in their country would symbolize a giant stride toward their goal.

In this, of course, they were sadly mistaken. In order to contribute to a country's economy, a steel mill requires not only raw materials and a skilled labor supply, but also such essentials as customers, a transportation system, and a complex of financial and marketing organizations.

In a very real sense, the industrialization of a country is more dependent on its economic and social institutions than upon its natural resources. How else explain the fact that countries with more or less comparable resources have industrialized at different times and different speeds?

This, in a nutshell, is why Point 4 faces no more difficult task than that of trying to promote the development of industry in the underdeveloped areas. Yet it is hard to quarrel with the conclusion that, in the long run, mankind's battle against his environment, and particularly against the shortage of food, can never be won without widespread industrialization. Even the development of agriculture itself requires a considerable degree of industrialization.

The United States and international agencies have done certain fairly obvious things which will, in the long run, help to promote the growth of industries. Perhaps most important in this respect is the widespread work in vocational and industrial training which has already been mentioned: a first essential for new and expanding industries is a supply of machinists, welders, lathe operators, and the like.

Surveys have of course been made in a number of countries, intended to find out in what directions those countries might most profitably pursue their efforts to industrialize.[3] Mineral surveys have been undertaken, and aerial mapping, all with a view to determining more precisely the resources that the countries have to work with. Such work is helpful, but when it is completed the real job of development has yet to begin. In a few countries —notably Indonesia, Burma and Formosa—the United States has provided general engineering services through contracts with large engineering firms, to make available top-caliber advice on industrial and public works projects.

Here and there, progress has been made in encouraging the development of small, local industries—some of the handicraft type, others slightly larger. In the Philippines, for example, United Nations Technical Assistance Administration experts have helped home weavers to meet the competition of machine looms. In Indonesia, seven research and training institutes in such fields as ceramics, tanning, wood-working, and furniture-making are in process of development, while twenty-one *centraals,* strategically located, will furnish tools and act as purchasing and marketing agencies for village industries. The United States Government, through E.C.A. and later T.C.A., contributed both technical guidance and shop equipment. In Ecuador, I.I.A.A. experts are teaching Indians how to weave marketable tweeds and other materials.

In the case of more highly developed industries, the principal effort has been to promote increased efficiency and productivity in existing plants, rather than to assist in the building of new plants. Production of Afghanistan's primitive coal mines has been sharply increased, and safety measures for the miners introduced, thanks to the efforts of two United States advisers. Indian steel foundries have been enabled to call on a metallurgist from the Armour Research Foundation to help solve their production problems. In three countries of Latin America, Chile, Brazil and El Salvador, industrial productivity servicios have been set up to make available expert assistance of all kinds to existing industry, much as various industrial research foundations do in the United States. The plan is that their operations should be largely self-sustaining, just as the industrial hygiene work in Peru has been. A somewhat similar Industry Institute has been established in Lebanon.

For the most part, the United States Government has not furnished expensive machinery or equipment on a grant basis for industrial plants in the underdeveloped areas—except for educational or demonstration purposes— but has left that to private industry and to the banks. The major departures from the rule were in Iran and Pakistan, where special considerations existed,[4] and under the terminology used in 1953, this type of project was considered special economic aid rather than technical cooperation. Similarly, the essential job of providing capital for the development of power and transportation facilities needed as a base for industrialization is one that the lending institutions are concentrating on and that must be left primarily to them.

One final category of grant aid, which indirectly benefits industry, should be mentioned. In India, Formosa, Indo-China and the Philippines, commodities such as steel, sulphur, and other industrial raw materials have been shipped in by the United States Government, either to relieve a foreign exchange deficit or to stimulate the production of badly needed products, e.g. farm equipment in India. Again, this type of assistance is almost purely economic, rather than technical.

All in all, in spite of these various activities, neither the international nor the United States agencies have yet discovered any very effective way to promote rapid industrialization in the less developed areas. The National Foreign Trade Council and other business spokesmen have urged that the government leave the entire Point 4 job in the industrial field to private enterprise. That would be an easy way out for those responsible. But, as the next chapter suggests, the job would hardly get done adequately that way either.

There is one approach which, in my view, has not been sufficiently explored, and that is in every possible way to encourage the growth of financial institutions which in turn may make new industry possible. One of the chief obstacles to the creation of new industries in the underdeveloped areas is the fact that wealthy individuals in those countries are unaccustomed to investing their capital in local private productive enterprise: they are more inclined to hoard it, put it into land, or invest it abroad. An industrial development bank or corporation, however, equipped with a reasonable amount of capital, can serve as a mechanism for attracting local capital into industrial enterprises, either on a partnership basis—the wealthy people lose some of their fears if they are partners with a government agency—or by getting an enterprise started and then selling it to private owners. Such methods of financing may seem somewhat socialistic to Americans, but they have often proved successful—in Puerto Rico, for example—and they are sometimes about the only means available in countries whose capitalists are not as risk-minded as ours. Moreover, such development banks or corporations are also in an excellent position actively to seek private foreign capital for investment within their countries, in much the way state development agencies and chambers of commerce do in the United States. If need be, technical advisers can help them to perform this task, as well as to select sound propositions for the direct investment of public capital.

Although a few such institutions exist in Latin America and elsewhere, the United States has to date done almost nothing to assist them or to encourage the creation of new ones by putting up part of the capital. We have also missed an opportunity in failing to support the idea of a similar institution as an international agency. In its April 1951, "Partners in Progress" report, the International Development Advisory Board urged that the United States help to establish an International Finance Corporation, which would put up part of the capital for promising industrial and other enterprises, on a loan or non-voting equity basis, and by its participation attract both local and foreign capital into the enterprises. As soon as a given company was on its feet, the Corporation would dispose of its investment to private holders, and use its funds elsewhere. In 1952, the International Bank made a study of the idea and reacted favorably. A number of United States Congressmen, notably Javits of New York, are interested, and an authorization of 10 million dollars for a starter almost got through the Congress in 1952.[5]

The reaction of the American banking and business community to all such plans, however, has been highly negative. Although American private enterprise is not now providing the underdeveloped areas with the equity financing they need, it takes a dog-in-the-manger attitude toward the idea of a national or international agency doing part of the job. If we mean what we say about the importance of strengthening the economies of the underdeveloped areas, "business as usual" is not enough of a slogan. A more imaginative, and more courageous policy is called for.

Joiners Wanted

Even though the job of trying to promote and strengthen useful governmental and industrial institutions is difficult, the problem with respect to private associations of all kinds is, if anything, even more delicate. Just how do outsiders go about trying to encourage the formation of free trade unions, farm organizations, civic groups, and the like, in countries where these things do not exist?

The labor situation in the city of Isfahan, Iran's principal textile center, is typical. One of the leading businessmen there made it quite clear to Warne and me that there were only two types of labor organizations in his plants: the communists and "my own people." He obviously had a labor spy system established that would have done credit to Pinkerton in his heyday.

And so it is in the vast majority of the underdeveloped areas' industrial centers: the militant, non-communist labor organization is practically unknown. United States and international labor experts can and do work with the managers of national industries and other forward-looking entrepreneurs, encouraging them to make improvements in working conditions and so increase productivity. But there seems to be very little that shirt-sleeve diplomats, who can act only pursuant to requests from their hosts, can do to build free labor unions where none exist. Once indigenous stirrings begin, of course, they can be nurtured: sizable groups of non-communist Indonesian labor leaders were brought to the United States in 1952 and 1953, on training grants, to see for themselves the operations of this country's trade unions, and they gave every evidence of being encouraged and inspired by what they saw. On the whole, however, Government agencies seem to be a clumsy instrument to carry out the injunction of the Mutual Security Act of 1951, that all foreign aid programs should be administered in such a way as "to encourage where suitable the development and strengthening of the free labor union movements as the collective bargaining agencies of labor within such countries." Perhaps American or international labor organizations, operating strictly on their own, could accomplish more. In any event, as long as life in the villages remains bleak and miserable so that thousands of people flock to the cities each year in search of work, true collective bargaining in the industrial market is a long way off.

In the farm organization field the picture is somewhat more hopeful, but not exactly bright. A number of specialists in farm cooperatives have been assigned to Point 4 missions, to work with the expanding extension services, and here and there a few cooperatives have been organized. But in many areas cooperatives are suspect because of past failures, or simply because the farmers tend to trust only members of their families. This reluctance to take group action exists even where there is an obvious desperate need for purchasing and marketing organizations. One experienced observer reported to me that he had seen potatoes selling in Indian villages for one rupee (twenty cents) a bushel, when the market price in a town a few miles away was twenty-five rupees.

The most promising approach to the task of promoting group action by farmers is through the encouragement of youth club activities. The youngsters learn how to run an organization and acquire the habits of give-and-take and group loyalty which are essential to democratic institutions. As yet there are few farm cooperatives in Costa Rica, for example, but the 4-S clubs are thriving. Their members will doubtless continue to work together for common objectives when they grow up. Indeed, as was noted in an earlier chapter, some of the grownups have already formed 4-S clubs of their own!

That it is possible to galvanize a community into action to meet some long-felt need, such as a village school, has been demonstrated again and again—in India, in Iran, in the Andes—as we have seen. The difficulties of building a village organization do not disappear after the first task is accomplished—village politics and factionalism often develop—but, once a community has found that it can get things done by working together, it may well keep on doing it, especially if some tactful and resourceful adviser is available to encourage it. The form of organization makes no real difference. In one case, it may be a wholly unofficial group, like one of our P.T.A.'s, that is inspired to make some improvement; in another, the work may be done under the auspices of the village committee—in India the *panchayat,* in Iran the *kadkhodas.* The important thing is that the respected leaders of the community should be involved in it, or at least give their blessing.

To date, not much has been done to develop similar self-help organizations in the towns and cities of the underdeveloped areas, in spite of the fact that there has been a great deal of talk about the necessity of tackling the urban problem. It is to my mind not at all impossible that the very unemployed intellectuals who tend to stir up political unrest in the urban areas could be organized in such a way that their energies would be channeled along specific, constructive lines. Civic responsibility, to be sure, is often not traditional, and it cannot be taught as easily as the use of a new tool, but if a nucleus of good citizens can be found, the notion of community action can be catching. There are already many Rotary Clubs with booster ideas. For example, such a club made quite a splash in Costa Rica early in 1953, by coming forward with a bold plan for the development of their city's port (Puntarenas). And in hundreds of cities and towns there are devoted women who work hard at their charities, often in an untrained, lady-bountiful kind of way. Most of them realize that they are dealing with the fruits of poverty, not with its causes, but they do not know what else to do. There are endless possibilities for imaginative action—adult education, recreation programs, youth clubs, health education and visiting nurse work, even housing improvement and the development or preservation of handicraft industries. Visible progress along any of these lines would give to people who might otherwise be apathetic and despairing a new sense of hope and of purpose in life.

To get such work started would be an extremely difficult task; it would require teams of highly trained and sensitive community workers,[6] with cultural anthropologists at least available for advice, but the possible rewards would be very great. I can see no more fruitful line of attack on the urban problem. In time, if other efforts to develop the economies of the less developed countries are successful and industries develop, so that the unemployed are put to work and educated young men and women see some light ahead, the problem may disappear. But there is no guarantee that we will have that much time.

10. The Role of Private Enterprise

POINT 4 IS NOT, of course, exclusively a Government operation. From the start it was conceived as a partnership of international and national agencies and of private groups of all kinds.

There are, in the first place, literally hundreds of religious, semi-religious, philanthropic, and educational organizations engaged in the process of helping the peoples of the underdeveloped areas to help themselves. Some of them are working with the United States Government on a contract basis, either carrying on a multi-purpose program in a particular area—as the Near East Foundation is doing near Teheran in Iran, and the American Friends Service Committee in the state of Orissa, India—or specializing on a particular type of activity. Several of the Land Grant Colleges, for example, are helping in the development of agricultural educational institutions: Arizona in Iraq, Oklahoma in Ethiopia, Arkansas in Panama, and Michigan in Colombia. But most of the private technical assistance work being done is entirely independent of the Government. One of the most remarkable groups, whose activities are not widely known in the United States, are the Seventh Day Adventists; their record of good works has made them welcome, for example, in many parts of Latin America where little is done without the sanction of the Roman Catholic Church. The Catholic Rural Life Conference and other Roman Catholic groups have done a great deal to promote the work of communicating skills to people who need them. Early in 1953 Catholic prelates from all over Latin America met at Manizales in Colombia to discuss rural development; one of the speeches was made by a peripatetic American named Raymond W. Miller, a consultant to F.A.O. and T.C.A. and a Point 4 enthusiast, who was introduced by Monsignor Ligutti, the Executive Secretary of the Catholic Rural Life Conference, as "my Methodist adviser." The Point 4 idea crosses all sectarian lines.

Some private Point 4 operations have no religious connections at all. An outstanding example is the American International Association for Economic and Social Development, which is working in Venezuela and Brazil on rural development, supervised credit, health education and the like. The A.I.A., which is Nelson Rockefeller's brain child, works through joint agencies much like the I.I.A.A.'s servicios which he originated. Several of the large oil companies have made substantial contributions to A.I.A.'s work in Venezuela.

These are but a few examples. The technical assistance work of the American missions has been going on for well over a century, and that of the foundations and associations for several decades.[1] It has not slackened because of the Government's activities, and it will doubtless continue for a long time to come. These groups are in general among the strongest supporters of the Government's Point 4 program, since they recognize that their own work can be no more than a drop in the bucket. In turn the United States agencies have done everything they could to encourage and support the private organizations, and not to duplicate or compete with them.

In addition to all the various non-profit organizations, many private companies are in effect conducting technical assistance programs in the underdeveloped areas. Almost every United States business concern which has overseas operations is constantly training local personnel to carry on those operations, and many are communicating specialized technical know-how to foreign concerns or governments on a straight fee basis. A few large concerns, such as Aramco in Saudi Arabia, United Fruit in Central America, and Firestone in Liberia, have undertaken splendid research and educational work, related to their business activities only in a long-range sense.[2] Finally, the United States Government has contracted with private corporations to carry on all sorts of operations, including aerial mapping and locust-spraying, movie-making, well-drilling, and economic and engineering studies and surveys.[3]

The main potential contribution of private enterprise to the underdeveloped areas, however, is not so much in providing technical knowledge, as in providing that other essential ingredient of development—capital. Almost without exception, the countries of Asia, Africa and Latin America are acutely short of capital, mainly because their small national incomes keep savings at a pathetically low level. To a limited extent, they can look to public sources of capital, such as the International Bank and the United States Export-Import Bank, but the great bulk of their capital needs, especially for industrial development purposes, must be met, if at all, by private enterprise.

It was always a part of the Point 4 scheme that private investment in the underdeveloped areas should be greatly increased. Harry Truman in his Fourth Point said: "in cooperation with other nations, we should foster capital investment in areas needing development," and the Government agencies have done what they could to that end. But the fact must be faced that this phase of the program has been a disappointment.

The basic difficulty with private capital, as a means for international development, is that it can do least where it is needed most. In Latin America, which is relatively far away from the Kremlin, the investment picture is fairly bright. By the end of 1951, total direct United States investment in Latin America had passed the 5.5 billion dollar mark, having increased almost half a billion during the year (taking reinvested earnings into account). While the increase was not quite as great as it had been in the years 1947 through 1949, the decline was more than accounted for by a sharp drop-off in the petroleum industry. Net capital outflow (not including reinvested earnings) to the non-petroleum industries went up from 70 million dollars in 1949 to 235 million dollars in 1951, about three-quarters of which was in manufacturing, distribution and agriculture.[4] While these figures are small in relation to the capital needs of the area, at least they compare very favorably with the United States Government outlay on Point 4 programs in Latin America of about 20 million dollars a year.

It is in the critical countries of Asia along the periphery of the communist world that private investment has been almost at a standstill. By the end of 1950, for example, *total* United States direct investment in India was 38 million dollars, or a little over ten cents per Indian. The figure for Pakistan was 7.8 million dollars, and for Burma, Ceylon, Iran and Thailand together 8 million dollars. The totals for the Philippines (149 million), Indonesia (58 million), and Egypt and the Sudan (40 million) were a little more respectable, but the only substantial investments in all of Asia were in the oil fields around the Persian Gulf, amounting to 726 million dollars.[5] While extractive industries provide a fine source of employment, of local expenditures, and of royalties to the government, they cannot and do not contribute as much to overall development as do manufacturing, service and distributive industries. As the local peoples are very well aware, the oil and mining companies are after all primarily engaged in taking wealth out, not in bringing it in.

The reasons for the failure of the private investment phase of Point 4, and possible remedies, have been the subject of a great deal of palaver in Washington, especially since early 1952. At that time (March 27, 1952) a staff study was prepared for the House Foreign Affairs Committee which said in effect that the Executive Branch could have done a lot more to promote foreign investment if it had really wanted to, but did not say just what. A little later, in the Mutual Security Act of 1952, the Congress directed the Department of Commerce to make a study of the impediments to foreign investment (although everyone knew pretty well what those impediments were). As to the big question of how to overcome the impediments, there have been a lot of ideas floating around, but no agreement.

One group, which includes a number of Congressmen, is certain that huckster techniques can solve the problem. T.C.A., for instance, was under constant pressure of a "Don't-just-stand-there-do-something!" variety, and was actually looking for ways to spend money on the private investment side of the program. Eric Johnston, Chairman of the International Development Advisory Board, organized big pep meetings on the subject, at which every one agreed that more investment overseas would be a fine thing, but even his super-salesmanship produced no concrete results. At one conference in San Francisco, Johnston virtually told the businessmen that it was their patriotic duty to invest in the underdeveloped areas, and this appeal was not kindly received at all. As businessmen themselves are fond of saying, they are not in business for their health. Nor, to put it more precisely, are they in business to carry out the foreign policy of the United States.[6] The private investment problem cannot be solved by exhortation.

This is not to say that some promotional techniques cannot be useful in stimulating the flow of investment dollars. For one thing, the interest of American companies, especially small ones, that never had thought seriously of venturing overseas, can be aroused. The United States Government, through F.O.A., the Department of Commerce and other agencies, can collect information about specific opportunities overseas and disseminate them to businessmen in this country. Private investment advisers can be, and in a few cases have been, sent out to the underdeveloped countries to help them identify promising industrial or other business opportunities and show them how to get in touch with potential investors through the use of carefully drawn prospectuses and other devices.[7]

But these techniques do not get to the heart of the problem. The difficulty is, in a few words, that the potential returns on most overseas investments are not enough to compensate for the risks of loss. Generally speaking, American businessmen do not need any help from the Government to find opportunities for investment if those opportunities are attractive enough. If we want really to speed up the flow of American investment dollars overseas, we must find some way of increasing the returns or reducing the risks, or both.

Many American businessmen would say that there is much the United States Government could do about improving the "investment climate" abroad. They point to the chilly attitude of some governments toward United States or any other foreign businessmen, to the exchange restrictions that make it difficult if not impossible to get earnings out, to the maze of regulations that often exist covering labor conditions, numbers of local employees that must be hired, etc., and to the occasional expropriations that occur. However, while these are indeed major impediments to the flow of investment, they are unfortunately not under United States control. When the businessmen say that the State Department should be tougher with other countries that take action unfavorable to United States business interests, just as the Foreign Office was in the great era of British foreign investment, they forget that we are no longer in the nineteenth century. The days of dollar diplomacy are over. These are proud governments we are dealing with. Many of them are newly independent and are particularly skittish about any action on the part of a western government that looks like the old imperialism. They would far rather risk domination by the Soviet than accept what they would consider to be domination by a western power. And some of them are simply not yet ready to discard their vaguely socialist notions about how a country can achieve industrialization; they are hostile to substantial private profits and regard them as wasteful.

These are the facts of life in the world today. We cannot change them overnight. Nor can we throw up our hands in disgust at what we may conceive to be the perversity of our friends overseas. We have too much at stake.

What we can do, and are doing, is gradually to break down the suspicion and hostility of the local governments and persuade them that they will gain by easing the regulations that are keeping the investors away. In part this can be done by our diplomatic representatives, shirt-sleeve and otherwise. For example, treaties of friendship, commerce and development, which will considerably improve the "investment climate," have been concluded with a few countries and are in process of negotiation with a number of others.[8] But, no matter how eloquent and persuasive are the official representatives of the United States Government, statesmanlike actions on the part of American companies in those countries where they are operating will speak much more effectively. The excellent records of Aramco in Saudi Arabia, and of Sears Roebuck in Brazil and Mexico, just to mention two outstanding examples, exert more influence in those countries and elsewhere than ten thousand diplomatic *aide-mémoires*.

An even more fundamental requirement for profitable enterprise than a favorable political climate, however, is a favorable economic climate. There must be, above all, a market. One reason why industries such as petroleum, mining, rubber and banana have gone ahead, in spite of relatively unfavorable conditions, when manufacturing, service and distributive industries have held back, is that their markets were outside, not inside, the countries. When 70-80 per cent of the country's population live on the land and have virtually no cash income, the prospects for most industrial investment are not apt to be bright.

This of course is where the Point 4 program can make its main contribution to private investment and industrialization: in helping the underdeveloped countries to attack their basic problems of hunger, disease and ignorance and so to lay a foundation for rising standards of living upon which to build. In addition to its work in agriculture, health and education, Point 4 can provide some direct assistance to industrial development, as noted in the previous chapter.

As for the power and transportation facilities which are needed, Point 4 can help with engineering problems and in the organization of government agencies, such as highway departments, capable of carrying on the work. In times past, the capital needs for some of these facilities have been met through private enterprise, but in most countries today that is no longer feasible, because the political climate will not permit profits high enough to make such investments profitable. This is the field in which the International Bank and (until 1953) the Export-Import Bank have been making most of their loans, again laying a foundation for further development by private capital.[9]

None of these various activities, which are designed to change the conditions of investment in the underdeveloped countries themselves, are likely to produce any spectacular results in the near future. There is an additional, and totally different, type of approach to the problem open to the United States Government, which if effective at all is likely to be quicker. It is sometimes known as the "push" instead of the "pull" technique. That is, through legislation enacted within the United States, to increase the potential net return from investment abroad, or reduce the risks, or both. Short of outright subsidy, which no one has yet seriously proposed, there are two main categories of techniques to achieve those purposes: insurance schemes and tax incentives.

The idea of insurance against some of the risks peculiar to foreign investment was part of the original Point 4 proposal, but was rejected by Congress at the time. In connection with the Marshall Plan, however, the Congress did authorize the E.C.A. to issue insurance for a fee against the risks of expropriation and of nonconvertibility (i.e. new and unfavorable exchange regulations making it impossible to convert earnings into dollars). In 1951, this plan was extended to cover investments in the underdeveloped areas as well. Unfortunately, it has not been much used. As of the spring of 1953, the total policies, or "guaranties," issued amounted to about 40 million dollars. Businessmen simply do not take to the idea. For one thing, a bad psychological mistake was made in using the term "guaranties," which sounds strange and somehow radical, instead of "insurance," which sounds familiar and conservative. For another, those companies with money already invested overseas claim that the plan discriminates against them and in favor of new investors, and hence vigorously attack it. For still another, the businessmen feel that the existence of the scheme suggests that we expect other governments to take unfavorable action against our investments and do not particularly mind. There are good answers to these objections, but there is no very good answer to the argument that the scheme is a failure because it is not producing the intended result. A thorough recasting of the plan by Congress—using the insurance terminology, extending the coverage to include all war risks, and making the policies available to old as well as new investors—might radically change the picture, but it is doubtful that such steps will be taken, in view of the hostility of the business community.[10]

The idea of providing some form of tax relief for overseas investors offers somewhat more promise, particularly because it is popular with businessmen. A few minor concessions have already been made, such as reducing the tax rate payable by companies operating in Latin America, but the United States Treasury, under both the Truman and Eisenhower administrations, has steadfastly resisted any major steps in this direction because of the loss of revenue that would follow.

The most drastic proposal, which is favored by the National Foreign Trade Council and by the International Development Advisory Board, is to eliminate all United States taxes on business income earned abroad. This is not such a fantastic idea as it might at first seem: most other countries do not in fact tax income earned outside their borders. But it is nevertheless highly controversial.

In considering this or any tax proposal, it is essential to keep in mind that, under the present United States law, corporations can take full credit for any income tax payments made to foreign governments. Thus, where the local tax rates are as high or higher than the United States, the companies do not now pay any United States tax on their foreign earnings, and even eliminating the United States tax altogether would afford no incentive whatever for businesses to go into those countries. The big advantage of eliminating or sharply reducing the United States tax on foreign earnings would be that it would provide an inducement to other governments to make tax concessions to United States investors in order to attract them, as Puerto Rico has done so successfully in recent years. As matters stand now, the other governments have no reason to make such concessions, because the United States tax collector promptly sops up any benefits.

On the other hand, as the Treasury points out, the great

disadvantage of the Foreign Trade Council's proposal is
that it would result in an unwarranted bonanza to companies already operating in countries with tax rates lower
than ours, and a corresponding loss of revenue—from 100
to 150 million dollars a year—to the Treasury. And it
would hardly be wise to attempt to discriminate between
new and old investors.

There is, however, another type of tax incentive, against
which the Treasury's case does not seem so strong. If the
cost of capital investments overseas could be rapidly
charged off to business expense, the risk of outright loss on
such investments would be greatly reduced. Five-year
amortization might be permitted, as has been done with
defense facilities in the United States, or the taxpayer
might even be allowed to deduct the total cost of the investment as a business expense in one year.[11] In most cases,
these changes would mean only a deferment, rather than
forgiveness, of taxes to be paid, yet they might well operate as a substantial incentive to investment abroad.

Most of the proposals of this kind have to do with direct
investments overseas by corporate enterprise. But there is
also a vast source of capital that might be tapped—as it was
quite indiscriminately in the twenties—if securities in foreign enterprise could once again somehow be made attractive to the individual and institutional investor.[12] If certain
types of foreign government bonds and industrial securities were made tax free, for example, they might be widely
purchased by high-bracket tax-payers, no matter how risky.
But it would be most unwise to issue a blanket tax exemption to all foreign securities, and standards for exemption
would have to be defined. The determination of whether
specific issues met those standards would be difficult, but
not impossible. Perhaps the Securities and Exchange Com-

mission could handle the job, making use of the State Department's economic counselors and F.O.A. private investment advisers as a field staff.

This type of proposal would doubtless have the strenuous opposition of the Treasury, on the ground that, if successful, it would cut into individual tax revenues. It might also be opposed by domestic security dealers and possibly by American corporate enterprise. But all of this opposition would be short-sighted in the extreme if by such means a real boost could be given to the economic growth of the less developed areas.

These are complicated and difficult questions, and there are no simple answers. Yet, sooner or later, the United States will have to decide whether it is serious about stepping up the rate at which Americans have been risking their money abroad, or not. If it is serious, it will have to find ways and means to make the idea more attractive.

Even under the best of circumstances, we should not be too hopeful about private investment being able to take the place of the Point 4 program and other types of public assistance. For one thing, private enterprise and government activities do not ordinarily cover the same ground, as we have seen. For another, so long as business conditions remain relatively favorable at home, and so long as communists rule the heartland of Asia, private United States capital is simply not going to start moving into the underdeveloped areas of the Middle East and Asia in quantities to meet their needs.[13]

No one can say exactly how great the needs are. In 1951, a group of experts appointed by the United Nations Secretary General estimated that the underdeveloped areas as a whole needed over 19 billion dollars of capital each year in order to raise their national incomes by 2 per cent a year, and that their savings amounted to only 5 billion dollars a year, leaving a deficit of some 14 billion dollars, most of it in South and Southeast Asia.[14] These estimates have been severely criticized as being exaggerated, but one could cut them by half or two-thirds, and the problem would still be enormous. Consider the case of India alone: as of 1950-51, India's national income was about 18 billion dollars, of which about 5 per cent or 900 million dollars was being saved. Even to double the amount of capital available each year would not give the country enough for a very rapid rate of development (12 to 15 per cent of income is considered minimum); yet this would require another 900 million dollars a year. As we have noted, the *total* United States investment in India as of the end of 1950 was 38 million dollars.

It would seem that other sources of capital will have to be found.

11. The Almighty Dollar Fallacy

In recent years a number of distinguished American liberals, sensing that private enterprise would not be able to meet the capital needs of the underdeveloped areas, have been calling for the United States Government to embark on a multi-billion-dollar aid program.

In July, 1950, for example, Walter Reuther proposed that the United States promise to contribute 13 billion dollars a year for a hundred years to "a United Nations Fund for Economic and Social Construction" to be used to help people to help themselves by developing their economic resources. He suggested that the aid be tied in with universal disarmament or, if that were not possible, to mutual defense arrangements whereby each nation was to agree not to use force except by direction of the United Nations.[1]

The same year, Senator Brien McMahon of Connecticut made his famous suggestion that the United States subscribe 10 billion dollars a year as our share of a fund to get the world's economy on its feet, provided a general agreement for disarmament was reached.*

In 1951, the United Nations Committee of Experts

---

* The idea of using "a substantial percentage" of the savings from disarmament for a world development fund was picked up by President Eisenhower in his speech of April 16, 1953, to the American Society of Newspaper Editors, but he did not indicate what he meant by "substantial."

urged that an International Development Authority be established to make grants-in-aid to the underdeveloped countries from "a sum of money which should increase rapidly, reaching eventually a level of about 3 billion dollars a year." Stringfellow Barr passionately supported the general scheme in his book *Citizens of the World* (Doubleday, 1952), and James Patton, President of the National Farmers Union, has expressed similar ideas.

Perhaps it is unfair to say that none of these proposals contained any specific indication as to how such sums could be expended wisely and with lasting good effects. When you are crying in the wilderness of an unimaginative era, attempting to open the eyes of the apathetic to their danger and exhorting them to take bold and drastic action, you do not call attention to all the obstacles in the way of making your program a success. On the other hand, there is no evidence that those who call for multi-billion-dollar programs have any real notion themselves as to what the difficulties are. Significantly, most of America's shirt-sleeve diplomats, who are on the firing line in the battle for world development, don't take the "big-money boys" very seriously. So far as I know, no one who has actually worked at the job of trying to help an underdeveloped country help itself has ever come out for a program in ten figures.

Let us pass for the time being the difficulties of international administration, which virtually all the multi-billion-dollar proposals have contemplated. The question of United States vs. international administration will be discussed in a later chapter. At this point, it is enough to say that most of the funds for a big-money program, probably at least 90 per cent, would have to come from the United States.

Perhaps the most generally overlooked fact about the capital shortage of the underdeveloped areas is that generally speaking, it is not so much dollars that are needed as, say, rupees, or rials, or cruzeiros. Major development projects, like dams, irrigation canals, highways, and construction work of all kinds cost a lot of money, but most of the bills must be paid in local currencies.

Dollars can be used to pay American personnel and to buy supplies and machinery in the United States, but they cannot be used as such to pay laborers in Nepal or Paraguay, or to buy local materials like cement. The American traveler who has found dollar bills accepted all over the world will challenge this, and to the extent that only a small amount of dollars are involved, he is right. But when a large number of dollars are pumped into a country's economy and changed into local currency, without any extra imports being brought in, the result is inflation. A lot more money has been put into the hands of the people to spend, but there are no new commodities for them to spend it on.

To visualize the problem in its simplest terms, think of a hundred thousand laborers working on a big earth dam in Iran; at the day's end, they are paid in dollar bills; they promptly go to the local bank to change their dollars for rials; to meet this unprecedented demand for rials, the government has to print extra currency; the laborers spend the rials on food, clothing, etc.; but the supply of food, clothing, etc., has not been increased; so prices go up and inflation is on.

The only way this inflationary process can be prevented is for the dollars to be used to buy consumers goods from abroad. But as we well know in this country, there is a limit to the amount a country can import; the rest of the world is begging us to import more, and we have plenty of money to buy imports with, but still we don't do it.

The inflationary effect of dollar aid has plagued the administrators of our big aid programs from the beginning. The E.C.A., and later the M.S.A., used the technique of shipping in commodities (instead of dollars) in the first instance, so that these commodities could be sold to produce the needed local currency (called counterpart). The T.C.A. did the same thing in Iran. But there is very definitely a limit to the use of this technique. If the amount of dollar aid is less than a country's normal imports, the technique works all right as long as those commodities are shipped in that the country would normally import (which means that the program administrator cannot be too fussy about what he ships in, whether it be perfume, whiskey, or opium). But once the amount of the aid goes over the level of normal imports, as it would in many cases under a multi-billion-dollar program, you have trouble; the administrator will find himself with commodities on his hands which can't be sold, just as T.C.A. did with the wheat in Jordan.

The difficulty can, of course, be avoided to the extent that the aid provided is in the form of capital goods, such as machine tools, textile machinery, rolling stock, electrical equipment, etc. But imports of this character can almost never be put to use unless substantial local expenditures are made in the construction of factory buildings, roads, dams and the like, which the recipient government may or may not be able to afford. Outside of the realm of straight industrial development, which is generally considered susceptible of private or at least loan financing, it is a rare project in which the larger share of the cost is not in local currency. In an undertaking such as India's community development plan, the ratio is about ten to one.

What this all boils down to is that, in a world economy where currencies are not freely exchangeable, the transfer of capital resources from one country to others is not a simple process. The fact is that, in the last analysis, a country can use dollars only to pay for imports, of commodities or talent, and there is a limit to the amount of either it can usefully import at any given stage of its development.

Another problem facing the administrators of a really big aid program is that of deciding whether to emphasize loans or grants. Each course has its disadvantages.

The difficulty about loans is that they are supposed to be repaid. Both the International Bank for Reconstruction and Development and the United States Export-Import Bank have taken this notion quite seriously, with the result that they have uncommitted funds and are actually scratching around for business. Any country's debt-servicing capacity is limited. While projects directly productive of increased exports add to that capacity, such projects are exceptional. Accordingly, the number of businesslike loans that a country can absorb is sharply limited, and there is no need whatever for a big new development agency to make sound loans.

On the other hand, if grants are to be the order of the day for all kinds of projects, there is a very great danger that private enterprise will be discouraged, rather than encouraged, and that the banks will be virtually put out of business.

The availability of a small amount of grant aid, falling far short of a country's capital needs, usually has a stimulating effect both on private investment and on loan operations. By providing money for those capital needs which cannot be met either by loans or by private capital, such a limited grant program contributes to a balanced development which strengthens the country's economy, enables it to borrow more money by increasing its capacity to service the debt, and contributes to economic and political stability so as to improve the climate for private investment. This conclusion has been confirmed by no less an authority than President Eugene Black of the International Bank.

If the amount of grant aid available were very large, however, and were to approach the level of capital needs, the effect would be quite the opposite. Loans would become unattractive when grant aid could be had instead. Private investment would not be encouraged by the recipient countries, since capital obtained from private sources has its price just as public loan capital does: interest and profits have to be paid out, thus using up precious foreign exchange, and eventually the capital may have to be repaid. Moreover, with plenty of grant aid available for industrialization, the natural tendency of some governments toward a socialist type of enterprise would be given full sway.

Presumably the announced policy would be that no grants would be made for projects which could reasonably be financed on a loan basis or privately, but such a policy would be virtually unenforceable unless grants were limited to strictly defined categories. If grants were to be made available for industrial development, for example, the factors that affect the private investor's decision are so many and complex that there would always be ways to make a proposition unattractive to private capital and hence eligible for a grant.

The United Nations Committee of Experts, incidentally, recommended that grants be limited to four categories of projects: research and education, including agricultural extension services, schools and universities; public health programs; subsidization of farm credit; and rural public works, including roads, water supplies, land reclamation, soil conservation, afforestation. While this policy would be enforceable enough, it would make even more acute the problem of spending dollars. For the foreign exchange costs of these categories of projects are all relatively low, and the local currency costs high!

There is a constant search in Washington and elsewhere for a technique of aid falling somewhere between a loan and a grant, but the magic formula has yet to be discovered. Most of the experts are agreed that fuzzy loans—loans which might or might not be repaid, depending on future circumstances—would create more problems than they would solve. If made in large quantities, they would have virtually the same effect as grants on the operations of the banks and of private enterprise.

Assuming that the administrators of a large aid program could somehow solve the dollar problem and the loan-grant problem, they would still have a lot of trouble spending their money at the expected rate. They could do so, of course, if they were willing to turn over commodities or currency credits to the recipient governments in accordance with their requests, without attempting to pass on the projects which the countries proposed to carry out, or to supervise the operations themselves. But this method would receive little serious support (except perhaps from some of the recipient nations), since only a small proportion of the funds would achieve any lasting benefits for the masses of the people: the temptation to spend money on flashy and politically popular short-range benefits, to say nothing of the temptation to corruption, would be too great.

The opposite extreme would be for the development agency to maintain complete control, not only over choice of projects, but over project operations as well. The agency would itself carry out all construction work, for example, and would turn over the completed product to the local government. Such a procedure would have the advantage of efficiency, and a fair amount of speed, but it might well be unacceptable to the host government for political reasons. Even if it were not, it would have overwhelming drawbacks: bearing all the earmarks of charity, it would be destructive of the self-respect and pride of the recipient peoples; it would do nothing to strengthen local institutions so as to enable them to carry on the development work effectively; in short, it would violate the self-help principle of aid programs, which is universally recognized as essential.

The obvious answer would be to steer a middle course between simply turning over cash and retaining complete control—by organizing servicios, joint funds, and other forms of partnership operations, and by encouraging local governments to do as much as possible to help themselves —but past experience indicates that by this method the money will not get spent very fast.

If the development agency insists on a sound program, it will inevitably encounter delays. For example, the agency would doubtless try to plan its aid on a global and regional basis so as to promote international specialization, rather than economic self-sufficiency. It might well decide that certain countries ought to stress agricultural and raw materials production, instead of industrialization. It would probably seek to encourage long-range development activity, as against projects which might increase the supply of consumers' goods in a relatively short time. But in all of these respects it would be bucking the desires of the countries themselves. If its attitude were too obviously one of impatience to get its money spent, its bargaining power to insist on the observance of desirable criteria would be correspondingly less.

In Lebanon in 1952, T.C.A. discovered how dangerous it was to be over-eager. The Point 4 program there got off to a bad start because the shrewd Lebanese gathered the impression that, if they were uncooperative, they would get what they wanted, which was a program involving a minimum of technical cooperation and a maximum of straight grant aid. Partly because of T.C.A.'s anxiousness to have some progress to talk about before Congressional committees, technicians were sent to Lebanon in response to informal Ministry requests, without waiting for project agreements to be properly executed and without adequate assurance from the Government as a whole that it would make the necessary effort to support a Point 4 program. The problem was complicated by political unrest and several cabinet shifts. Finally, it became necessary to say to the Lebanese that, unless the proper agreements were signed by a certain date, the technicians would be sent elsewhere. In other words, the United States had to assume a more dignified posture—saying in effect: "This is what we have to offer, on these conditions; we don't really care whether or not you take it. It's up to you." Once that was done, good progress began to be made, but still slowly.

Perhaps the most difficult of all the problems facing a development agency with billions to spend would be what is sometimes called the dilemma of reform vs. non-interference. This dilemma confronts all aid program administrators, but it is most acute in the case of a program involving large-scale capital grants. To take a simple case, assume that in the country of Deserta there are only two river valleys suitable for development, and that the area to be irrigated in each case is owned by one or two big landlords. If the Government of Deserta, in which the landlords and their friends may be powerful, declines to undertake any redistribution of the land or otherwise to spread the benefits fairly, what can the agency do but refuse to go ahead? A more difficult case would arise where the government gave every assurance that land reform would be carried out and then, when the work was almost completed, the agreement was repudiated by a new cabinet.

Or let us assume that the development agency's program would include grants-in-aid for the construction and equipment of industrial plants. To what extent should it attempt to dictate the scale of wages and other labor conditions that would obtain at the plants? And if it did secure the country's agreement to certain conditions, should it attempt to exercise continuing supervision over the plants' operations to make sure that the agreement was being observed?

Such questions have no totally satisfactory answers, and reasonable men would differ about how the program should be administered. It seems a fair assumption, however, that those very idealists who are most enthusiastic about a multi-billion-dollar program would be the ones who would want to insist most strongly on imposing conditions that would slow down the spending of the money and, in some cases, probably block it completely.

If Thurman Arnold ever gets around to writing *The Folklore of American Liberalism,* he will surely devote a chapter to the liberal's touching faith in the dollar. It used to be that dollar worship was practiced by those who believed that making money was the *summum bonum,* but in the last twenty years a new type of devotee has appeared in the temple. Although liberals are generally non-materialistic in their personal lives, they have somehow developed the belief that plenty of government dollars can solve almost any kind of social and economic problem, whether it be in the field of state or national government, or in the field of international affairs.

The truth is that dollars, no matter how many, will not solve the problems of the underdeveloped areas. In the long run a country's institutions and attitudes will be more important in its development than the amount of wealth it can command. Those institutions and attitudes cannot be bought with dollars, or with any other kind of money; indeed, the availability of too much money may actually be harmful to their growth.

As a practical matter, of course, there is no danger whatsoever that too much money will become available for international development programs. The danger is that there will not be enough.

12. The Bargain Basement Delusion

"YOU CAN'T EXPECT to get something for nothing" is a good old adage which few Americans ever take very seriously. We are a nation of bargain-hunters, of senders-for-free-samples.

After the start of the war in Korea, when billions of dollars were again needed for the defense of the free world, and when billions more were being spent to put Europe back on her feet economically, the idea that a program costing 100 million dollars or so a year could really accomplish something to promote prosperity and peace was almost irresistibly attractive.

This was the picture that had been created in the minds of a lot of Americans, in many walks of life, but especially in the halls of Congress:

> the main reason the underdeveloped areas are in a parlous state is lack of American know-how;
>
> by sending out a few hundred American technicians, and by bringing a few hundred people from abroad into the United States for training, we can accomplish marvels of progress;
>
> there is no need for hand-outs or give-aways.

Tales of how crop yields had been doubled in this area, quadrupled in that, through the show-how efforts of one or two technicians, were told and retold (the tales were often true, but they did not tell the whole truth). The story of Etawah in India was repeated over and over, and glib predictions were made that India's food production could be doubled within ten years by the application of the same simple techniques and at very little expense. Even such an authority as Dr. Bennett sometimes let his enthusiasm run away with him: referring to Etawah in a speech given in August, 1951, he said:

> "Here the significant things are that progress is achieved swiftly and at a cost that seems unbelievable to the average American. You will agree with me, I think, that it would be unusual in this country to expect to increase wheat production from 13 to 27 bushels an acre with nothing more expensive than a $1.75 steel point for an ancient, bullock-drawn plow. But that is the way it is being done in India. That is the way it must be done."

Of course, Dr. Bennett knew that putting a steel point on a wooden plow was only one of many things that an Indian farmer had to do in order to double his wheat production, and that the process of teaching and persuading him to do these things required a lot of effort on the part of trained people and not inconsiderable expense. He would have maintained, I feel sure, that he did not intend to suggest otherwise. Yet, perhaps unconsciously, he gave his hearers the impression that it was relatively easy to enable an Indian farmer to double his production of food.

Often the spectacular stories of successes achieved by one or two men had to do with control of plant diseases. For example, in the lead paragraph of a story on a world-wide survey of Point 4 appearing in *The New York Times* of

January 12, 1953, the statement was made: "Ecuador's potato crop, a main food crop, has been increased sixfold." In the body of the story on the inside pages, it appeared that most of the increase was the result of introducing chemical control of a "blight which in recent years had ruined 75 per cent of the crop." Obviously, the achievement was a very great one, and had meant an enormous amount to the farmers of Ecuador, but there had been little net gain in Ecuador's food supply. Surely without intending to, *The Times'* writer had created a misleading impression of what Point 4 could accomplish.

For those who, like myself, believe in the Point 4 idea and want to persuade other people of its value, the temptation to talk in terms of isolated success stories is almost irresistible. One reason is that, in most countries, Point 4 has not been going long enough to achieve results which can be assessed quantitatively, and that, even where it has been, there are always other factors at work which mess up the statistics. If only *The Times* had been able to say: "After five years the average Ecuadoran has 10 per cent more to eat, and half of that increase is due to Point 4," that would have been quite different. In the few cases where statistics like that are beginning to appear (such as in extensive malaria control programs), the facts are that quite a lot of money was required to do the job. Again, the tendency is, among the supporters of pure Point 4, not to talk much about those cases, but to keep trotting out the one-man miracle stories.

Many of the Americans who have pushed the idea of a small Point 4 program have been connected in one way or another with missionary work. These people have a picture in their minds which they cherish: the picture of a man, or perhaps a couple, going out to a village and living there, devoting their lives to teaching the village people better agricultural methods, the rudiments of sanitation, and how to read and write. They see Point 4 in that image, in effect as an expansion and extension of the kind of work American missions and other private groups have been doing for decades.

Now this group speaks with authority; many of them have had experience in the underdeveloped areas and they do not underestimate the difficulties of helping millions of people to raise their standard of living. I think the explanation of their attitude is that they know the work as they see it requires an individual, person-to-person approach which is impossible on a large scale and which a big program would tend to overshadow. Further, and this is even more speculative, the missionary attitude, being mainly altruistic and humanitarian in motive, tends to be satisfied with small, scattered achievements. It is a wondrous thing to hear these good people talk about the success of a lifetime's work in half a dozen villages in some Asian country. They have had a profound effect on the lives of several hundred human beings, they know that it is good, and they are content. They do not worry about all the millions whom they did not reach; why should they? One does what one can; others must shoulder the burden elsewhere.

Perhaps this indicates a fundamental difference between the humanitarian approach to Point 4, and the approach of "hard-headed self-interest" which Dean Acheson used to talk about. The humanitarian is content to "do what one can," by the person-to-person approach. The realist is not content with that, because he is aware that it will accomplish such a very little; he is oppressed by the urgency of the world situation, and believes that a way must be found to help more people help themselves faster than can be done by the missionary's methods.

It is significant that the mission groups who favor a very limited approach are also the ones who hate to see Point 4 included in a "mutual security" program. They believe that it should be carried on for humanitarian reasons, and they deprecate any effort to justify it as necessary in the interest of the United States. (Perhaps in their hearts they realize that the Congress would never have launched the program for purely humanitarian reasons, but they prefer not to think of that.) The two things seem to go together; since they regard the program as a humanitarian endeavor, they are content to think of it as attacking only a small segment of the total problem, even over several decades.

One more word should be said about the "pure Point 4" enthusiasts. They believe that, so long as the program is kept small, it will continue to enjoy almost universal popularity, and they are mortally afraid that, if it becomes too big and expensive, it will lose that popularity and be killed by the Congress. Therefore, they tend to oppose actively the idea of "big grants," even where those grants are proposed as supplementary to the Point 4 program, rather than in place of it.

Now put yourself in the position of the average Congressman in the spring of 1952. On the one hand, here is the unpopular State Department asking for a Point 4 program of 150 million dollars for India and Pakistan alone. Here, on the other, is a group of obviously sincere people, with experience in these matters, who say that any such amount is unnecessary to accomplish the objectives of Point 4 and represents just another give-away which will serve no good purpose. This group reminds you that the late Dr. Bennett had been opposed to big grants and that he had known how India's food problem could be tackled inexpensively. There is even a suggestion that the people now running T.C.A. are New-Dealish and like to spend other people's money; you have heard there is a group even within T.C.A. who disagree with them. And then you remember how your constituents have been hollering about taxes and hammering at you to stop all those hand-outs to foreigners. What do you decide? Is it really any wonder that the requests for India and Pakistan were cut almost two-thirds? or the Point 4 program as a whole about a third?

In the 1953 session, the situation was somewhat different, for two reasons. First, the new Administration was in a stronger position with the Congress. Second, following a decision reached in the closing months of the Truman regime, parts of the large programs for the Middle East and South Asia had been separated out from the regular Point 4 budget and called "special economic assistance," so that the Point 4 request as such was less than half the size of the previous year's. Even so, the House of Representatives, following the lead of its Appropriations Committee, cut the Point 4 proposal to ribbons, and a major disaster was averted only in Conference, after extraordinary pressure from the White House had been reportedly brought to bear in the Senate. The final figure of 118 million dollars (which included 11 million dollars of "unobligated balances" reappropriated) was not too bad, especially in light of the fact that the requests for "special" aid had come through surprisingly well: 135 million dollars was appropriated for the Arab states, Israel and Iran—a cut of only 5 million dollars—and 75 million for India and Pakistan, as against a request of 94.4 million.

When Point 4-type programs are under consideration,

the economy bloc is always in a strong position. In the case of the Marshall Plan, no one said Europe could be rehabilitated after the war for a few millions of dollars. Nobody expects the military side of our national defense to be inexpensive. But when it comes to the development of the less developed areas, at least some of the experts say it can be done cheap.

Thus, the contest is an unequal one. A small Point 4 program has everything: it appeals to all kinds; it gives even the most isolationist legislators something to talk about in the foreign affairs field which makes them sound like internationally minded statesmen. As a result, it isn't even controversial any more. But a 200-million-dollar program for India, say, no matter what its content, no matter how much it may be based on the self-help principle, immediately looks like a give-away; it becomes intensely controversial. Although most of the Congress are agreed on the importance of keeping India in the free world, it takes courage for a politician to say that the job will take a lot of effort and money when others are saying it can be done painlessly. If you have one doctor who says you need an operation and another who says you don't, which do you believe? As I said before, everyone loves a bargain.

At this point the simple question "why *won't* a small program do the job?" demands an answer.

First, it is necessary to be a little more specific about what we mean by the word small. There is one group, especially on Capitol Hill, who mean by this a program costing less than 50 million dollars a year and consisting exclusively of straight technical assistance without program funds or supporting supplies and equipment in any quantity, a program in the image of those carried on by the

United Nations and its specialized agencies. This is the extreme view. It was never supported by Dr. Bennett or by anyone else in the T.C.A. organization. It would mean abandoning the approach that has been so successful in Latin America, for the key to the servicio idea is that both countries contribute program funds for jointly operated activities. And yet it is the position maintained by no less an authority in the field than Norris E. Dodd, former Director General of F.A.O. Indeed he used to accuse T.C.A. of operating a "bargain basement" program, because by providing program funds and supplies and equipment, it was underselling F.A.O.

The basic flaw in the approach of Dodd and his ilk is that the technician in the field is in the position of a bystander giving advice. Often, he can only submit reports and recommendations, and the reports and recommendations simply get filed away. Sometimes, he can establish a close continuing relationship with the local authorities. But fundamentally he is in the position of a kibitzer; he is not himself playing any cards. The analogy suggests the trouble with this kind of technical assistance: sooner or later, the kibitzee gets fed up and decides he doesn't need any more advice. I believe the time is coming when the governments of the underdeveloped countries will have had enough of programs which offer only advice.

Even those mission groups who favor a program of "pure Point 4" do not really favor "pure technical assistance" because they know that with a program of advice you cannot "get out to the people" as they so much want to do. They know that at least some program funds are needed—in a village development program, for example. A technician who is just an "adviser" is expected to advise government people, not to help ordinary people.

This is not to deny that, on many occasions, advice can be extraordinarily valuable, especially when it is given on the basis of on-the-spot research. Indeed, some of Point 4's most spectacular accomplishments have been in this category. Moreover, in all kinds of developmental programs, advice will always be an invaluable factor. But its role is limited. It cannot ordinarily provide the leverage that is needed to get joint activities under way. It lacks the trigger quality of "seed money."

Many, perhaps most, of the advocates of "pure Point 4" concede the necessity of providing program funds or supplies and equipment to give the technicians something to work with. They are in favor of a program ranging perhaps from 100 million dollars to 150 million dollars a year for all the underdeveloped areas. But they are either indifferent, or actively opposed, to grant aid which goes beyond the concept of training and demonstration.

In discussing the problems of the underdeveloped areas, these purists are always inclined to slide over the knotty question of where the crucially needed capital is going to come from. If compelled to face up to the problem, they will concede that technical cooperation alone cannot promote international development except at a painfully slow pace, and that capital is a necessity, even for the effective communication of knowledge and skills to millions of people. If further forced into a corner, they will say that private investment will provide most of the capital, and that any gap can be filled in through the use of loans. If you point out that up to now these two sources have failed to meet the need—by an appalling margin—they begin to back away, muttering that we could do more than we have done along those two lines.

There is no doubt that we could—within limits. In a

previous chapter, possible ways and means to step up private investment have been considered, and the conclusion was reached that the prospects were far from bright for a substantial flow to the areas where it is most needed. So far as loans are concerned, the banks could probably have been somewhat more flexible and less businesslike in their approach than they have been, but unless a fuzzy loan policy is adopted, the problems of repayment in dollars set a severe limit to what can be done. The argument is sometimes made that projects for which capital aid is needed can always be made self-liquidating and that therefore all such aid should be in the form of loans rather than grants. The facts are, however, that many worthy projects, such as the construction of schools, health centers, and even highways, are not self-liquidating, and that even those projects which may be self-liquidating in terms of local currency often will not produce any additional foreign exchange. Thus, even when everything conceivable has been done to step up the rate of private investment and of international loans, there will remain a series of acute needs which can be met only through the use of grants in one form or another.

In the first place, there are certain countries, such as Formosa, Indo-China, and Israel, which need help for current purposes, largely unrelated to Point 4, even in the broadest sense of the term. In the case of Formosa and Indo-China, this assistance is essential to enable these countries to carry a burden of military expenditures far beyond their economic capabilities. Israel, suffering acutely from its humane policy of hospitality to all Jewish immigrants, has had to face a fearful gap in its balance of payments, even after taking account of all outside assistance from private sources. Although both the Israeli and the United

States governments would have preferred it otherwise, only a fraction of the United States grant aid to Israel to date has been used for long-range developmental purposes.

In the second place, there are other countries where the need is for developmental aid, but where a program of technical cooperation simply will not do the job fast enough.

Consider the case of Iran, for example. Even though we were not in sympathy with the way the Mossadegh Government handled the oil dispute, we could not stand idly by and watch the country slide over the brink. This is not to say that financial aid should necessarily be provided to a government to enable it to meet its operating deficits, even though it may threaten to commit national suicide by turning to the Soviets for help if we do not. That would be a kind of blackmail operation to which there might be no end. But the people of Iran could not safely be left with the feeling that they had been utterly abandoned by the West and that they had no hope of making any progress except through moving in the direction of communism.

The usual kind of technical cooperation program was not adequate for this kind of situation. For one thing, the Mossadegh Government was so desperately short of revenue that it could not make substantial contributions to the Point 4 operations, and the United States Government had to put up most of the money for the necessary local currency expenses of the program in Iran, as well as for the dollar costs.[1] In addition, in order to have an immediate quantitative effect on the country, it was necessary to do things on more than a pilot project basis. In the highly successful malaria control program of 1952, for example, the United States put up some 2.5 million dollars for D.D.T. and other supplies so that a quarter of Iran's villages could be protected. One could say that this was demonstration in the sense that it was showing the people of Iran how to protect themselves from malaria, but certainly the economic aid component was an unusually large one. Similarly, although one might argue that the provision of a water treatment plant for Teheran would demonstrate the value of clean water, that project was mainly of value for its psychological effect on the people of the riot-torn capital city. When American dollars were used to make possible the completion of nearly finished industrial plants, the accomplishment per dollar was very great, but here again the technical assistance element was minor.

The net result of "beefing up" the Point 4 program in Iran has been a set of achievements which are probably more impressive than in any other country, and the impact on the Iranian people has been correspondingly great. In spite of the Government's financial difficulties, tens of thousands of Iranians, especially in the rural areas, have been given a sense of hope for the first time. It is indeed quite conceivable that, had it not been for this program, Iran would have slipped behind the iron curtain by now.

The replacement of the weeping Mossadegh by a government both more friendly to the United States and more responsible only intensifies the need for substantial economic aid to Iran. Much of the aid will doubtless have to be of a character to meet a critical financial emergency, but it should be possible for a sizable proportion of it to be designed to promote Iran's economic and social development.[2]

The need for a program comprising a considerable amount of economic aid as a supplement to the work of the technicians is also acute in some of the Arab states. Point 4 enthusiasts have pointed to the program in Jordan, where the servicio device is being used, as in many ways a model program, which indeed it is. But it is also a relatively costly program. The United States Government has been putting in almost 2.5 dollars a year per Jordanian. (If that rate of expenditure were in effect throughout the less developed areas, the annual outlay for Point 4 would be some 2.5 billion dollars.)

And even more substantial aid will have to be given to the Arab states than has been to date. Large amounts of capital are needed for the development of the region's meager water resources and inadequate transportation system. Although some of this capital can be obtained in the form of loans, and some from the United Nations agency for the relief and resettlement of the refugees from Palestine, these sources will not be enough.

In addition to the economic factors calling for grant aid to the Arab states, there is a compelling political reason. Until one has visited in the Arab world, and has talked, not only to Arabs but to Americans who have long been exposed to the Arab point of view, it is difficult to imagine the depth of bitterness toward the United States because of its part in the establishment of the State of Israel. This bitterness has unfortunately been accentuated by the large sums given to Israel, which have made the programs in the Arab states look puny by comparison and which have been regarded by the Arabs as proof of the fact that we were not, as we claimed, impartial. In spite of the efforts of the United States Government to make our large contributions to the United Nations agency for the relief and resettlement of the Arab refugees from Palestine look like a counterbalance to the grants to Israel, the Arabs have refused to regard them as such. Their attitude is, "These eight hundred thousand unfortunates happen to be living within our borders, but they are not our responsibility, they are yours." Whatever one may think of the reasonableness of this attitude, it exists.

Considering how crucial the Middle East is for the security of the free world, the situation is an alarming one. As Moslems, the Arabs tend to be hostile to communism, but this barrier would scarcely be enough to prevent them from turning for help to the communist bloc if they once became convinced that they could not expect fair treatment from the West. And the occasional anti-Jewish outbursts among the communists are well calculated to make the Arabs look upon them as natural allies.

Of course we could mollify the Arabs by withdrawing our support from Israel, but that is unthinkable. Not only are we deeply committed in a moral sense to Israel's survival, but the crushing of this brave and hopeful new state would be an appalling and wholly intolerable tragedy in human terms. That being the case, the only way we can demonstrate our impartiality is by providing the Arab states also with a certain amount of grant aid to be used for developmental projects, in such fields as transportation and water development. Hopefully, a beginning will be made in the present (1954) fiscal year with some of the 135 million dollars provided by the Congress as special economic aid for the Near East region. How much will be available will depend on how much has to go to Israel and how much to Iran for emergency and developmental purposes.

The area in which pure technical assistance is most obviously inadequate is the Indian sub-continent. In both India and Pakistan, there is a desperate shortage of time and capital for the development job that has to be done.

No one can prove beyond a doubt that India is in danger of going communist in the 1956 elections. But most Americans who have lived there in the last year or two, including experienced newspapermen and Foreign Service officers, believe that there is a very grave danger of just that, especially if Nehru's Government fails to meet its Five-Year Plan goals and the masses of the people feel that they are making no real progress.

If India had adequate sources of capital, the necessary rate of development could perhaps be achieved with technical assistance from United Nations and United States agencies. But India is desperately short of capital, simply because her national income is so low that savings, the prerequisite of capital, cannot be accumulated. At the present time, India's savings are less than 5 per cent of her national income, which is barely enough to keep the existing capital plant intact and to stay abreast of an annual population increase of 1 to 1.5 per cent. The Indian Planning Commission is hoping that the rate of savings can be pushed up to 6.75 per cent by 1955-56, and after that rapidly to 20 per cent in 1967-68 by saving half of all increases in national income. In a country with a vaguely socialist political climate such as India's, this kind of saving and capital investment cannot be accomplished (as it was in most cases of rapid industrial development such as occurred in England, the United States, Germany and Japan) by the plowing back of large private profits, because no government which permitted such profits to be earned could survive at the polls. The only alternative is a rigorous policy of holding down levels of consumption (as was done in the U.S.S.R. in the twenties and thirties), either through heavy taxation, forced savings, or their equivalent for this purpose, inflationary financing. As the Indian Planning Commission has said, with British-like understatement, such an effort "will necessitate a great deal of hard work and austerity." [3]

But the effort can scarcely begin—the increases in national income of which half are to be saved cannot be achieved—if the immediate goals of the Five-Year Plan cannot be met. And the difference between the projected cost of the Plan (some 20 billion rupees, or about 4 billion dollars) and India's foreseeable resources is about 700 million dollars. Since the five-year period started on April 1, 1951, and runs only until March 31, 1956, that means a gap of about 200 million dollars a year, calculating from the summer of 1953. This was approximately the level of aid which Chester Bowles and Clifford Willson, the able Point 4 director in India, recommended for the fiscal year 1953-54. The Eisenhower Administration cut the request almost in half, and the Congress then sliced it another 20 per cent or so, to less than 90 million dollars.

One of the most important objectives of the Plan is to make India self-sufficient in food grains by 1956. In recent years, India has had to import 4 to 5 million tons of grain annually, thus using up an inordinately large proportion of her precious foreign exchange which might otherwise have been used for capital goods contributing to industrial development. Taking into account a population increase of some twenty to twenty-five million during the five-year period and taking into account also the fact that some of any increase in food production is inevitably consumed by the cultivators themselves, the Planning Commission calculated that an increase of 7.6 million tons, or about 15 per cent, in food grain production would be necessary to achieve the goal of self-sufficiency. Most of the United States aid to India up to now has been devoted to helping India achieve this food production increase, whether through assistance to the ambitious community development program and to large and small irrigation projects, or through imports of commodities such as fertilizer and steel for farm implements.[4]

The situation in Pakistan is in many ways similar to that in India, except that the country is about one-quarter the size, in terms both of population and area. Until recently, Pakistan was considered to be self-sufficient in food, but in the spring of 1953, an acute shortage of grain developed, which led the United States Government to make an emergency grant to Pakistan of one million tons of wheat out of United States stocks. A request put in terms of food for the starving is always more appealing to the Congress and to the American people than any other type of help, especially when our warehouses are bulging, but we should not delude ourselves as to the real nature of the request. Since there was no world shortage of grain, and since Pakistan could therefore readily have bought the wheat if she had chosen to draw on her scanty reserves of foreign exchange, the problem was essentially a financial one; that is, the issue facing the United States was not the simple one of whether or not to allow millions of Pakistani to starve, but the complex and difficult one of whether to force Pakistan to pursue dangerous fiscal policies that would threaten her economic stability and rate of development. The same was largely true, by the way, of the 190 million dollars wheat loan we made to India in 1951.

Obviously the only way to prevent such appeals for emergency help from being made again and again in the future is to help the Pakistani and the Indians to increase their food production and indeed their rate of development generally. Giving or lending them wheat will contribute to that end to the extent that they sell the wheat and devote the proceeds to developmental programs, but other types of aid will be needed in addition. Certainly, a small Point 4 program, consisting of a hundred or so technicians and a few million dollars of program funds, will not fill the bill.

No one can say with confidence just how much money the United States should spend for developmental programs in the less developed areas of the world. In 1950, a careful study was made at the direction of President Truman by an able group headed by Gordon Gray and Edward Mason; they concluded that "a needed, feasible and effective program" of grants for technical assistance and development in the underdeveloped areas "would require funds of up to about 500 million dollars a year for several years, apart from emergency requirements arising from military action." The following year the International Development Advisory Board, then chaired by Nelson Rockefeller, confirmed the conclusion of the "Gray Report" as to the need for about 500 million dollars for United States grant aid, and further recommended that the United States subscribe 200 million dollars to the capital of an International Development Authority empowered to make partial grants for public works, and another 150 million dollars to the capital of an International Finance Corporation to encourage private investment.[5]

Whether these figures are precisely correct or not, they

indicate an order of magnitude which is commensurate with the problem. My own feeling is that anything over 1 billion dollars a year would be difficult to spend wisely and with lasting results, and that anything much less than 500 million dollars is inadequate to the needs.

13. The Role of the United Nations

IN ANY GROUP discussing the problems of international development, there is almost always at least one bright-eyed idealist who will argue that we ought to channel all our aid to the underdeveloped areas through the United Nations.

This position is a very appealing one, but it is scarcely realistic. In the first place—on a strictly practical level—the Congress, which is already unhappy over the fact that we have been contributing 60 per cent of the funds for the present modest United Nations technical assistance program, would scarcely be willing to raise the United States contribution to 90 or 95 per cent. Yet that is what it would have to be if all our present aid for the underdeveloped areas were to be handled on a multilateral basis.

In the second place, and on a somewhat higher plane of argument, if the contribution of one country was to be so great a part of the total, the program would inevitably tend to lose some of its international character, so that part of the point of turning United States funds over to a multilateral agency would be lost.

But there is a third consideration which seems to me decisive. In brief: the total job of administering aid for the less developed areas would be too hot to handle for the United Nations, especially in these early crucial years of its existence.

There would, on the one hand, be a grave danger of log-rolling. If the international development agency were organized as a subsidiary of the United Nations Assembly, or of the Economic and Social Council (E.C.O.S.O.C.), or if it were set up in the notably democratic pattern of the specialized agencies, it would tend to be dominated by the underdeveloped nations themselves. No matter what fine criteria for aid were adopted at the outset, there would be a strong temptation for country A to say to country B: "Of course, your pet project would be a waste of money, while ours fits the criteria perfectly; but since there seems to be opposition to ours for some unaccountable reason, we will support yours, if you will go along with ours." If this kind of politicking were in fact to develop, so that the funds were going down the sewer of politically motivated "pork barrel" projects, it would not take long for a world-wide stink to arise. The American taxpayer, who would be carrying the main load, would justifiably rebel, and the net effect would be harmful to the whole United Nations concept.

The danger of log-rolling might be minimized if the agency were set up either as a subsidiary of the International Bank or along the same lines, as has often been suggested. The Bank has a strong executive, and the actual decision-making power tends to reside in the contributors to its capital, more or less in proportion to their contributions. But this kind of organization would give the United States such a dominant voice in the affairs of the agency as virtually to destroy its international status.

Moreover, there is another even more disruptive problem which any international agency, no matter how organized, would face if it were given sole responsibility for developmental programs. As we have seen in previous chapters, the need for assistance is most urgent in those areas of the world which lie along the periphery of the communist bloc. Thus, any administrator of a United States aid program is going to give higher priority to India, Pakistan and Iran, for example, than to many other countries. But how could an agency affiliated with the United Nations make any such distinction? How could it, especially now that Russia has agreed to contribute to its developmental programs, adopt criteria which would be other than purely economic and social? An international agency in these circumstances would be faced with a fearful dilemma: either it must use its funds in a uniform way, ignoring factors of time and urgency, or it must open itself to attacks of partisanship.

As a corollary to this, it must be added that the United States in its own security interests cannot afford to surrender control of all the funds it is prepared to spend for assistance to the underdeveloped areas. We could not take the chance that the countries in the most acute danger would not be given the amount of aid we felt they needed in order to survive as free nations. Moreover, there are times (such as following Mossadegh's ouster in Iran in August, 1953) when an unforeseen emergency will be so great as to require that funds originally intended for long-range developmental purposes be diverted to attain short-range objectives. As suggested in a later chapter, this is a most unfortunate thing to have to do, and it could be avoided if the Congress would appropriate funds for such contingencies. But the Congress has consistently refused to do this, and has insisted that at least tentative programs be submitted in support of all appropriation requests. Accordingly, we have no reserves for contingencies unless we keep control of at least some of our available aid funds. In today's world, we cannot do without such protection.

None of these arguments against an international aid program applies to anything like the same extent if one is talking, not about giving the United Nations the whole job, but about giving it a larger share of the job. The present state of affairs, in which the United Nations programs are seriously overshadowed by what the United States is doing, is unhealthy for the United Nations and therefore for the United States, and is bad for the self-respect of the underdeveloped countries themselves.

This is of course not to say that the international agencies—the U.N.T.A.A., F.A.O., W.H.O., U.N.E.S.C.O., I.L.O., the International Bank, and the others—have not made important contributions to the development of the less developed areas through technical assistance projects of many kinds. (A very few of their achievements have been mentioned in earlier chapters.) But by any standards, the disparity in size between the United States and the United Nations developmental programs is very great. In terms of personnel, the ratio is probably nearly two to one, and in money terms it is about ten to one.

On a logical basis, considering purely the relative advantages of the two types of organization, there is no justification whatever for such a disproportionate allocation of responsibilities. Indeed most of the intrinsic factors favor the international agencies. Underdeveloped countries quite naturally prefer to get help from a multilateral agency to which they have themselves contributed and in which they therefore feel a sense of proprietorship. A

United Nations agency can more easily recruit experts from all over the world, experts whose background and special skills may well equip them to tackle the problems of the countries requesting assistance far better than any American experts could do. In addition, international agencies have certain obvious advantages where regional programs, such as for the control of locusts or communicable diseases, are concerned. Most important of all, when the social, economic or political situation in a particular underdeveloped country demands action that may be difficult for the country to take, experts with international status can make the necessary recommendations forcefully, without fear that their motives will be misconstrued.

It is true that there are certain intrinsic disadvantages to multilateral operation, as compared with bilateral. In the first place, the language problem is apt to be greater. When shirt-sleeve diplomats cannot speak the language of the country they are working in, the problem of communication is acute enough, but when technicians working on the same team cannot understand each other, the difficulties are multiplied. In the second place, an organization which has a number of sovereign bosses is almost bound to be more cumbersome, less flexible, and slower to take action than an agency which is a part of only one government.

The present United Nations technical assistance program has certain other disadvantages relative to the United States programs which, while not intrinsic, were probably difficult to avoid under all the circumstances. Based on observations here and there, I would venture a guess that a higher proportion of the personnel of the multilateral agencies sought their jobs for economic reasons than is true of the United States agency personnel, and that this in turn has led to a cautious and unidealistic job-holding attitude in some missions. Probably not all observers would agree with this conclusion, but hardly any would deny that the multilateral program has suffered from bureaucratic jealousies. The specialized agencies, while affiliated with the United Nations and represented on the Technical Assistance Board of E.C.O.S.O.C., are independent entities, with memberships varying from each other and from the United Nations itself. They are afraid of becoming involved in the United Nations' political battles, and tend to resist direct control by any central authority. Acting on the advice of a series of consultants and unbiased observers, officials at the United Nations headquarters have sought to bring about a greater degree of coordination and integration of the various programs by appointing resident representatives of the United Nations in many underdeveloped countries, and by appointing a full-time Executive Chairman of the Technical Assistance Board.[1] But some of the agencies, notably F.A.O., have resisted these efforts, clinging to the untenable principle that a country's problems can be broken down into arbitrary compartments—agriculture, health, etc.—and dealt with separately by separate agencies. It is curious, and depressing, that international agencies in so short a time should develop to such an intense degree the empire-building (or empire-preserving, if you prefer) proclivities usually associated with long-established old-line agencies of a national government.

If the achievements and prestige of the United Nations developmental programs have suffered somewhat from these difficulties and weaknesses, they have suffered far more from the fact that the programs have been limited to the purest kind of technical assistance. To a certain extent this has been due to a rigid idea of what developmental programs should properly consist of, but in the main it has been due simply to paucity of funds. With only a few million dollars available, an agency cannot spend much on program funds or supplies and equipment, or even on transportation for its own personnel.[2] Since the launching of the Expanded Technical Assistance Programme in the fall of 1949, many of those concerned with it have come to realize the importance of being able to contribute something besides advice. In 1951, the Technical Assistance Committee of E.C.O.S.O.C. recommended that ways and means of meeting needs for supplies for certain types of projects be studied and that greater emphasis be given to the establishment of training and demonstration centers and pilot plants, and the General Assembly welcomed the move.[3] But the possibilities for moving in that direction have been severely limited, except where the international agencies have been able to find supplementary funds from other sources. W.H.O. has worked out some excellent projects in conjunction with the more adequately financed United Nations Children's Fund, and both W.H.O. and U.N.E.S.C.O. have gladly joined forces with the United States in attacking particular problems, with the United States supplying most of the funds for needed supplies and equipment.

It is of course not fair to pin the blame for the small size of the United Nations funds on the United States alone. At least within the Executive Branch during the Truman Administration, there was a disposition to make available to the multilateral programs all the funds they could use, provided the United States contribution did not go above 60 per cent of the total. This attitude was not matched by many other United Nations members— even the United Kingdom, for example, has contributed only a little over 1 million dollars a year and Canada less than a million, and most of the other countries have been less generous. While the Soviet Union's promise in mid-1953 to contribute 4 million rubles to the U.N.T.A.A. was highly significant in view of its previous failure to contribute anything to the United Nations program, the sum involved is relatively small in terms of Russia's resources. On the whole, in spite of general enthusiasm for the program, tangible support for it from non-United States sources has been meager (although steadily improving).

One reason for this, undoubtedly, has been the rule early adopted by E.C.O.S.O.C. and the General Assembly that no nation could specify how or in what area its contribution should be used. Not only has the United States wanted to retain control over the disposition of a large part of its aid funds, but also the Commonwealth nations have been more open-handed in their allocations to the Colombo plan than to the United Nations program.[4] It is possible that a system might be worked out which would permit contributing nations to specify how at least a part of their contribution should be used. There are some risks, particularly of politicking, in this sort of approach, but with proper safeguards it might provide an effective means for expanding the scope of the United Nations developmental work beyond the present low level.

While the United States may not be responsible for the financial stringency facing the United Nations technical assistance program, we must bear a large share of the blame for blocking the idea of a moderate international grant aid program to be administered by an International Development Authority organized along the lines of the International Bank or under its control.

The idea of such an international program was included among the recommendations of the International Development Advisory Board under Nelson Rockefeller's chairmanship in its 1951 "Partners in Progress" report, and has been enthusiastically pressed by a number of countries at every recent session of the General Assembly and ECOSOC. Regrettably, the United States has consistently opposed it. The argument of the American representatives, acting under State Department instructions, has been that no nation had any substantial funds to put into such an organization and that therefore it was misleading to the underdeveloped areas even to talk about its creation, since such talk could only give rise to false hopes. Our position has inevitably created the unfortunate (but correct) impression that we wanted to hold complete control over all funds we might have available for foreign aid, which in turn suggested (not correctly) that we had undisclosed and nefarious motives for giving aid to the underdeveloped countries.

Even assuming that we do not want to make any large sums available for such an authority, we could accomplish our objective much more tactfully by announcing that of course we are in favor of an international development fund, and that we would be willing to match any other contributions to it, but that we feel strongly that no one nation should provide more than 50 per cent (or perhaps 60) of the whole amount. No one could quarrel with this latter conclusion, which is an eminently reasonable one if the agency is to be kept truly international, and we would appear before the world in a far more favorable light. The sincerity of our protestations of faith in the United Nations and of our wish to help the less developed nations according to *their* desires, rather than ours, would be re-established.

The result would of course be a relatively small operation. Even assuming that the development fund and the technical assistance program funds were combined, and that the British Commonwealth nations could be persuaded to add to the fund the contributions they have been making to the Colombo Plan,[5] the total from all nations other than the United States could hardly be more than 50 million dollars a year. This would call for a maximum of, say, 70 million dollars from the United States, which could be subtracted from the amount we would otherwise contribute to our own and the United Nations technical cooperation programs.

We would seem to have everything to gain and nothing to lose by doing this much. It would not inhibit our own programs in critical areas such as India and Iran, it would probably increase the total benefit to the underdeveloped areas, especially to the extent that new contributions from other countries might be forthcoming for a more dramatic program, and it would certainly enhance the prestige of the United Nations.

If something like this is not done, the multilateral technical assistance program may eventually lose its momentum. Although at the present time, interest in the program is at a new high, and far more requests for help are received than can be filled, the time is not far off, in the opinion of many observers, when the less developed countries will have had enough of experts able to furnish nothing but advice.

Whether the United States should do more than offer to match other contributions to such an international fund is a much more difficult question. I personally would doubt the wisdom of our doing so, at least until the operation had proved itself effective after several years of experience.

In any event, it seems clear that we should not now attempt to limit our activities in the less developed areas either to a purely multilateral or a purely bilateral set of operations. The prospect of continuing with both types of programs for an indefinite period may seem unattractive because of the difficulty of coordinating the two, but this problem is not as troublesome as might be imagined. In the early stages of Point 4, when both the United Nations and United States were desperately trying to get their programs off the ground, there was a certain amount of competition between them. The difficulty was multiplied by the tendency of some governments to shop around for the best possible terms, playing one agency off against another. But experience has led to the solution of most of these problems. In many countries technical assistance committees have been established, usually including the chiefs of the United States and United Nations aid missions, and the question of which organization should undertake a particular project has been settled on a sensible basis by deciding which could handle the job more easily and more effectively. The host government, of course, must make the final decision, but a good working relationship between United States and United Nations representatives, such as now exists in most countries, can effectively influence that decision in the right direction. Moreover, there has been a wholesome tendency for the agencies to seek ways of working together on joint projects and to work out together their respective roles in an integrated, overall country development program, rather than simply trying to stay out of each other's way.[6] A relative increase in the size and scope of the United Nations program should not interfere with this trend toward better cooperation, coordination and mutual support.

Returning to the practical level of argument suggested at the beginning of the chapter, the danger is that the role of the United Nations will be cut down, rather than increased. There has been a strong tendency in the Congress to limit the United States contributions for the multilateral technical assistance program to one-third of the total (as in the regular United Nations budget), which would just about wreck the program, since the contributions of others would probably be reduced rather than increased if we took such a step. Even if this did not happen, the amount available would drop from about 20 million to about 12 million dollars.

Americans who believe in the Point 4 concept, as well as those interested in the future of the United Nations, must make their voices heard on the subject of giving the United Nations a more important role to play in the international development field. The short answer to the question of what that role should be is that it ought to be as big as is feasible under all the circumstances. As stated in the original Fourth Point, the enterprise should be a cooperative one in which all nations work together through the United Nations and its specialized agencies "wherever practicable."

Certainly there should be no room for the argument

that we should get credit for whatever we do, and not let the United Nations have too much of the glory. After all, the more glory the United Nations can acquire, the better for us. The purpose of foreign aid in the underdeveloped areas is not to win gratitude, but peace.

14. The American Way of Life Is Not the Only Way

IN A SENSE it would be a lot easier if we *could* turn over the whole job of helping the less developed areas to the United Nations. The task is an awesome one, and we are perhaps not yet mature enough as a nation to handle it wisely. Since, however, we seem to be stuck with a huge share of the responsibility, for a few decades at least, we must pray, first of all, for humility.

Everybody agrees in principle that the American way of life is not the only way and that a program like Point 4 must aim to help other nations develop in the ways that are right for them. But deep down, most Americans have a tendency to believe that our way *is* the only way—or at least the best way, not only for us, but for everybody.

Sometimes this arrogance is painfully obvious. One has only to read a few speeches in the Congress of the United States on the subject of a Point 4 appropriation to find plenty of embarrassingly critical or patronizing comments about our neighbors in the underdeveloped areas. Frequently the implication is that if the peoples of these areas are poor, it is their own fault; that if they really wanted to, they could solve their problems by being industrious and thrifty, like Americans. In the spring of

1952, the appropriation for aid to South and Southeast Asia was cut in half in the House, right after Representative Davis of Georgia had made a shocking speech, the gist of which was: "Why should we spend good taxpayers' dollars on stupid, superstitious people who waste most of what we give them on cows and monkeys?"

Henry Hazlitt has established some sort of record for carrying this kind of argument to its most absurd extremity. In his book *Illusions of Point Four* (The Foundation for Economic Education, 1950), Hazlitt quotes Harry Truman's statement that, if the peoples of the underdeveloped areas are "frustrated and disappointed" in their aspirations for a better life, "they may turn to false doctrines which hold that the way of progress lies through tyranny," and then comments upon it as follows:

> "Is not this, perhaps, a reversal of cause and effect? Is it not in many cases precisely because they have *already* turned to false doctrines that they are frustrated and disappointed? If, instead of adopting a caste system or ancestor worship, say, they had adopted a system of free markets, free entrance to work and enterprise, free competition, free initiative, equality of opportunity, stability of currency, security of life and limb and private property, and voluntary restraint in population growth—would they be today as frustrated and disappointed and underdeveloped as they are?" *

But it is not only the Hazlitts and Davises who are convinced of American superiority in all things. Some of our own representatives abroad feel the same way and take no pains to conceal the fact. In a mixed Pakistani-American

---

* Hazlitt's basic approach to Point 4 is revealed by the fact that he attributes the idea to Earl Browder. Actually, of course, the communists have been fighting the program with every propaganda weapon in their arsenal, and often with violence, ever since it started.

group sitting around Ambassador Avra Warren's living room in Karachi, I heard an American communications expert and his wife bitterly complain about everything and everybody in Pakistan. When they finally left, the Ambassador stormed that he would never have them in his house again, but the damage had been done.

This particular expert had been appointed by the United Nations Technical Assistance Administration, but the United States agencies, in spite of all their efforts to screen out the lemons, have made mistakes too.

Still another form of American arrogance is displayed by those who favor sending out thousands of young Americans more or less indiscriminately to work in the towns and villages of Asia and the Middle East. Deputy Secretary of Defense Roger Kyes, for example, thinks the young lads in the Future Farmers of America could handle the job nicely. This notion overlooks the fact that untrained Americans in large numbers simply would not be welcome: the local governments would not want them wandering around, trying to do the work the local ministries are responsible for, and the ordinary people would tend to look on them with suspicion, if not hostility.

But an even more fundamental fallacy in the idea is the assumption that just being an American is enough of a qualification for a shirt-sleeve diplomat. Probably the greatest single problem confronting Point 4 today is that of finding the right people to work at these extraordinarily delicate and difficult jobs. Not only must the expert be technically qualified, so that he can command the respect of the ministry officials with whom he will be working, but he must be tactful, imaginative and flexible in his approach, free from all national or color prejudice, and physically and mentally equipped to stand the strain of living under strange and difficult conditions for a protracted period of time. Besides all this, his wife must have most of these qualities, too! [1]

Even the very best people will make occasional blunders and will sometimes find themselves up against a stone wall in trying to induce some change in local methods that seems to them obviously desirable. Both T.C.A. and M.S.A. came increasingly to the conclusion that each of their missions overseas needed at least one cultural anthropologist to advise it on problems of this kind. A trained anthropologist can usually tell what local practices are subject to change if a better way is demonstrated, and what habits are so deeply engrained that they are best let alone. He can often suggest ways of getting around difficulties that seem insuperable to the technician.

One of the trickiest questions in all self-help programs is that of motivation. While it may be an oversimplification to say, as some experts have said, that development is a state of mind, there is no question that incentives are crucial. Economic considerations may not be controlling. In India, for instance, even the poorest people are reluctant to switch from their standard diet of rice or wheat to tapioca, which is cheaper and more nourishing, but which they are not used to. Faced with rigidities of this kind, the administrators of India's community development plan are anxious to have some of their workers trained in cultural anthropology.

In a program such as Point 4, the effort must always be to introduce change which is acceptable within the indigenous cultural pattern. A famous case in Point 4 annals was that of the blue cow in India. In one area, herds of antelope were doing a lot of damage to crops; the antelopes were inaccurately known as blue cows and the Hindu farmers refused to kill them, on religious grounds; someone had the bright idea that the Government should issue a decree changing the antelope's name to blue horse. The farmers promptly began to take action to protect their crops. A horse was not sacred, and could be killed.

There is no doubt that India *is* overpopulated with cows and monkeys. But the problem, which the Indian Government is fully aware of, is not going to be solved by American insults or demands. It is in the process of being solved gradually by the Indians themselves: more and more states are now giving bounties for monkeys, and the free roaming cattle are beginning to be regulated. What the American technicians can do is make suggestions for improvement that take account of, and show respect for, the Hindus' religious sensitivities. The discovery and introduction of a legume crop that the cows would not eat has already been mentioned. Also, the thought can be conveyed to Indian farmers that they will be kinder to their cattle if they prevent indiscriminate breeding and take better care of the calves that are born.

Precisely the same hands-off attitude must be maintained by Americans towards India's caste system. Almost all educated Indians are opposed to it, and in the cities caste distinctions have almost disappeared, but the system remains strong in many rural areas. To the extent that the community development scheme can promote a kind of civic-mindedness among the villagers, it will doubtless tend to break down the barriers. And Americans can have an influence by being friendly to all and by not being afraid to get their hands dirty at any kind of a task. Horace Holmes tells of a farewell ceremony that was given in his honor at Etawah in a Hindu temple: for the first time in the history of the village, Brahmans, untouchables and Moslems were gathered together. But American criticism of the caste system to those who still believe in it will only stiffen their backs.

In the Moslem world, a devout man must perform ablutions five times a day. In places where the water supply is limited and foul, this practice results in transmission of disease. But it would be fruitless, and probably dangerous, for Americans to urge that the holy ablutions be suspended on sanitary grounds. (Would American Christians be likely to listen to anyone who said that men must keep their hats on in church to avoid catching cold?) Obviously, the answer to the Moslem ablution problem is to clean up the water supplies, and in many places that is being done.

In Latin America, virtually nothing can be done by our Point 4 teams without the approval of the Roman Catholic Church. And in Israel the Sabbath customs must be respected.

The essential point is, as one anthropologist has stated it, that our technicians "are going among people who have a developed culture, if not a developed technology; people who value their way of life and want to keep its essence undisturbed." If the Point 4 program tends to give these people a means of realizing to a greater degree the goals that they themselves recognize, it will be a success. If it attempts to substitute new, American-type goals, it will surely fail.[2]

15. Neither a Stick nor a Carrot

ONE OF THE CLASSIC YARNS about American politics concerns the district leader who was disappointed to find that a long-time supporter had deserted him in a primary fight. "How could you do this to me?" the leader wanted to know. "Didn't I get you a nice soft job at City Hall a couple of years ago? And what about those World Series tickets last year? And didn't I keep your boy out of jail a few months back?" The renegade's chilly reply was: "And what have you done for me lately?"

Some of our Ambassadors and State Department policy-makers would do well to have that little story framed and hung in front of their desks. For it seems to be remarkably easy to forget that gratitude is just as much of a will o' the wisp in international affairs as it is in ward politics.

The primary objective of Point 4 is not, of course, to win the gratitude of foreign governments or peoples, and most shirt-sleeve diplomats keep this well in mind. Oddly enough, it is rather those professional diplomats and political officers who consider themselves hard-headed realists who are apt to want to use Point 4 in whatever way will please the recipient governments most. If they had their wish they would end up by justifying the catcalls of Point 4's opponents who call it "Operation Rathole."

For once you start trying to win the support of foreign governments by giving them aid, there is no end to it. They can always say: "What have you done for me lately?"

Admittedly the temptations to make Point 4 a method of "winning friends and influencing people" are very great. There are so often things that we are trying to get a government to do. It may be a commercial treaty that we want; or a favorable vote on a crucial issue in the United Nations; or a commitment to join a collective defense arrangement of some kind. Those who have the responsibility for conducting our foreign relations have to look for blue chips to play with. To them an appropriation of a few million dollars for a Point 4 program in a given country often looks like a very nice blue chip.

The temptation is all the stronger because many a government in the underdeveloped areas would much rather have a slice of grant aid to use as it sees fit, than a technical cooperation program which may require considerable effort on its part. If it gets an idea that it may be able to get the candy, it will refuse the spinach.

These problems are by no means hypothetical. The administrators of T.C.A. a number of times had to resist proposals from Ambassadors to use Point 4 funds for the achievement of short-range political objectives. Sometimes they were successful in doing so, sometimes not.

In one case, T.C.A. lost the first round, but won the last. The Ambassador to country X had become worried that communists were going to score successes in an upcoming election because of widespread unemployment, and he persuaded Washington, over T.C.A.'s protest, to transfer Point 4 funds from elsewhere to country X so as to launch several projects that would put a lot of people to work. Because of bureaucratic delays, the W.P.A.-type projects never got started before the election, the communist threat turned out to have been exaggerated, and the money was eventually put to constructive use.

One must of course admit that there may occasionally be times when such raids will be justified from the standpoint of the security interests of the United States. What T.C.A. tried to do was to keep before the top policy-makers the long-range considerations: the fact that each time Point 4 funds are used for short-range purposes or to obtain a *quid pro quo* of some kind, Point 4's reputation as a non-political program to help others help themselves is tarnished; that each time candy is substituted for spinach, a precedent is created which will make future requests for candy harder to resist. One of the dangers of the new highly centralized F.O.A. set-up is that there may no longer be any influential group in the Government to fight for this long-range point of view.

Unfortunately not all the professional diplomats are alive to these considerations. Some of them are shockingly cynical about the "hopelessness" of "backward peoples" and therefore tend to think that Point 4 is a waste of money and effort. (One often wonders if even their suave exteriors can effectively conceal their feelings of superiority when dealing with the acute and sensitive representatives of these "backward peoples.") This type often argues that the peoples of the underdeveloped areas have no influence on their own destinies anyway, and that the rise and fall of their governments depend entirely on the machinations of various ruling cliques, all of which are more or less corrupt. I have even heard one or two Foreign Service Officers strenuously deny that poverty and hunger tend to make people any more susceptible to communist propaganda!

On one occasion the preconceptions of key officers in an American Embassy led them to attribute desires to the local government leaders which did not at all reflect the latter's feelings. The Embassy reported that a sizable grant to the government as an indication of United States good will and support was essential, and that the government wanted it in the form of rice, because of a desperate shortage. The T.C.A. stuck to the belief that, if the government leaders knew that the money could be used instead for a Point 4 type of program which would help to raise the living standards of a sizable segment of the country's people, they would prefer that course. The Embassy at first declined to let T.C.A. even suggest such an idea to the local officials, on the ground that the latter would feel that an attractive offer was in effect being withdrawn, and would be offended. When a T.C.A. representative arrived on the spot, however, the Embassy apparently decided that it could not prevent him from communicating T.C.A.'s idea to the government. It turned out that the government was in fact much less interested in getting the grain than in a long-range developmental program.

Admittedly, this was an exceptional case, but it nevertheless reveals an attitude of near hostility to Point 4 on the part of certain career diplomats, who have a kind of snobbish distaste for anything that looks even vaguely like social uplift. Some Congressmen have a tendency to believe that "new dealish" bureaucrats must be behind anything in the nature of a hand-out, but in fact those who press for that type of program are apt to be politically very conservative. Perhaps it is because charity from up down fits into their scheme of things.*

I hasten to add that the great majority of the Foreign Service Officers do not share these views. Most of them realize that the United States Government is fundamentally much more interested in helping free and friendly governments hold the support of their peoples, than in trying to keep those governments obligated to the United States. They know that a cabinet overthrow can wipe out in an hour all the credit that the United States may have established with a government, whereas operations carried on at the level of the people achieve benefits which no cabinet crisis can destroy. In short, they have been concerned with the peoples to whom they were accredited, and not just with the governments that happened to be in power. Among the Ambassadors who were outstanding in their vigorous and understanding support of Point 4 during my tenure were Harold Minor in Lebanon, Loy Henderson in Iran, General Philip Fleming in Costa Rica, Angier Biddle Duke in El Salvador, and of course, Chester Bowles in India.

While most members of the United States Congress have shared the T.C.A. view that international give-aways do not win lasting gratitude from the recipients, the Congress has nevertheless from time to time displayed an unwarranted faith in Point 4 as a political weapon. That is to say, the Congress has insisted that recipient countries meet certain political conditions, not, presumably, in order to punish them like naughty boys if they did not

---

* A few Chiefs of Mission have shown a total misconception of Point 4 in a different way, by insisting that technicians behave like traditional diplomats. One career ambassador actually criticized his T.C.A. director in a formal report to Washington for coming to a conference on a blistering hot day in shirt sleeves.

comply, but in order to induce them to comply. The outstanding example was the Kem Amendment, followed by the Battle Act, intended to stop countries receiving foreign aid of any kind from supplying strategic materials to communist countries. The one country in the Point 4 area which had been engaged in such commerce, Ceylon, has not been induced to stop by the hope of receiving Point 4 assistance.

Another political condition, imposed in 1951 by the Congress, was that each country receiving economic or technical aid must agree "to join in promoting international understanding and good will, and in maintaining world peace, and to take such action as may be mutually agreed upon to eliminate causes of international tension" (Section 511-b of the Mutual Security Act of 1951). This was innocuous enough—indeed it was argued for a while that any country which had signed the United Nations Charter had already agreed to these terms—but its very innocuity made it suspect. Governments could not understand why they were being asked to sign something so meaningless, and a great deal of time and effort was spent on negotiating the agreements, in one form or another. It is difficult to see what good purpose was served by this "exercise" (to use an expressive bit of Washington jargon) and the condition may have kept at least one country, Syria, out of the Point 4 program.

Aside from the fact that Point 4's psychological value is lessened by tacking political conditions on to it, the plain truth is that Point 4 is not attractive enough to most countries to serve as an effective inducement for any kind of action that is in the least obnoxious. If we want to use our foreign aid to get Ceylon to stop shipping rubber to communist China and to persuade Syria to be less standoffish, we will simply have to be freer with our taxpayers' money than we have been. Point 4 is not intended for such purposes and does not serve them very well. It is just not a big enough, or a sweet enough, carrot.

Precisely the same can be said about the conditions Justice William O. Douglas would impose on Point 4 aid. Douglas argues in effect that our aid agencies should stay out of any country that is not taking steps toward land reform and other social improvements as fast as he or someone else might think it ought to.[1]

He himself admits that this would be intervention, but he argues that giving aid without seeking to disturb the status quo is also intervention. The difficulty with this argument is that the one course is regarded as intervention of a most impermissible kind by the people concerned, and the other is not. Any serious attempt to follow the Douglas formula would in most cases result in Point 4 being kicked right out of the country. In other words, there would be no reforms, and no program either. Practically all the people who have worked as shirt-sleeve diplomats would, I believe, agree with this conclusion. Doubtless if Justice Douglas had been exposed to any responsibility in connection with the development of the underdeveloped areas, he would agree also.

When large amounts of grant aid are desperately needed by a country to which we have peculiarly close ties, the situation may be different. In Formosa, for example, where American military and economic assistance is absolutely essential to the Government, the United States is in a position to impose virtually any conditions it chooses, (actually it has used the power perhaps too sparingly). In the Philippines, when an economic crisis caused the Quirino government to turn to the United States for advice and help in 1950, the E.C.A. was able to say: "if you will take the steps we recommend, particularly in connection with taxes and land reform, we will ask our Congress to appropriate aid for you in the amount of 250 million dollars over a period of years." The deal was acceptable to the Filipinos, substantial fiscal reforms were instituted, and the islands' economic situation began to improve almost immediately. The commitment to proceed with land reform was not as faithfully carried out, at least so long as the Quirino government was in office.

In most of the hypersensitive countries of Asia and the Middle East, it is highly doubtful that we could achieve much except resentment by seeking to insist on speedier reform measures as a condition of our aid, no matter how many millions of dollars we were talking about. In India and Pakistan especially, where the primary responsibility for measures like land reform is in the hands of the state governments, we would probably be told in no uncertain terms to peddle our wares elsewhere. Justice Douglas' assumption that our interference would be welcomed by the local partisans of reform seems to me wholly unwarranted: they would be more likely to accuse us of hindering their efforts by putting a propaganda weapon into the hands of the conservative elements.[2]

Justice Douglas enjoys enormous personal popularity in the Middle East and Asia, so that in those areas one rarely hears him criticized for anything. Moreover, out of sheer politeness, many local people have probably told him they agreed with him on this matter of interference. But what the result would be if the United States Government tried to put his views into effect is something else again.

All this is not to say that our representatives overseas

should not do all they reasonably can to encourage social reforms, and especially to try to assure their success when these are instituted. In earlier chapters, we have seen what has been done along these lines in various parts of the world, but it must be reported that a good many opportunities have been missed.

The main trouble is that many State Department and Foreign Service people are opposed to our saying or doing anything at all to encourage reforms. Even after the United States has officially gone on record at international gatherings in favor, let us say, of land reform measures, these people would prefer to let the subject drop. This same hush-hush treatment was given the provision (Section 528-b) of the Mutual Security Act of 1951 to the effect that Point 4 should seek to encourage the establishment of fair wage rates and working conditions.

The reluctance to speak out for any principles of social justice has been much more pronounced in some embassies and State Department offices than in others (those concerned with Latin America seem to be the most timid). Moreover, it is traceable not so much to any opposition to reform, or lack of awareness that reforms might be badly needed, as to a fear of offending those in power. Here again, short-range political considerations seem to dominate the thinking of many of those concerned with the conduct of our foreign relations. A typical comment would be: "We are trying to get this government to send troops to Korea, and the Defense Minister is a big landowner who is allergic to any mention of land reform."

In considering the degree to which aid of the Point 4 type can be used as a lever for political action of one sort or another, it is important to bear in mind that many of the free Asian countries are not full-fledged allies of ours, but are seeking to steer a more or less neutral course between the communist bloc and the West. They accept Point 4 aid from us because they do not regard it as involving a military or political commitment. In other words, Point 4 can do the essential job it has to do in these countries only so long as its long-range, non-political character is maintained.

With the merger of M.S.A. and T.C.A. into a new agency, the Foreign Operations Administration, it becomes more than ever important that Point 4's integrity in this respect be maintained. It would be a serious error, for example, to make the development of supplies of strategic materials the over-riding objective of a program of the Point 4 type. Such activity is of crucial importance to the security of the free world, but it must nevertheless be kept separate so far as possible from programs which are offered as being designed to help other peoples develop their own economies. So long as minerals development work can be justified from the point of view of contributing to the local economies, it is of course entirely within the Point 4 concept. The difference may be narrow in practice, but is tremendously important psychologically, i.e. from an international public relations point of view.[3]

This is not to say that Point 4 must be presented to the world as a purely altruistic expression of American idealism. No one would believe the claim, and there would be all sorts of speculation as to what the hidden motive really was. Our motive can be made perfectly comprehensible by constantly restating our belief that the economic and social progress of free nations contributes to our security.

If Point 4 cannot be *used* as a political weapon, it nevertheless *is* a formidable one. The good will generated by operating on an open-handed basis, without extracting *quid pro quos,* has been demonstrated again and again, and good will is far more durable than gratitude.

The change in the attitude of Latin America toward the United States in the last twenty years is little short of miraculous. We are no longer the dreaded and hated "Colossus of the North." Point 4 and the similar work that preceded it can take much of the credit; they have been symbols of the Good Neighbor Policy.

In 1952, when T.C.A. first launched sizable programs in the Middle East, the political climate was far from auspicious and the newspapers in countries like Jordan and Lebanon were full of carping criticism of Point 4. By the next year, although the problems of Zionism and oil were still just as troublesome, the hostility toward Point 4 had largely disappeared.[4]

Perhaps the most dramatic evidence of the psychological effect of American developmental aid programs has been furnished at the annual meetings of the Economic Commission of Asia and the Far East (E.C.A.F.E.), a regional offshoot of the United Nations Economic and Social Council. As might be expected, the Soviet delegate regularly attacks Point 4 and similar programs in the most vitriolic terms as imperialism, a cover for espionage, etc., etc. With each passing year, the response of the free Asian governments, including those that attempt to be neutralist, has been more violent. The United States, they say, is truly helping them to develop their own economies, without seeking to exact unreasonable conditions, while all the communists are doing is attempting to sow the seeds of discord and unrest. "If Point 4 be imperialism," their theme is, "let us have more of it."

16. The Communists Don't Worry About Malthus

WHEN A MEMBER of the Executive Branch appears at a Congressional hearing to defend an administration proposal such as an appropriation for Point 4, he never knows what aspect of the subject he will be called upon to discuss. The hearings are necessarily much too short to permit anything like a complete discussion of a complex topic, and the number and character of the questions asked will depend on a multitude of factors, such as, for example, the hour of the day or the political slant of the particular Senators or Congressmen whose constituents have left them alone long enough to attend the committee session. The fact that a particular Senator is running for office that year may have a bearing (when Senator Connally of Texas decided not to seek re-election in 1952, his attitude as Chairman of the Foreign Relations Committee toward the pending Mutual Security bill changed abruptly from hostile to friendly). A legislator may open one of the voluminous "presentation documents" that lie before him on the committee table, pick out a minor item at random, and spend half an hour probing into it, knowing perfectly well that the harassed witness probably knows nothing about that particular item.

But there is one question which, in one form or another, is almost sure to come up in any hearing on a Point 4-type program. More often than not, it is raised by people who are opposed to Point 4 anyway. But sometimes it is brought up by supporters of the program who are seriously concerned about the problem. Since the question always leads into an area of discussion which most politicians want to avoid, the colloquies are sometimes left off the record. But here is the way the questions and answers might go at a typical session:

Senator (who has just entered the committee room and wants to establish his presence on the record): This whole program reminds me of Hercules and those stables. We're just pouring money down a rat hole.

Administration Witness: I'm not sure I get your question, Senator.

S.: I didn't ask any question yet. What I want to know is this: isn't it true that increases in population are going to wipe out any gains you may be able to make under this Point 4 program?

A.W.: Are you referring to any particular area, sir?

S.: Any area. I don't care.

A.W.: Well, the population problem varies a great deal from country to country. Some countries, especially in Latin America, are definitely under-populated.

S.: I'm talking about all these Asiatic countries that are so over-crowded.

A.W.: Even in Asia, Senator, there are big areas that are not crowded. A country like Iraq used to have two or three times as many people in Old Testament times as it does today. Parts of Indonesia and the Philippines are terribly over-populated, but there are other parts that are relatively empty, so that large-scale resettlement programs are possible and desirable. But I presume you refer especially to Egypt and India, where the population seems to be out-running the food supply.

S.: Of course. Let's hear about India. The more Indians you feed now, the more there will be to starve later on. How can you deny that?

A.W.: Well, Senator, I think we have to look at this problem from two different angles, the short-range and the long-range. It is true that India's population has been growing fast—the rate of increase is lower than ours in America, but the numbers are much greater—and that food production has been standing still. But we are certain that we can reverse that trend, for a while anyway. If the Five-Year Plan goal can be met—and I see no reason why it can't be, with our help—India's grain production will increase about 15 per cent, while her population will go up only about 5 per cent.

S.: How can you be so sure?

A.W.: The results at Etawah and elsewhere have shown that food production increases of 50 per cent or more can be obtained through introduction of better seeds, better methods, green manure, and so forth. Of course, it takes a lot of trained people to teach the farmers about these things, but it can be done. In addition, the various irrigation projects—not only big dams, but thousands of drilled wells and pumps—will make it possible to grow two crops instead of one in large areas, and in some places to grow food where none was grown before.

Right now we have our eye on the elections that come up in 1956. If we can help the Indian people to eat a little better by that time, they will be less likely to vote communist.

S.: That's all very well, but what good will it do in the long run? Sooner or later India's population will catch up, and you will be right back where you started from.

A.W.: The long-range picture is not at all clear, Senator. It's true that as you increase the production of food on any acre of land, each percentage point of increase becomes harder to achieve. And somewhere there is a limit to what you can do with a fixed amount of land, at least as far as our present scientific knowledge is concerned. But at the same time, if the Indian people can achieve a higher degree of development, their birth rate is bound to go down. That has been proved again and again. A higher standard of living means a lower birth rate.

S.: Yes, but all this health work you are doing is going to push the death rate down. And more babies will survive.

A.W.: There is no doubt that our health programs will have a tendency to push the death rate down, even if we try to concentrate our efforts on keeping adults strong and healthy and able to work. And there are always strong pressures for maternity and child care activities. You can't blame the people for wanting their babies to live. So that, even if Point 4 was to stay away from this kind of work, the local authorities would probably do it anyway.

S.: Well, that means that the population increase will be even faster than it has been.

A.W.: For a while, that is undoubtedly true, Senator. We cannot deny it. Just how long it will take for the effects of a higher standard of living to bring down the birth rate, nobody knows. The experts disagree. Some of them, like DeCastro of Brazil, are very optimistic. Others like Vogt are just the opposite. The only answer is to increase production enough so as to tide us over that interim period, however long it is.[1]

S.: It seems to me you are not paying enough attention to this problem of population in your programs.

A.W.: Are you suggesting, Senator, that the Congress might want us to include methods of birth control in our educational programs?

S.: No, no, of course not. What an idea!

A.W.: I may say, Senator, that there are no religious difficulties about population control either in India or Egypt, but that present methods of birth control are economically out of the question for most of their people. Some of the governments are doing some research in the field, studying the possibilities of the rhythm method, for example.

S.: That's *their* business.

A.W.: Quite. And we don't feel it would be appropriate for us to lecture the people of any country about abstinence, either.

S.: No, I can see your point about that. But there must be *something* you can do.

A.W.: Not a great deal, Senator. Where resettlement in less crowded areas is a possibility, we can help with that, as we have been doing in the Philippines. As I have indicated, we can try not to emphasize health programs which have a direct impact on the rate of population increase. And in our community development work, we can try to help the local authorities develop adult education programs and other community activities to provide the people with something to do in the evenings. The experts say that simply the introduction of kerosene lamps in the village homes has a perceptible effect on the birth rate.

S.: Harrumph. This is getting us pretty far afield.

A.W.: On the contrary, Senator, if I may say so, I believe it is quite pertinent.

S.: Sooner or later, you're going to lose the race, kerosene lamps and green manure or not.

A.W.: I don't think that follows necessarily, Sir. Malthus himself thought civilized man was rapidly losing the race with his food supply a hundred and fifty years ago, but he was proved wrong. There are huge sources in the sea, for instance, which have hardly been tapped at all. And when that runs out, the scientists will probably find a way to make food cheaply out of the atmosphere. Who knows? Perhaps this man-made subsidiary planet they talk about will materialize and provide the answer by way of weather control.[2] Dr. Henry Bennett used to say that, even with our present knowledge, the world could keep ahead of its population problem until the year 2000, and that beyond that he just wasn't going to worry: something would surely turn up.

S.: Well, I'm certainly not going to aggravate myself too much about what happens in the year 2000 either. But how am I going to explain this thing to my constituents, when you admit that the population problem will get worse before it gets better, and that it may get out of hand altogether in half a century?

A.W.: I think, Senator, that the whole question boils

down to one of alternatives. What are we going to do if
we *don't* try to help these countries raise their production?
Even though we may not be able to see ahead all the way
to the millennium, it seems to me we have to do the best we
can to improve things here and now.

If I may suggest an analogy, we may be a little like a
man who has survived a plane crash in a forest. He finds a
path which looks promising, but he hesitates to start out
on it because he is afraid it may lead to impassable rivers
and mountain ranges or his energy may give out before he
reaches civilization. The man has two choices: he can stay
put and hope for a miracle, or he can start out on the path.

In our case, a miracle is not very likely. If we do nothing
to help countries like India and Egypt tackle their problems, we are in effect saying to the communists: the field
is yours.

Of one thing we can be very sure, Senator. The Kremlin's
operators do not stay out of countries with serious population problems. On the contrary, those are their happiest
hunting grounds. Old Malthus' threat doesn't worry the
communists at all, even in the case of a country such as
India. At least, not until *after* they have taken the country
over.

17. No Simple Answers

THE JOB OF running any part of the United States Government is complicated. Contrary to the opinion of some who have never taken a crack at it, the job is not just like managing a business. The decisions are not as clear cut, nor is it as easy to find out who has the power to make them.

In many ways the task of administering a program like Point 4 is no different from that of a hundred and one other operations in the Government. The average day of the Director of such a program is apt to be filled with items like the following:

a staff conference on next year's budget for the Washington office. The budget proposed is slightly larger than last year's, but every single division chief is certain that he can't do his job properly with the meager staff provided for—

a telephone call from the head of a powerful old-line bureau to the effect that if his bureau can't get better cooperation he will simply have to wash his hands of the whole program. The Director tries to soothe the ruffled feelings of the old bureaucrat, who has a lot of influence on "the Hill"—

a note from the Director's secretary, saying that the management staff are most anxious to have his signature on the

attached ten-page, single-space Office Procedures Memorandum, which describes a new system for dealing with outside organizations on a contract basis—

an unscheduled visit from a division chief, new to the Government, who insists that he must be able to fire his present
deputy or he won't be able to get anything done. The only
complaint against the deputy seems to be a personality
quirk which the Civil Service Commission would never
recognize as grounds for discharge. Perhaps a transfer can
be arranged—

telephone calls from three different people in the office
saying that if the security clearance of X (or Y or Z) to go to
A country (or B or C) does not come through pretty soon,
the whole program in that country will be endangered. The
Director promises to see what he can do with the security
people—

a formal hearing at the Budget Bureau on part of the proposed program for next year, at which the young exami-
ners suggest that the written material prepared in support
of the request would not be convincing to the Congress and
should be entirely recast along different lines[1]—

a call from Senator McCarthy's office wanting to know
whether it is true that a contract has been made with a
private foundation which was once connected with a Bun-
dles for Russia drive and, if so, what individuals on the staff
had anything to do with making the contract. The Director
promises to look into the matter—

an interdepartmental meeting (one of a series) called to
decide who is going to do what about the private investment phase of the program. There is no agreement. The
possibility of getting the President to resolve the matter is
suggested but quickly discarded as impractical. Another
meeting is scheduled for next week—

a bitter argument with the Departmental personnel office
which has declined to approve the salary recommended for
a technician to go to Deserta. The Director points out that

it took six months to find this man and that he can be persuaded to give up a comfortable home and considerable
security only if he will be earning a little more money.
The personnel office insists that this would be a violation
of the rules and create a dangerous precedent—

drafts prepared in the Information Office for two speeches
to be delivered next week in the Middle West (the drafts
are uninspired and don't sound like the Director anyway)—

letters from (1) the President of the Women's Club of Mid-
dletown wanting to know how the Club can play "an active
role in this wonderful humanitarian work you are doing"; [2]
(2) an influential businessman of no particular talents who
is most anxious to serve his country "in a worth-while capacity" (a penciled note of unknown source is annexed to
this one, reading: "White House interested in this man");
(3) a college student who is doing a term paper on the
program and would like to interview "the key people";
(4) the irate sales manager of a pump manufacturing company which didn't get a particular piece of business (the
sales manager says his Congressman is certainly going to
hear about this); (5) a congenital letter-writer, who has
some rather interesting ideas about the philosophy of the
program (five pages, hand-written); (6) a Senator, who believes that a young constituent of his should be given a
chance to prove himself, even though he may not have the
qualifications for any particular job—

and so forth and so on.

These, as I said before, are the kind of headaches that
plague any government official from day to day. They are
headaches, it will be noted, which have to do solely with
the United States end of the Point 4 operation. None of
them is traceable to the difficulties of helping the peoples
of the underdeveloped areas to move toward a better life.
And yet, as I hope this book has made clear, those difficulties are, shall we say, not inconsiderable.

Although most of the operating problems in the field are in the hands of the shirt-sleeve diplomats to solve as best they can, the Washington office is constantly confronted with questions for which there are no certain answers. Consider, for example, the basic question that faces an aid program administrator in one form or another almost every day: how big, in the interests of the United States, should the program for Deserta or any other country be?

The obvious way to go at the problem is to decide what are the specific objectives to be pursued, and then to calculate what will be required to achieve these objectives in a given period of time. This is a relatively simple process when one is dealing with military assistance: the military experts can estimate what forces country A should have in order to be able to resist aggression by country B for long enough to allow help to arrive, or whatever else the military objective may be. They can then calculate with reasonable exactness how much in the way of recruiting, training and equipment country A will need in order to develop the requisite forces. Likewise when a balance of payments program is in question, such as was involved in the Marshall Plan, the objective is definite (to meet the foreign exchange deficit) and the amount of aid that will be required to achieve that objective can be estimated with at least some degree of accuracy.

But in the case of a program for the development of an underdeveloped country, there are almost no bench marks at all. In the first place it is difficult to establish any quantitative objectives that are not wholly arbitrary. For example, if country X decides that it wants to eliminate malaria in five years, there are usually no good answers to the questions, why not three years? why not ten? Or if a plan is worked out jointly whereby country Y can achieve a 5 per cent increase in its per capita income in five years, no one can say for sure whether the country's people would be satisfied with less or would demand more.

Even if sensible objectives can be agreed upon, the task of determining how much aid, and of what types, a country will need to achieve those objectives is an enormously complicated one, involving all kinds of variable and unknown quantities. Estimates have to be made of the country's own resources, of the amount of capital it can reasonably expect in the form of loans from the banks and in the form of private investment from overseas. The nature of its deficiencies have to be carefully considered— whether they are most grievous in the form of capital, or technical skills, or organizational capabilities. And the answers to these questions will vary widely from country to country.

One might suppose that it would be possible to work out a set of criteria for program figures from statistics such as per capita income, caloric intake, incidence of various diseases, illiteracy, etc. Such statistics are usually unreliable, however, and in addition they fail to reflect such vitally important factors as the attitude of a country toward change and development, the scale and intensity of its own efforts in that direction, and the degree to which it is in acute danger of communist attack or subversion.

Because of the difficulties of calculating program totals by these methods, the tendency has been to follow the project, or building block, approach. That is, the country missions recommend individual projects that they know would be helpful and worth while. The Washington office reviews the recommendations, prunes them some, and calculates its requests to the Congress accordingly, emphasizing that the project proposals are only illustrative, i.e. tentative.

The trouble with this approach is that the total amount for country X may be greater than for country Y, not because the need is greater, but because the government of country X may be more persuasive or because the Point 4 team there has more drive and imagination. Moreover, when this project approach is followed, the administrator of the program never can answer the inevitable Congressional question of "why won't less do?" or occasionally, "how can you be sure this amount will be enough?"

The weakness of the project approach has been recognized in Washington, but not much has yet been done to get away from it. When a country has calculated reasonable objectives for itself—as in the case of India's Five-Year Plan—it is possible to key an aid program to the attainment of those objectives and to justify it accordingly. As more and more governments work out rational plans for their own development, with the help of outside experts, the task of deciding on the size of aid programs should become somewhat simplified.

In spite of the difficulties of comparing non-comparable situations, it is easier for an administrator to make judgments as to relative figures between countries, than as to absolute totals, either over all or for any one country. For this reason an administrator will often wish that some higher authority would say to him: "The total amount for technical and economic aid is X million dollars; you decide how to allocate it." But the trouble is, no one higher up is in a position to decide on any intelligent basis how much X should be.

In practice, of course, providing the Executive Branch

with an "X" figure is about what the Congress does. Officially, the Congress is supposed to decide what the figure should be, not by looking into a crystal ball, but by considering the evidence the Administration has brought before it, in support of its requests. Actually, the process is more intuitive than that, especially when the measures are past the committee stage and have reached the floor of the Senate or House. Totals get talked about in the cloakrooms; they look reasonable or unreasonable, in terms of (a) a vague hunch as to the need, (b) a somewhat clearer idea as to how much money can be wisely spent, and (c) a very distinct notion as to what the home folks will swallow. (This means, incidentally, that the better the home folks understand the importance of helping the peoples of the underdeveloped areas to help themselves, the more adequate the funds voted by the Congress are likely to be.)

The question of proper program totals is, of course, only one of the extraordinarily difficult and complex questions having to do with the programs themselves which Washington has to decide. While it is clearly essential in a program such as Point 4 to give to the country missions as much responsibility as possible, there are times when Washington's very remoteness from the scene of action makes for calmer judgments and a better perspective. Even though most elements of a developmental program are supposed to be determined by what the host government wants, there are always times when a no is in order. And it is always easier to say no at a far-away Washington desk than face to face with an able local official who has become a close friend. One of T.C.A.'s best directors once supported a country's request that would have diverted most of his program funds into a bottomless pit of local government deficits; later he admitted that he was glad he had been unable to get Washington to go along.

The relative emphasis that should be given to various types of activities is another question which depends in large part on the judgment of Washington officials. In the first instance, it is up to the Point 4 director in any country to coordinate and integrate the various activities of his specialists and to ensure that no one phase of the program gets disproportionately large (or small) because one particular specialist happens to be especially energetic (or the opposite). But here again it may be inordinately difficult for the director on the spot to resist unsound preferences on the part of local officials. In country Z, for example, there may be a great desire for hospital facilities and equipment, which would not help to solve any fundamental problems, and at the same time a reluctance to take steps to improve agricultural production.

One question which is constantly in the minds of Washington officials, and only rarely in the minds of the shirt-sleeve diplomats in the field is, "what will they think on the Hill?" I recall one case where a proposed program included provision for a demonstration ski lift. The country director was insistent in that case that the development of resort facilities attractive to tourists was of extreme economic importance to the country. We in Washington were ready to concede that, but we still said "nothing doing." We could just visualize the fine time a hostile Senator would have had on the Senate floor with that one!

Because of Congressional preoccupation with the sanctity of technical assistance, Washington has had to keep the heat on some missions to introduce at least a respectable element of technical assistance in programs largely economic in nature. One or two other missions have themselves been too hidebound by the pure Point 4 concept and have had to be pressed to embark on action programs.

The factor which, perhaps most of all, makes the Point 4 task so enormously complex is the lack of uniformity in the problems that arise from country to country. What is needed in Ethiopia may not be at all what is needed in Brazil, and what is needed in Brazil may be just the opposite of what is needed in India. That is one good reason why no simple, words-of-one-syllable formula can be worked out.

This is perhaps unfortunate from a public relations point of view within the United States. Undoubtedly it is easier to make simple, black-and-white ideas appealing and inspiring. But I do not believe that fundamentally the American people want to be fed glib talk and over-simplified pap.

Certainly the search for answers to the subtle questions inherent in international development programs should continue. Each year of experience with Point 4 will cast more light on what is possible and what is impossible. Perhaps the social scientists and the anthropologists will learn more about rates of development—what the highest feasible rate is for a given country and what the minimum rate is that will give people a sense of hope and of satisfaction with their government. Increased knowledge along these lines would make it possible to arrive at much firmer program figures.

But at best there will always be gray areas and qualifications and unanswerable questions. Does that mean that the American people will toss out the whole idea of helping our neighbors in the world as a mass of uncertain values from top to bottom? Surely not. Our every-day lives are full of uncertainties too. A man may not be able to find out even roughly how much his house is worth until he tries to sell it, but he does not conclude from that that his house is of no value. Our minds may be full of questions about what is good and what is bad in education, and we may not be able to arrive at any uniform answers for all kinds of children, but we do not therefore decide to keep our kids out of school.

18. Risking Dollars or Risking Lives

OF ALL THE QUESTIONS about Point 4 and our international development work, the most insistently asked is, can we afford it?

Obviously every American can afford to contribute a dollar, or five dollars, a year to an investment in peace, if it is a *good* investment. The question therefore is not, can we afford it? but rather: is this expenditure going to contribute measurably to the chances of peace? And if the answer to that is yes, then the final question is: can we afford *not* to do it?

If communist China were to attack India tomorrow, how much would we be willing to spend in military aid to help India to help herself? Almost an unlimited amount, I should think—as much as India could profitably use. We would hardly count the cost, any more than we really counted the cost of the billions we spent to help our allies during World War II.

Indeed if India were to abandon her more or less neutral position today and join with us in a collective defense arrangement like the North Atlantic Treaty, we would probably not boggle at giving her a billion dollars or so worth of tanks, planes and guns. Yet India has in fact

joined with us in a collective defense arrangement against
subversion, and has asked us for help in a war against the
enemy within. Are not our interests as great in the one case
as the other?

Of course, the technical and economic aid we give a
country like India is not sure to prevent it from going
communist. Neither would the guns and planes we might
give the Indians in the event of an attack guarantee their
safety.

Nor can we be sure that India will go communist if we
give her no more aid. When one buys a fire insurance
policy, one cannot be sure that there is going to be a fire.

What we have to do is try to balance the risks. In the
case of a program like Point 4, we must try to weigh the
risk of losing our money today against the risk of losing
our lives or our children's lives tomorrow.

It is true, of course, that we have other, much heavier
burdens to carry in the interest of our security. No one
would doubt that we could afford to spend a billion dollars
a year on helping the less developed countries achieve a
better life if that were all we had to do to protect ourselves
and the free world against communism. Clearly, no discussion of what we can or cannot afford makes sense except
in terms of what all our obligations, and our resources, are.

Some experts say that our own defense plans are inadequate; they say that we must and can afford to spend more
than we are spending on arming ourselves and our allies.
Others take the opposite point of view, and talk darkly of
the danger of bankrupting the nation.

This is not the place to discuss the adequacy or inade-
quacy of our total security program in terms of our resources. It is enough to point out that even those who

argue for cutting back our Air Force, for example, do not dare admit that the lower level would be unsafe. They must of necessity argue that the economies can be made without unduly endangering our security. They would never be so foolish as to say: we need these additional aircraft, but we cannot afford them.

Therefore, as I suggested, the real question is not what we can afford, but what we need for our security.

It is hard indeed to compare the relative importance for that purpose of a dollar for military equipment and a dollar for a Point 4 program. Who would say with any confidence that a new 20 million dollar destroyer, which will grow quickly obsolete, is any more or any less important than a 20 million dollar program which in the space of one year can help a sizable segment of the Iranian people make permanent improvements in their standard of living and so bind them more firmly to the cause of freedom?

But this can be said: all the other security measures we are taking are defensive and negative in character. They are not characteristic of democracy any more than of totalitarianism; they express nothing of our ideals. The only offensive program we have in the cold war, the only positive answer to communism that we are offering to much of the world, is Point 4.

Of course, there is no guarantee that the Russians will remain as inactive on the technical assistance front as they have been to date. In fact their recent pledge of 4 million rubles to the United Nations T.A.A. may mean that they are beginning to realize the power of the Point 4 idea. While it seems inconceivable that they should be able to carry on the kind of disinterested, non-political work that is needed for success, nevertheless the threat is there.

At least we have a big head start in the field. Let us not lose it.

As Dean Acheson and many others have pointed out, there is a kind of revolution going on today in the less developed areas of the world, whether we like it or not. The people, many of them organized into newly independent and highly nationalistic states, are restless and stirring. They see that other nations are better off, they do not understand why this should be, and they are determined to narrow the gap. They are therefore not going to stand still, patiently waiting for things to improve, but are going to move—in one direction or another.

We cannot stop this revolution, and we will ignore it at our peril. But perhaps we can guide it in the direction of freedom instead of slavery.

We believe with a burning conviction that human beings can achieve a decent standard of living without surrendering their liberties. We have proved that this is true in a country as fortunate as ours, but can we prove that it is true in Paraguay or Iraq or Indonesia? This is perhaps the greatest challenge of our time.

Point 4, in its broadest sense, is our answer. It may not be the perfect answer, but this much can be said: no one has yet come up with a better one. Until someone does, we had better cling to it with all our might and main.

This will mean sacrifices, of course, not only through substantial expenditures for program operations, not only through the personal sacrifices that our shirt-sleeve diplomats will have to go on making, but in other ways as well. While we will no doubt be able to export more to the less developed countries as they make economic progress, we must also be prepared to import more from them. In the long run, a more liberal trade policy on the part of the

United States is a *sine qua non* for a successful Point 4 program.[1] But this cannot be done painlessly. For some, the sacrifices will seem disproportionate to what is to be gained. But the country as a whole must have the strength to resist the pleas of the few who are hurt, in the long-range interest of all of us.

It is still too early to say what the present Administration is going to do about Point 4. Quite naturally, it has tried to bury the name, but that is unimportant. More ominous, most of the key members of the former T.C.A. staff in Washington—a remarkably able and selfless group—have been summarily dismissed.* This was done allegedly on grounds of economy, but it is inconceivable that most of these people should not be replaced. For if they are not, the program will grind to a virtual stop, in a dreadful chaos of cables unanswered, supply requisitions unfilled, requests for technicians unmet, and program decisions unmade.[2] The men and women in the field cannot do their jobs without adequate backstopping from Washington. On the other hand, if those dismissed are to be replaced, it will be extraordinarily difficult to find equally capable and devoted people, and impossible to find them quickly or among the ordinary run of job-seekers, no matter how "deserving." In either event, the wholesale dismissals are tragic, not only because of their impact on people who regarded themselves as career civil servants, and some of whom have never worked outside the Government, but far more importantly, because of the inevitable damage to the program in the field.

* I am of course not referring to my own departure or that of Stanley Andrews, former T.C.A. Administrator. As Presidential appointees, we submitted our resignations automatically in January, 1953, and it was entirely proper that they be accepted.

Most disturbing of all is the evidence that under the new, highly centralized F.O.A. set-up Point 4 will no longer be kept distinct from military and emergency economic aid. Although he professes great interest in the preservation of the Point 4 program as such, Administrator Stassen has appeared to lean toward a more spectacular and dramatic type of aid. Overlooking the enormous value of stressing cooperation and joint operations, instead of charity and American achievements, he has given orders that each "Technical Cooperation Mission" overseas drop that name and call itself instead "United States Operations Mission." Many of the American church groups and other private agencies which have been among the strongest supporters of the Point 4 idea have been deeply worried by these indications of a trend away from the original long-range, non-political concept of Point 4, and it would certainly not be surprising if this attitude of mistrust spread to many of the less developed countries themselves.[3]

If these facts bode ill for Point 4, it must at the same time be recorded that in 1953 the Republican Administration effectively persuaded the Congress to appropriate more money for developmental programs in the underdeveloped areas than its predecessor ever succeeded in doing. And President Eisenhower, in his fine speech to the American Society of Newspaper Editors on April 16, 1953, clearly expressed his conviction that the United States should, within the limit of its resources, help the peoples of less fortunate lands to achieve a better life.

In the last analysis, it will be up to the American people to decide what is to be done—whether the Point 4 ideal is to be vigorously pursued, or whether it is to be thrown into the discard, either outright or indirectly. This is an awesome responsibility. A short-sighted pinchpenny attitude will lead us straight into the hopeless morass of isolationism and eventual war. On the other hand, it will take courage, determination and wisdom to make the sacrifices needed for progress and peace.

Appendix A

FOURTH POINT OF PRESIDENT TRUMAN'S
INAUGURAL ADDRESS, JANUARY 20, 1949

FOURTH, we must embark on a bold new program for making the benefits of our scientific advances and industrial progress available for the improvement and growth of underdeveloped areas.

More than half the people of the world are living in conditions approaching misery. Their food is inadequate. They are victims of disease. Their economic life is primitive and stagnant. Their poverty is a handicap and a threat both to them and to more prosperous areas.

For the first time in history, humanity possesses the knowledge and the skill to relieve the suffering of these people.

The United States is pre-eminent among nations in the development of industrial and scientific techniques. The material resources which we can afford to use for the assistance of other peoples are limited. But our imponderable resources in technical knowledge are constantly growing and are inexhaustible.

I believe that we should make available to peace-loving peoples the benefits of our store of technical knowledge in order to help them realize their aspirations for a better life. And, in cooperation with other nations, we should foster capital investment in areas needing development.

Our aim should be to help the free peoples of the world, through their own efforts, to produce more food, more clothing, more materials for housing and more mechanical power to lighten their burdens.

We invite other countries to pool their technological re-sources in this undertaking. Their contributions will be warmly welcomed. This should be a cooperative enterprise in which all nations work together through the United Nations and its specialized agencies wherever practicable. It must be a world-wide effort for the achievement of peace, plenty, and freedom.

With the cooperation of business, private capital, agricul-ture, and labor in this country, this program can greatly in-crease the industrial activity in other nations and can raise substantially their standards of living.

Such new economic developments must be devised and con-trolled to benefit the peoples of the areas in which they are established. Guaranties to the investor must be balanced by guaranties in the interest of the people whose resources and whose labor go into these developments.

The old imperialism—exploitation for foreign profit—has no place in our plans. What we envisage is a program of develop-ment based on the concepts of democratic fair-dealing.

All countries, including our own, will greatly benefit from a constructive program for the better use of the world's human and natural resources. Experience shows that our commerce with other countries expands as they progress industrially and economically.

Greater production is the key to prosperity and peace. And the key to greater production is a wider and more vigorous application of modern scientific and technical knowledge.

Only by helping the least fortunate of its members to help themselves can the human family achieve the decent, satisfying life that is the right of all people.

Democracy alone can supply the vitalizing force to stir the peoples of the world into triumphant action, not only against their human oppressors, but also against their ancient enemies —hunger, misery and despair.

SUMMARY OF U.S. DEVELOPMENTAL PROGRAMS

	Area (thous. sq. mi.)	Population (millions)	Per Cap. Income ($)	Program Totals FY 1952	FY 1953	FY 1954 (millions of dollars)	U.S. technicians (FY 1954)
LATIN AMERICA							
Bolivia	416	4	55	1.4	1.4	1.4	56
Brazil	3,288	53.4	127	2.6	3.2	3.3	129
Chile	286	5.9	190	1.0	1.3	1.6	35
Colombia	440	11.3	243	.7	1.0	1.6	50
Costa Rica	19	.8	180	1.3	.9	1.0	41
Cuba	44	5.6	332	.1	.2	.2	17
Dominican Rep.	19	2.2	136	.2	.4	.5	19
Ecuador	106	3.6	45	1.2	1.2	1.2	51
El Salvador	8	1.9	163	.4	.8	.7	36
Guatemala	42	2.9	130	.2	.2	.2	9
Haiti	11	3.7	48	.6	.7	.7	27
Honduras	59	1.8	128	.6	.7	.9	29
Mexico	760	26.3	166	.7	.8	1.2	51
Nicaragua	58	1.2	90	.6	.7	.6	28
Panama	29	.8	155	1.3	.8	1.1	45
Paraguay	157	1.5	118	1.1	1.2	1.4	55
Peru	482	8.7	100	1.7	1.8	1.9	69
Uruguay	72	2.4	330	.4	.3	.5	15
Venezuela	352	5.6	392	.1	.1	.2	9
Carib. Dep. Terrs.	180	4	n.a.	.07	.02	.2	8
Regional Projs.	..	..	..	.8	1.3	1.1	80
Subtotals	7,000	150	..	17.8	18.9	22.3	850
NEAR EAST, AFRICA							
Egypt	386	20.7	121	.3	12.9	9.1	153
Ethiopia	350	15(?)	40	1.1	1.4	1.3	76
Iran	628	19.1	85	23.8	23.2	23.4*	255
Iraq	168	5.1	85	.6	2.1	1.7	104
Israel	8	1.6	720	.8*	2.6*	1.2*	72
Jordan	35	1.3	98	3.4*	2.9	1.7*	69
Lebanon	4	1.3	125	3.4	.9	2.2*	70
Liberia	43	1.6	40	.8	1.7	1.0	81
Libya	679	1.1	40	1.5	1.4	1.2	51
Saudi Arabia	700	6	40	.2	1.7	.6	31
Syria	72	3.3	108	0	0	2.3*	42
Regional Projs.	..	..	..	2.2	1.7	.8	26
"Special" Aid	..	..	..	32*	35*	62*	..
African D. Ts.	9,000	135	n.a.	n.a.	n.a.	12.0*	70*
Subtotals	12,000	210	..	70*	88*	113*	1,100
So. & S. E. ASIA							
Afghanistan	251	12	50	.3	.7	1.2	51
Burma	262	19	34	14.0	7.0	0	n.a.
Formosa	13	9.5	n.a.	27.5*	29.3*	30.4*	109
India	1,220	360	53	52.7	44.2	90.0	245
Indo-China	287	28.5	50	7.5*	7.3*	9.5*	70
Indonesia	583	76.5	40	8.0	4.3	3.4	137
Nepal	54	7	n.a.	.2	.5	.5	25
Pakistan	366	75.8	50	10.6	12.0	22.8	163
Philippines	116	20.6	170	23.4*	20.1	14.6	194
Thailand	200	19.2	75	7.0	6.3	4.3	83
Pacific D. Ts.	400	10	n.a.	n.a.	n.a.	.9	10
Subtotals	3,500	650	..	148*	132*	177*	1,100
Totals	22,000	1,000	..	236*	259*	312*	3,000

* Figure arbitrary or misleading; see comments on following pages.
n.a. = not available. .. = not applicable.

COMMENTS ON PROGRAM STATISTICS

THE PROGRAM FIGURES shown in the table on the preceding page do not include loans, or emergency economic aid (e.g., to meet an acute food shortage, as in Pakistan in 1953; military needs, as in Formosa; a serious foreign exchange deficit, as in Israel; or a serious local budgetary deficit, as in Iran), or contribution to U.N., O.A.S. or other multilateral programs.

In the case of most of the countries listed, the figures shown are for Point 4 programs carried out under the Act for International Development. This is true of all the Latin American countries, and of the countries of Africa and Asia unless otherwise indicated in the comments that follow. Of the totals shown at the foot of the table, the Act for International Development programs account for the following amounts: for Fiscal Year 1952, $120 million (or 50%); for FY 1953, $141 million (or 55%); for Fiscal Year 1954, $118 million (or 38%).* The balance is accounted for by similar developmental programs carried on by E.C.A. and later M.S.A. and F.O.A. in various Far Eastern countries, and by "Special Economic Assistance" insofar as that assistance may be for long-range development purposes.

I have followed the usual government practice of giving program figures which represent "obligations"—i.e., those sums which the U.S. Government in a given year obligates itself to spend by contract or otherwise. In the early years of any program, these figures tend to be larger than the figures for sums

---

* It is possible that some of the $118 million for FY 1954 will be spent under authority other than the Act for International Development. See comment on the Philippines program.

It must also be recognized that the three figures given for Act for International Development programs are not strictly comparable one with another because of organizational shifts. Thus, whereas the FY 1952 figure does not include any part of the amounts shown for Burma, Formosa, Indo-China, Indonesia, the Philippines, or Thailand, the FY 1953 figure does include the sums for Burma and Indonesia, and the FY 1954 figure includes the amounts for Indonesia, the Philippines, Thailand and the Pacific Dependent Territories. On the other hand, the FY 1952 and 1953 figures include the entire amounts for India, Pakistan and Iran, while the FY 1954 figure includes only a portion of the amounts for those countries.

actually expended, so that they may give an exaggerated notion of how much assistance has in fact been extended.

The program figures for FY 1952 and FY 1953 are actual, while those for FY 1954 are estimated. These estimates are based on the proposed programs submitted to the Congress in the spring of 1953, reduced pro rata by the percentage of cuts made in the requests for each of the three major areas. Since the Administration is not bound by its proposals, but may shift funds as between countries and even, within limits, as between areas, these estimates may prove to be very inaccurate in some cases.

The figures given for U.S. technicians represent the estimates of the Executive Branch in the spring of 1953 as to the numbers that will be at work in the various countries by June 30, 1954. If past experience is an indicator, these figures will prove to be on the high side.

The area, population and per capita income, as well as the program, figures are based for the most part on material submitted to the Congressional Committees by the Executive Branch in support of the Fiscal Year 1954 Mutual Security Program. Where this material was incomplete, the information has been obtained from standard reference sources or on inquiry from the F.O.A.

A word should be said about the per capita income figures. While they are probably as good as any figures available to suggest relative living standards, they are notoriously unreliable. Not only are the statistics on which they are based scanty and inaccurate, but there are various factors which may distort the comparative results, such as the different and sometimes artificial rates at which local currency figures are translated into dollar terms.

In a few cases, the population figures are also in the nature of educated guesses. Moreover, both per capita income and population figures represent estimates made in different years.

As will be observed, subtotals and totals have been rounded off to a certain extent. The presence of a decimal point in any figure indicates that the figure is intended to be accurate to the nearest tenth.

FY 1952 means the fiscal year July 1, 1951 to June 30, 1952; similarly with FY 1953 and FY 1954.

Latin America. As noted above, all the programs in Latin America are carried on under the authority of the Act for International Development. In most countries in this area, salaries and expenses of American technicians, and training awards to local nationals, account for more than half the U.S. outlays.

Bolivia. In FY 1953 the principal fields of activity were agriculture (about 40%) and health and education (each about 25%). Plans for FY 1954 called for no change in emphasis. Servicios have been organized in all three major fields. Total local contributions for FY 1953 were about 1.4 times the U.S. outlay. The FY 1954 figure does not reflect the emergency aid granted to Bolivia in the fall of 1953.

Brazil. The outstanding segment of the program has been in health and sanitation; while this work accounted for less than a quarter of U.S. expenditures in FY 1953, the Brazilian contributions were many times that amount. An account of the work of S.E.S.P., the health servicio, appears in Chapter 6. Other sizable programs were in agriculture (about 20%), and in education (13%) and industry and labor (12%). Plans for FY 1954 called for increased emphasis on agriculture and education. Servicios exist not only in health, but also in vocational education, elementary education, and industrial productivity. Total local contributions for FY 1953 were about four times the U.S. outlay.

Chile. As of FY 1953, the principal fields of activity were agriculture (about 40%), health (30%), and industry and labor (20%). Servicios have been organized in each of these three fields, the last being concerned with industrial productivity. A considerable increase across the board was planned for FY 1954, with particular emphasis on developing an educational program. In FY 1953, total local contributions were estimated to be about 2.5 times the U.S. outlay.

Colombia. Work in agriculture accounted for almost half the program in FY 1953, a considerable part of it being done under contract by Michigan State College. The only other major program was in health and sanitation, operating through a servicio. The total local contributions were more than three times the U.S. outlay. Considerable expansion was planned for FY 1954, with particular emphasis on developing programs in natural resources, industry and labor, and transportation.

Costa Rica. Agriculture (more than 50%) and health (more than 25%) are the two main elements of our program in Costa Rica, which is a large one in terms of the country's size. Servicios exist in both major fields. Mention of some of their accomplishments has been made in Chapters 5 and 6. Public administration is a growing program activity, and is expected to account for more than 10% of the program in FY 1954. Total local contributions in FY 1953 were about 20% greater than U.S. outlay.

Cuba. This has been a relatively small program, the principal activity being technical assistance to further the development of the fiber *kenaf* as a substitute for jute. As of FY 1953 Cuba's contribution was only about two-fifths that of the United States.

Dominican Republic. The major program activity has been in vocational education, in which a servicio has been organized. Plans for FY 1954 called for an expansion of activity in agriculture, health and sanitation, and in elementary education. Total local contributions have been running less than 40% of the U.S. outlay.

Ecuador. The principal fields of activity in FY 1953 were health and sanitation (33%), agriculture (28%) and education (23%). Servicios operated in all three fields. No great change in emphasis was planned for FY 1954, but it was expected that there would be some expansion of a small-industry program. As of FY 1953, total local contributions were almost twice those of the United States, in spite of Ecuador's great poverty.

El Salvador. Agriculture and health have each been accounting for about one-third of the program, with increasing activity in the field of industry and labor, especially industrial productivity. Servicios exist in health and in industrial productivity. Total local contributions have been exceeding U.S. outlay by about 40%.

Guatemala. This has been a small program in agriculture

and health only, which has not been increased in recent years along with programs in neighboring countries. A servicio exists in the health field. Local contributions have been three times U.S. outlay.

Haiti. Program has been mainly in agriculture (60%) and in health (33%), with servicios operating in both fields. Intensive work in the Artibonite Valley, concentrating on irrigation, has led the Government to embark on full-scale development of 100,000 acres under a $14 million Export-Import Bank loan. Local contributions have been exceeding U.S. outlays by about 40%.

Honduras. Servicios have been operating in the three main fields of agriculture (40%), health and education (each over 20%). The agricultural servicio has in effect been operating as the staff of the newly formed Ministry of Agriculture. Total local contributions in FY 1953 were 2.4 times the U.S. outlays.

Mexico. This has been a small program, relative to the country's size. Principal activities have been in health, through a servicio, and in mineral resource development. As of FY 1953, work in the field of agriculture and fisheries was concerned largely with rubber and the shrimp industry. Plans for FY 1954 called for a broadening of the program, in part under a contract with Texas A. & M. University. As of FY 1953, the Mexican Government was not quite matching U.S. contributions.

Nicaragua. As of FY 1953 the three principal fields of activity were agriculture (37%), health (29%) and education (26%), with servicios in the latter two. The local government's contributions were running 30% higher than U.S. outlays.

Panama. Relative to population, this is one of the largest programs in Latin America. As of FY 1953, the three principal fields of activity were agriculture (33%), industrial and vocational education (30%), and health (25%). Servicios exist in all three. Plans for FY 1954 called for a sharp increase in agricultural work, part of which is carried on by the University of Arkansas under contract. Panama's contributions have been running about 50% higher than U.S. outlays.

Paraguay. Three fields—agriculture, health and education— have accounted for more than 80% of the program. Servicios exist in all three. The pioneering work done in the farm credit field is described in Chapter 5. Local contributions amounted to only 55% of U.S. outlays as of FY 1953. It was expected that the ratio would improve in FY 1954. For that year a sizable program in public administration, amounting to 14% of the total, was planned.

Peru. Work in the agricultural field, including forestry and fisheries, accounts for almost half the program. Two agricultural servicios exist, one for development (S.C.I.P.A.) and the other, more recently established, for research. Some of S.C.I.P.A.'s work is described in Chapter 5. The programs in health and education are also sizable, operating through servicios; each accounted for about 20% of the program in FY 1953. As of that year, total local contributions were running about 10% higher than U.S. outlays.

Uruguay. As of FY 1953, the main emphasis was on agriculture (45%) and health (35%), with a servicio organized in the latter field. Plans for FY 1954 called for less emphasis on agriculture and more on industry and labor. Uruguay has been about matching U.S. outlays.

Venezuela. A small program in an oil-rich country, with activities in health and sanitation (through a servicio) and public administration only. Local contributions have been running five times U.S. outlays.

Caribbean Dependent Territories. Activities to date have included technical assistance to encourage low-cost, self-help cooperative housing in several British islands and in Surinam, and assistance to a vocational school in Puerto Rico to enable it to provide training for students from other Caribbean areas.

Regional projects. This category includes contracts with various institutions in the U.S. to provide research work or training for more than one Latin American country, and also provides for specialists in various fields who are assigned to a regional pool. About one-third of the work is in agriculture, forestry and fisheries, about one-sixth in health and sanitation, and another sixth in industry and labor.

Near East and Africa *

Egypt. The FY 1953 program was increased during that fiscal year by $10 million, to provide for an intensive development program in two provinces, including resettlement of landless peasants, farm credit, fundamental education, health work, etc. Almost half of the FY 1954 program was slated for a similar project in a third province, but this may be deferred. These projects are set up on a matching-fund basis. Of the remainder of the program, work in agriculture and irrigation accounts for more than half. Another large program is in health and sanitation, with emphasis on the drilling of sanitary latrines. About 10% of the FY 1953 program was for technicians and training awards.

Ethiopia. Agriculture accounts for about half the program, with particular emphasis on the development and strengthening of agricultural educational institutions. A team from Oklahoma A. & M. is engaged in this work, under contract. The program is operated under a "joint fund" arrangement. Ethiopia's cash contributions are slightly smaller than U.S. outlays, but local contributions in kind (services, rent, etc.) are estimated to be substantially greater than the cash contributions. Plans for FY 1954 included a project for the stimulation of private investment through the collection of data, the setting up of a Development Service in the Ministry of Commerce and Industry, etc. About 15% of the FY 1954 funds were to be used in Eritrea, which federated with Ethiopia in 1952. About two-thirds of the funds are used for technicians and training awards.

Iran. The FY 1954 figure is based on an announcement made in the late summer of 1953. Presumably some $10 million of the "special economic assistance" funds for the Near East area will have to be used for this program, to supplement the funds available under the Act for International Development appropriation for the area. (In the two previous years, all funds for Iran were provided under that act.) The FY 1954

* Does not include Greece and Turkey, or the countries of the Indian subcontinent. This grouping corresponds with that used in the Mutual Security Act and Appropriations Act of 1953 in providing funds for "the Near East and Africa."

figure does not include any of the $45-million emergency aid announced in September 1953 (but see comment below on "special" aid). As of FY 1953, there were large programs in health and sanitation (26%), agriculture (17%), industry (13%) and education (11%). In FY 1953, the cost of U.S. technicians and training awards amounted to about 10% of the total program cost. Plans for FY 1954 called for considerable expansion in the field of water resources, especially dam construction. A cooperative bureau, somewhat similar to a servicio, has been set up in the health field. U.S. Government figures indicate that Iran has been contributing about two-thirds as much as the United States, but this figure depends on a very broad interpretation of the term "contribution." Chapters 5, 6, 7 and 9 contain considerable information about program activities in Iran.

Iraq. Because Iraq has large sums from oil royalties available for developmental work, about two-thirds of the United States aid has been for technicians and training awards. More than half of the program has been devoted to rural development and resettlement, water development and agriculture. Other sizable programs are in health and education. U.S. Government figures show Iraq's contributions running several times greater than U.S. outlays, but these "contributions" include expenditures for development which the Iraqi Government would probably be making anyway, though perhaps less effectively.

Israel. The figures shown are for the technical cooperation program only, and do not include the much larger figures for economic aid ($63.5 million in FY 1952, and $70.2 million in FY 1953, and an unknown amount in FY 1954). An arbitrary proportion of that economic aid is included in the table under the heading "Special" aid (see comment on that item, below). The main technical cooperation projects are in agriculture, vocational education, industry and health. Israel contributes to these operations on approximately a matching basis.

Jordan. The figures do not include any part of the economic aid received in FY 1952 through a shipment of wheat in the amount of $1,260,000, or any aid that may be received in FY 1954 under the "special economic assistance" authority.

As of FY 1953, the principal fields of activity were water development (33%), education, agriculture and health (each about 15%). Cooperative services similar to servicios have been organized in each of these fields, and a fifth cooperative service has been organized to carry on the work in industry, transportation, mineral development, etc. In FY 1953, about one-third of the U.S. funds went for technicians and training awards. In that year local contributions amounted to about one-third of the U.S. outlay, but for the following year were expected to be on a matching basis.

Lebanon. The figure for FY 1954 does not include whatever part of the "special" aid for the area might be allocated to Lebanon. The relatively small figure for FY 1953 reflects the fact that the FY 1952 program was slow in starting and was largely carried over into FY 1953. Of the proposed FY 1954 program, about one-third was for technicians and training awards. Activities in agriculture, water development, and intensive rural development account for about 70% of the total program. Lebanon's direct contributions to joint programs have been only about 25% of the U.S. outlays, but the country's total expenditures for development are substantial.

Liberia. The major fields of activity have been agriculture (25%), health (25%) and transportation, communications and public works (20%). About two-thirds of the funds are spent for technicians and training awards. The local government has been devoting 20% of its revenues to cooperative development activities, and has been almost matching U.S. outlays.

Libya. Agriculture and education each account for about one-third of the program, with health work and water resource development comprising most of the balance. Somewhat more than one-third of the funds are spent for technicians and training awards. Local contributions amount to about one-half U.S. outlays. The program is operated on a cooperative basis under the name of L.A.T.A.S. (Libyan-American Technical Assistance Service).

Saudi Arabia. Like Iraq, Saudi Arabia has large sums available for developmental work from oil royalties. The proposed FY 1954 program consisted solely of technicians and training awards, mainly in agriculture (30%), health (25%) and public

administration (13%). Estimated local contributions are said
to exceed U.S. outlays.

Syria. No program has yet commenced in Syria. Provision
was made in the FY 1954 proposals for activities mainly in
agriculture, water resources and health, in case Syria should
prove willing to enter into the standard agreements. In that
event, Syria would probably also receive a portion of the
"special" aid funds.

Regional projects. Under this heading funds are provided
for locust control operations in the Near East, for regional
training facilities at the American University at Beirut, for
the production on a regional basis of audio-visual aids for
technical cooperation work, and the like.

"Special" aid. The figures represent *one-half* of the economic aid available in the Near East region ($64 million for
Israel and Jordan in FY 1952; $70 million for Israel in FY
1953; and $125 million for the area as a whole in FY 1954,
after deducting from the total of $135 million available for
"special economic assistance" the $10 million allocated to the
technical cooperation program in Iran, as indicated above). The
one-half represents an arbitrary and very rough estimate of
the proportion of such economic aid which may contribute to
long-range development. This estimate is probably too liberal
insofar as aid to Israel and emergency aid to Iran are concerned, but may well be too small insofar as grants may be
made to certain Arab states in FY 1954. Such grants would
presumably be for projects such as dam and highway construction and would accordingly be entirely for long-range, rather
than current, purposes.

The figures do not include any of the amounts contributed
by the U.S. to the United Nations Relief and Works Agency
for Palestine Refugees.

African Dependent Territories. Before FY 1954, developmental work in these British, French, Belgian and Portuguese
dependencies was carried out on a limited basis as an indistinguishable part of the regular E.C.A. (later M.S.A.) program in
Europe. The present $12 million appropriation, just 50% of the
requested amount, is the first to be made specifically for that
purpose. Being included in the category of "special economic

assistance," it can be used for capital projects as well as technical assistance. The Executive Branch proposal listed "illustrative" technical assistance projects amounting to $1.5 million (two-thirds for technicians), and also developmental projects, mainly in water and transportation development, amounting to four times the appropriated amount. The number of technicians given in the table (70) is derived from the $1 million requested for that purpose, and will probably prove to be an overestimate.

South and Southeast Asia. For this area, the Congress in the Mutual Security Act and Appropriations Act of 1953 provided three kinds of program funds (aside from straight-out military aid) for FY 1954: (1) $84 million for "defense support, economic and technical assistance" for Formosa and Indo-China, (2) $94.4 million for "special economic assistance" for India and Pakistan, (3) $72.1 million for "defense support, economic and technical assistance" for non-communist countries (other than Formosa and Indo-China) in "the general area of China," which has been interpreted to mean all of South and Southeast Asia. The figures in the table include all of categories (2) and (3), and about one-half of the category (1). The "defense support" and "economic" assistance in category (3) can be given only to those countries like the Philippines and Thailand which are cooperating with the U.S. in a mutual defense program. That means that only programs authorized by the Act for International Development can be carried on with category (3) funds in Afghanistan, Burma, India, Indonesia, Nepal and Pakistan.

Afghanistan. Over two-thirds of the program in FY 1953 was in agriculture, resettlement and community development, particularly in the Helmand Valley, where loans from the Export-Import Bank have made possible an extensive reclamation program. Other projects include assistance in coal mining methods and in technical education. Two-thirds of the funds are used for technicians and training awards. Total local contributions to developmental projects on which the U.S. is assisting amount to several times the U.S. outlay.

Burma. For political reasons, the Burmese Government terminated the program in mid-1953, and accordingly no funds were requested of the Congress for FY 1954. However, some technicians are still in the country, winding up previously launched projects, and it is not impossible that program operations may be resumed before the end of FY 1954, especially if the Nationalist Chinese guerrillas are successfully evacuated from Burmese territory. The program in Burma, which was operated by M.S.A. in FY 1952 and by T.C.A. in FY 1953, emphasized activities in the health field, including medical education. It also included an outstanding low-cost housing project, with the U.S. providing technical help only.

Formosa (Nationalist China). The figures given include $12 to $16.5 million a year for fertilizer imports, but do not include $37.5 to $40.7 million a year for other commodity imports described as "Maintenance of Essential Supply." Nor do they include large sums for "Common Use Items" needed by local military forces. Of the figure shown for FY 1954, agriculture (including fertilizer) accounts for over 40%, manufacturing, mining and other industry about 30%, and transportation, power and other public works, almost 20%. Technicians and training awards require less than 10% of the total shown. This program has been operated at all times by E.C.A., M.S.A. or F.O.A. Economic assistance of a "defense support" character is authorized. No local "contributions" as such are solicited; local expenses are met from "counterpart" funds. The work of the J.C.R.R. is described in Chapter 5.

India. Until FY 1954 the entire program was carried on under the Act for International Development. For FY 1954, some $26 million is to be used in accordance with that act, and the remaining $64 million is provided as "special economic assistance." The two segments of the program are, however, interdependent and in some respects indistinguishable. According to the plans submitted for FY 1954, some 80% of the combined program was to be aimed at increasing the production of food, and includes projects such as community development (see Chapter 8), steel imports for farm implements, expansion of fertilizer production, and river valley development. Other large programs were in health (especially malaria control) and education. There is some reason to believe that the F.O.A. is now moving toward greater emphasis on industrial development, presumably through financing imports needed by local industries. Up to now, India has been spending about twice as much as the United States on the various programs to which we have been contributing. Considerably less than 10% of U.S. outlays has been used for technicians and training awards.

Indo-China. The figures shown do not include substantial sums for "Common Use Items" for local military forces, or about $16 million a year for commodity imports designated as "Maintenance of Essential Supply." For FY 1954, the proposals submitted called for emphasis on transportation, power and public works (over 50%), health (about 20%) and agriculture (about 15%). Technicians and training awards account for slightly more than 10% of the program total shown. As in the case of Formosa, this program is operated under "defense support" authority. Local expenses are met from "counterpart" funds derived from sale of commodities imported under the program.

Indonesia. This program was transferred to T.C.A. in mid-1952 and has since been carried on under the authority of the Act for International Development. According to plans submitted for FY 1954, a third of the program was to be devoted to agriculture and fisheries (see Chapter 5), most of the rest being divided among health, education, small industries (see Chapter 9) and general engineering services provided by a private U.S. firm under contract. Up to now, most of the local contributions to the program have been derived from "counterpart" funds previously deposited. Technicians and training awards account for two-thirds of the U.S. outlays.

Nepal. Agricultural and village development work, including tube well drilling and malaria control, account for three-quarters of the program. Nepal is to meet the local expenses, on more or less a matching basis. Almost half the U.S. funds are used for technicians and training awards.

Pakistan. In FY 1952 and 1953, the total program was carried on under the Act for International Development, but in FY 1954 about half the amount shown will be provided under the heading of "special economic assistance." The figure for

FY 1953 does not include the $15-million wheat loan made in
that year. According to plans for FY 1954, some 80% of the
combined program will be directed toward village development work and agriculture, including water resource development, fertilizer imports and expansion of fertilizer production.
It is expected that Pakistan's contributions will exceed the
amount of the combined program. As of FY 1953, less than
10% of U.S. outlays were being used for technicians and training awards.

Philippines. The FY 1952 figure does not include $8.6 mil-
lion for commodity imports designated as "Maintenance of
Essential Supply." This program, started by E.C.A. and carried
on by M.S.A. and later F.O.A., has been moving in the direction of a "beefed-up" technical cooperation program. Nevertheless, it has not been carried on under the authority of the
Act for International Development, but under the more flexible statutory authority permitting economic aid in support of
mutual defense programs. The Act for International Development is of course available, if F.O.A. wishes to use it, and
would, I believe, permit the carrying out of all programs proposed for FY 1954. For this reason, the figure for the Philippines, as well as that for Thailand, which is in the same
category, was included in the total given on page 246, above, as
the FY 1954 total for Act for International Development programs. The principal fields of activity are agriculture including fertilizer imports (about 33%), transportation, power and
other public works (25%), health, and education (each 12%).
About 20% of the FY 1954 total is expected to be used for
technicians and training awards. As noted in Chapter 9, the
largest group of technicians will be in the field of public administration (57 out of 194). Local expenses for the program
have been met from "counterpart" funds, rather than through
the making of contributions.

Thailand. Like the program in the Philippines (see comment above), the program in Thailand has been carried on by
M.S.A. and now F.O.A. under the "defense support" provisions for economic aid provided by the Mutual Security Act of
1951, and accordingly the provisions of the Act for International Development have, so far as is known, not been used.

Nevertheless, the program has become more and more of the Point 4 type. Under the program proposed for FY 1954, more than one-third of U.S. outlays will be used for technicians and training awards, and the principal activities are to be in agriculture (42%), health (24%), transportation, power and public works (15%), and education (11%). Local expenses have been met not only with "counterpart" funds, but also from the Thai Government's own budget.

Pacific Dependent Territories. In FY 1952 and 1953, limited developmental work in these areas was carried on as part of the E.C.A./M.S.A. program in Europe. Of the $1 million requested for FY 1954, 40% was for technical assistance in the area, and the remainder for a dam and road development in Malaya. Congressional criticism of these proposals was sharp, however, and they may not be carried out.

Appendix C

ORGANIZATION OF U.S. DEVELOPMENTAL
PROGRAMS

As of January, 1949, when Point 4 was enunciated, and until September, 1950, various United States agencies—including the Institute of Inter-American Affairs, the Federal Security Agency, and the departments of Agriculture, Commerce, Interior, and Labor—were carrying on modest programs of technical cooperation overseas. Their work was supposed to be coordinated in Washington by an Interdepartmental Committee on Scientific and Cultural Cooperation, but the Committee was mainly concerned with budgetary matters, such as the allocation of funds among the agencies, and had little to do with operations. (See "United States Organization for Point Four," by Haldore Hanson, Executive Secretary of the Committee, in The Annals of the American Academy of Political and Social Science, March 1950.) While the technicians in the field were nominally under the Ambassador or Minister, in actual fact they often operated quite independently. The I.I.A.A., for example, usually maintained separate offices from the Embassies, and frequently no single American official in a country knew what technicians were at work in the country or what they were doing.

This was obviously excessive decentralization, and in September of 1950, three months after the enactment of the Act for International Development, the Technical Cooperation Administration was set up within the State Department to supervise and coordinate all Point 4 activities. Throughout its existence, T.C.A. tried to follow the policy of drawing upon the experience of the other Government agencies for the technical aspects of the program, rather than seeking to set up within itself a whole new body of experts in agriculture, public health, etc. Most experts going overseas were recruited by the technical agencies and remained on their payrolls, but in each country the responsible head of the program was a Director of Technical Cooperation, appointed by T.C.A. and reporting directly to the Ambassador or Minister. This attempt to compromise the issue of centralization vs. decentralization gave rise to a good deal of bureaucratic bickering in Washington, but worked reasonably well in the field, where the Point 4 people tended to coalesce into good working teams.

At first the I.I.A.A. was considered as one of the technical agencies, but late in 1951 it was made a part of T.C.A. itself and became the regional operating arm for the Latin American area. It thus had responsibility not only for running its own programs, but also for coordinating the work of experts from other agencies. T.C.A. established two other regional divisions, namely a Near East and African Development Service, and an Asian Development Service.

During the period from 1949 to 1951, while the Point 4 program was expanding in Latin America and gradually getting under way in the Middle East and South Asia, the Economic Cooperation Administration (or "Marshall Plan" agency) was establishing "Special Technical and Economic Missions" in six Far Eastern countries, pursuant to different legislation. It began operations on Formosa in the spring of 1949, under the authority of the Foreign Assistance Act of 1948, and in Burma, Indo-China, Thailand and Indonesia in 1950, and in the Philippines in April 1951, under the authority of the Foreign Economic Assistance Act of 1950. Because of the close connection of the dependent territories of the Caribbean, Africa, and the Pacific to the European metropolitan powers, E.C.A. also had the primary responsibility for any aid programs affecting those areas.

In 1950 and 1951, T.C.A. launched a few educational projects in countries where E.C.A. was operating, but in October 1951 the newly created Director for Mutual Security, Averell

Harriman, laid down the "one country—one agency" rule which meant that E.C.A. and T.C.A. would not both operate in any given country. T.C.A. turned over its educational projects in E.C.A. countries, and E.C.A. gave up its plans of setting up missions in India, Pakistan and Iran. The following year, pursuant to Congressional mandate, T.C.A. took over responsibility for the work in Burma, Indonesia, and the Caribbean dependencies.

From October 1951 until May 1953, T.C.A., while a part of the State Department, received its allocations of funds from the Director for Mutual Security and operated under his general supervision. The Mutual Security Agency (successor to E.C.A.), on the other hand, was immediately under the Director for Mutual Security, but was supposed to take its policy direction from the State Department. Either system was capable of working reasonably well, given a minimum of mutual confidence and give-and-take. The division of the underdeveloped areas between T.C.A. and M.S.A. looked arbitrary and illogical, increasingly so as M.S.A. moved from its original emphasis on commodity imports over to programs of the Point 4 type, but it caused no particular difficulties. Indeed there was a distinct advantage in having an agency to work in countries such as India and Indonesia which was not involved with the "defense support" programs of a distinctly military tinge in Formosa and Indo-China.

However, President Eisenhower's committee on reorganization, headed by Nelson Rockefeller, recommended that all economic and technical aid operations be brought within a single agency,* and on June 1, 1953, the President sent to Congress a Reorganization Plan incorporating this recommendation. The decision was not entirely popular on the Hill, where a number of legislators felt that foreign aid of all kinds was an aspect of our foreign policy and belonged under the direct control of the Secretary of State. Had Mr. Dulles been inclined to make a fight to retain control of such operations, he

* It was hardly surprising that such a recommendation should come from a committee headed by Nelson Rockefeller. In April, 1951, the International Development Advisory Board under his Chairmanship had likewise recommended the "single agency" approach to the same problem.

doubtless would have succeeded. But he was obviously happy to shed these operational responsibilities, and no organized opposition to the Reorganization Plan developed.

Accordingly, as of the end of July, 1953, the Foreign Operations Administration came into being, with responsibility for all types of foreign aid, except for loans which remained in the hands of the Export-Import Bank and the International Bank, and except for the operating end of the military assistance programs which was a function of the Department of Defense. It would still have been possible for T.C.A. to be kept more or less intact, as a sort of Point 4 division of F.O.A., but the Director, Harold Stassen, wanted it otherwise.

Any agency operating in the foreign field has to decide whether to organize mainly along regional or mainly along functional lines, and Mr. Stassen chose the former. He gave full responsibility for all types of programs to four regional divisions of F.O.A., corresponding to the four regional offices of the State Department: Europe; the Near East and Africa (including India and Pakistan); the Far East; and Latin America. A technical services division was established, but it was to serve only in an advisory or "staff" capacity, and would not have operating or "line" responsibility. It remained to be seen how far T.C.A.'s partnership system of operations with the other government agencies would be continued, or whether here too the trend would be in the direction of centralization, after the M.S.A. pattern, with most experts being hired by the F.O.A. itself or by private agencies operating under contract with F.O.A.

There is a danger that, in this kind of centralized foreign aid operation, the peculiarly idealistic quality of the Point 4 program will be lost sight of and that the relatively small and long-range technical cooperation programs will be overshadowed by "big-money" psychology, that is, by the idea that the importance and the effectiveness of aid programs depend on their size. On the other hand, this need not be the case. It is perfectly possible that programs of larger size than the previous T.C.A. programs can be operated with the same emphasis on self-help, joint action, long-range development, and the communication of knowledge and skills.

As in all cases where more than one government agency is necessarily involved in the performance of a given governmental task, the problem of organizing for various kinds of foreign aid programs is a complex and difficult one to which there is no perfect solution.* The questions involved, however, are not really so important as the bitter inter-agency struggles in Washington would suggest. No form of organization will work without goodwill and teamwork on the part of the individuals involved, and almost any form, within reason, can be made to function adequately if those elements are present. As Alexander Pope said:

> "For forms of government let fools contest;
> That which is best administered is best."

* The organization of a military assistance program, in which both the State and Defense departments are vitally interested, presents even more serious problems than the organization of technical and economic aid. The same is true of organizing for the task of encouraging the flow of private investment overseas, which is closely related to the industrial phases of Point 4, but which also impinges upon the sacred territory of the Treasury (fiscal policy) and the Department of Commerce (foreign trade). In situations like these, it is almost impossible to put the chief responsibility in the hands of one old-line agency, over-riding the others, and equally impossible to give the job to a new outfit of less than cabinet status like F.O.A. Obviously, the President cannot give sustained personal attention to such problems. The new Administration seems to be moving in the direction of giving the National Security Council a lot of inter-agency coordination to do, but this may well be a mistake. If such a group as the N.S.C. gets overloaded, the principals have to delegate their responsibility to subordinates, and the group quickly degenerates into just another inter-departmental committee susceptible to the disease of excessive talk and insufficient decision.

Notes, Bibliographical
and Otherwise

THE FOLLOWING NOTES are intended for those with some particular interest in Point 4. They are not essential to an understanding of the text and can safely be skipped by the casual reader.

I have not attempted to cite authorities for every statement and have not done so at all where my information came from reports received in Washington or from conversations with persons involved in the program. The listing of books, articles and other materials is principally intended to provide leads for anyone wishing to pursue a particular topic farther. They constitute by no means a complete bibliography of the subject. For further and more comprehensive bibliographical material, see "International Economic and Social Development," a selected background reading list prepared for the National Conference on International Economic and Social Development, Washington, 1952; "Point Four, a selected bibliography of materials on technical cooperation with foreign governments," United States State Department Division of Library and Reference Services, Bibl. No. 54, and three supplements, Nos. 55, 56, and 57, dealing with the Near East and Africa, Latin America, and the Far East, respectively.

General works not mentioned in any of the following notes include: *Point 4 Program,* edited by Walter M. Daniels, a "Reference Shelf" volume, H. W. Wilson, 1951; *International Technical Assistance,* by Walter S. Sharp, Public Administration Service, 1952; "Aiding Underdeveloped Areas Abroad" and "Formulating a Point Four Program," *The Annals of the American Academy of Political and Social Science,* March and July, 1950; "Technical Cooperation with Underdeveloped Countries," by Philip C. Newman, John E. Ullman and Robert S. Aries, Chemonomics Inc., New York, 1952; *The Only War We Seek,* by Arthur Goodfriend, Farrar, Straus and Young, 1951; *Raising the World's Standard of Living,* by R. T. Mack, Citadel, 1953; *Door to the 20th Century,* a periodical edited by Andrew E. Rice at 816 21st St., N.W., Washington, D.C.; "Technical and Economic Assistance under Point 4," by Eugene Staley, *Academy of Political Science Proceedings,* May, 1952; "Point 4 Program—Promise or Menace?" by H. Olden and P. Phillips, *Science and Society,* Vol. 16, No. 3, page 222, 1952; "Point 4—Four Years Later," a series of four articles in *The Nation,* January 17, 24, 31, February 7, 1953; "Point Four and the Battle for Asia," by Clarence Decker, *New Republic,* December 1, 8, 22, 29, 1952, January 5, 12, 19, 1953; articles and news items in the *Department of State Bulletin* and the *United Nations Bulletin;* annual reports and other publications of the Organization of American States, F.A.O., W.H.O., UNESCO, I.L.O., I.C.A.O., etc.

Chapter 2—The Challenge and the Response

1. Ben Hardy first put the idea into a memorandum to his immediate superior in the State Department, Mr. Francis Russell, dated November 23, 1948. He later prepared an expanded version of the same memorandum, dated December 15, not addressed to anyone in particular, but presumably intended for the White House.

Hardy became the first information chief of the Point 4 program. On December 22, 1951, he was killed in the same airplane crash as his chief, Dr. Bennett.

In statements issued on that occasion, both President Truman and Secretary of State Acheson gave Hardy credit for originating the Point 4 idea.

2. A concise account of the development of United Nations technical assistance is contained in "United Nations Technical Assistance," Background Paper No. 74 (January 1, 1953),

issued by the United Nations Department of Public Information.

The origins of the Colombo Plan are described in a report of the Commonwealth Consultative Committee, "The Colombo Plan for Co-operative Economic Development in South and Southeast Asia," London, H.M. Stationery Office (1950). For later developments, see "Colombo Plan: new promise for Asia," by Willfred Malenbaum, United States State Department Bulletin (September 22, 1952).

Outside of her own dependencies, France's technical assistance efforts have been largely concentrated in Syria and Lebanon. Switzerland, in addition to participating in the program of the United Nations (of which Switzerland is not a member), has had a three-man mission in Nepal. Norway has embarked on an ambitious technical aid program in India with funds provided partly by private contributions.

3. *The Act for International Development* was enacted as Title IV of Public Law 535, 81st Congress, 2d Session, which also included the Economic Cooperation Act of 1950 (Title I), the China Area Aid Act of 1950 (Title II), and the United Nations Palestine Refugee Aid Act of 1950 (Title III).

Hearings on various bills intended to implement the Point 4 program had been held before the House Foreign Affairs Committee in the fall of 1949, and in January, 1950, and before the Senate Foreign Relations Committee on March 30, and April 3, 1950.

The bill as originally proposed by the State Department was narrow in scope and was entitled Act for Technical Cooperation, but contained an unlimited authorization for the expenditure of such sums as might later be appropriated. Later a limit of 45 million dollars for the first year was proposed, which was reduced by the Congress to 35 million dollars, of which about 12 million was to be used as the United States contribution to the United Nations technical assistance program. The title of the bill was changed and its provisions were considerably broadened by the House Foreign Affairs Committee, with Representative Christian Herter, Republican of Massachusetts, playing a leading role.

Debate took place in the House toward the end of March, 1950, and in the Senate in April and May.

As finally enacted, the Act for International Development contained some remarkably broad statements of policy, including the following:

> It is declared to be the policy of the United States to aid the efforts of the peoples of economically underdeveloped areas to develop their resources and improve their working and living conditions by encouraging the exchange of technical knowledge and skills and the flow of investment capital to countries which provide conditions under which such technical assistance and capital can effectively and constructively contribute to raising standards of living, creating new sources of wealth, increasing productivity and expanding purchasing power.

The Act authorized the President to carry out "technical cooperation programs," which were defined as "programs for the international interchange of technical knowledge and skills designed to contribute to the balanced and integrated development of the economic resources and productive capacities of economically underdeveloped areas," including "economic, engineering, medical, educational, agricultural, fishery, mineral, and fiscal surveys, demonstration, training, and similar projects that serve the purpose of promoting the development of economic resources and productive capacities of underdeveloped areas."

The Act also authorized the President to make "grants in aid of technical cooperation programs," (a provision which was much relied upon by the Executive Branch in the operation of the program on a flexible basis), and also suggested in a backhand way—Section 403 (b) (3)—that capital grants might be made under certain conditions (a provision which the Executive Branch never tried to use).

Certain conditions were laid down for the granting of aid, such as that the recipient country should pay "a fair share of the cost of the program" and should give the program "full publicity."

The Act created the International Development Advisory

Board and authorized the establishment of joint commissions (with underdeveloped countries) for economic development.

For more information about the legislative history of the Act, see: Hearings before the Foreign Affairs Committee of the House on H.R. 5615, 81st Congress, 1st Session, and on H.R. 5615, 6026, 6834, 6835, and 7346, and House Report No. 1802, Part 4, 81st Congress, 2d Session; Hearings Before the Foreign Relations Committee of the Senate on an Act for International Development, and Senate Report No. 1371, Part 2, 81st Congress, 2d Session; Congressional Record, 81st Congress, 2d Session, especially pages 4047-4552, 5484-6148, 6426-6569, 7602-7848.

The Administration's case for the program was stated at considerable length in a booklet entitled "Point Four—Cooperative Program for Aid in the Development of Economically Underdeveloped Areas," Dept. of State Publication 3719, released January 1950.

4. The report of the First National Conference on International Economic and Social Development was printed in Washington in June, 1952, under the title: "World Neighbors Working Together for Peace and Plenty."

5. As reported in *The New York Times* of March 28, 1952, Senator Taft said in a speech the previous day in Milwaukee:

> We must be a good neighbor, but there is a limit to our ability to spend abroad. I do not think economic assistance to the rest of the world is a necessary part of our foreign policy. The Marshall Plan is necessary as an emergency measure to help the war-devastated countries of Europe to recover and ward off communism. I believe that the Point 4 program is sound in that we can give technical assistance and help other people to bring their economies to a level that will assure their welfare.

6. In 1951, 1952, and 1953, funds were authorized and appropriated for the Point 4 program as a part of the much larger Mutual Security Program, and were not always clearly identifiable. The requests made by the different Administrations in each year can be identified by an examination of the

various Committee Hearings and by documents printed each year for the use of the Committees entitled "The Mutual Security Program For Fiscal Year 1952 (or 1953, or 1954)— Basic Data Supplied by the Executive Branch." The subsequent course of the legislation can be traced in the Congressional Record, in the various Committee Reports, in the Conference Reports, and finally in the laws themselves (Public Laws 165 and 249, 82d Congress, 1st Session; P.L. 400 and 547, 82d Congress, 2d Session, and P.L. 118 and 218, 83d Congress, 1st Session). See Appendix B for program statistics.

CHAPTER 3—Learning by Doing—in Latin America

1. For a summary of this activity, see the State Department's "Point Four" booklet, Publication 3719, January, 1950, pp. 129-41. For more detail see, e.g., "Technical Collaboration in Agriculture in the Western Hemisphere," by Benjamin J. Birdsall, printed in the *Soil Science Society of America Proceedings*, Vol. 13, 1948; "Teamwork in World Agriculture, Agricultural Information Bulletin 21," United States Department of Agriculture, 1950; a series of articles in the Department of State Bulletin on the work of the Interdepartmental Committee on Scientific and Cultural Cooperation (September 28, October 12, 19, 26, November 16, 1947); annual reports of various agencies.

2. Many articles describing the I.I.A.A.'s program in favorable terms have appeared in American newspapers and magazines. Two of the best, "We're Building a Better Hemisphere" and "Miracle on the Amazon," by John W. White, appeared in *Collier's* (January 27, and February 3, 1951).

Late in 1951, a special Inter-American Study Mission of the House Foreign Affairs Committee, consisting of three politically conservative members—Chairman James P. Richards of South Carolina, Omar Burleson of Texas, and Donald L. Jackson of California—visited Haiti, Venezuela, Colombia, Peru, Panama, El Salvador, and Mexico. Their report, dated January 21, 1952, contained the following "general observations" about the Point 4 programs in Latin America:

If any foreign aid programs merit the title "grass roots" it is the technical assistance programs in Latin America. Apart from some necessary administrative centralization, the operational phases are scattered throughout each of the countries. Touching as they do the daily life of the peoples, these projects dramatically convey the ability and the willingness of the United States to share its know-how. From the point of coverage they are one of the least expensive and most effective forms of advertising. * * * They have become so much a part of the developmental programs of the host countries that any curtailment would be a marked disservice to these countries and a sharp set-back in United States relations with them.

A comprehensive account of the early history of the I.I.A.A. is contained in Chapters VIII, X, and XI of the *History of the Office of the Coordinator of Inter-American Affairs,* one of the "Historical Reports on War Administration," G.P.O., 1947. As this volume makes clear, the I.I.A.A. was originally concerned almost exclusively with the health work, while food supply and education were handled by the Office of the Coordinator. First food supply and then education were later brought into the I.I.A.A.

Considerable information about the I.I.A.A. is also contained in its "Building a Better Hemisphere" series of reprints, especially No. 1, "The Servicio in Theory and Practice," and No. 2, "Ten Years of Point 4 in Action in Latin America."

CHAPTER 4—Diplomat Goes to Work in the Middle East

1. The policy paper here quoted is a composite of various memoranda and other documents circulated from time to time in T.C.A. I made a somewhat similar listing of policy principles in my testimony before the Senate Foreign Relations Committee and the House Foreign Affairs Committee in the spring of 1952. See Hearings on the Mutual Security Act of 1952, Foreign Affairs Committee of the House, 82d Congress, 2d Session, pp. 959-60, and Foreign Relations Committee of the Senate, pp. 617-19.

2. In most cases, an "umbrella agreement" laying the foundation for a technical cooperation program was negotiated with each recipient country before activities were begun. See Dr. Bennett's testimony in Committee hearings in 1951— Hearings on the Mutual Security Act of 1951, House Foreign Affairs Committee, 82d Congress, 1st Session, pp. 1436-1439, and Senate Foreign Relations Committee, pp. 410-412.

3. This telegram, while fictional, is not exaggerated. I was on the sending end of some just like it.

The initials MSP stand for Mutual Security Program, TA for technical assistance, FY for fiscal year, TCA/W for T.C.A. Headquarters in Washington.

The phrase "sums obligated" stands for sums which the agency has obligated itself by contract, agreement, or otherwise to spend. There may be, and usually is, a considerable lag between obligations and expenditures (when the money is actually paid out).

CHAPTER 5—The Free World Marches on Its Stomach

1. The figures on food production and consumption contained in the text are taken from various publications of the United Nations Food and Agriculture Organization, including the following: Second World Food Survey (November 1952); The State of Food and Agriculture, *Review and Outlook* (October 1952).

2. The most vivid picture of the Etawah experience is given in *What Can A Man Do?* by Arthur Goodfriend, Farrar, Straus & Young, New York, 1953, which consists mostly of beautiful photographs. See also Horace Holmes' testimony before the House Foreign Affairs Committee and the Senate Foreign Relations Committee in 1951 (House Foreign Affairs Committee Hearings on the Mutual Security Act of 1951, pp. 1004-20, and Senate Foreign Relations Committee Hearings on the same, pp. 457-71, 642-7); and "Point Four Pioneers," State Department Publication 4279 (October 1951), pp. 27-36.

3. For a more complete account of Frank Pinder's achievements in Liberia, see "Point Four Pioneers," State Department Publication No. 4279, pp. 3-11.

The speech by Secretary Acheson, in which he referred to Frank Pinder, was called "What is Point Four?" and was delivered at the Roosevelt Day Dinner of the Americans for Democratic Action in New York City, 1952 (Department of State Publication 4487, released February, 1952). It contained a clear and impressive statement of his views on the meaning of Point 4, its objectives and purposes, and the way in which they should best be pursued.

4. The best account of locust control operations is an illustrated article in *The National Geographic Magazine* of April, 1953, by Tony and Dickey Chappelle.

5. For a first-hand account of S.C.I.P.A.'s achievements in this field, see an I.I.A.A. mimeographed release entitled "Plant Insect and Disease Control in Peru," by Raymond Russell (November, 1952).

6. An example of excellent newspaper coverage of the Point 4 program was *The New York Times* story on the water-spreading demonstrations in Jordan (February 16, 1953). As mentioned elsewhere, *The New York Times* ran an extraordinarily comprehensive survey of the entire program in its issue of January 12, 1953.

7. For a detailed account, see "Point Four Brings 4-S to Costa Rica," by Carolyn L. Gaines, *Journal of Home Economics,* April 1952, reprinted as No. 13 in I.I.A.A.'s Building a Better Hemisphere Series. No. 15 in the same series reprints a letter Ambassador Philip B. Fleming wrote to President Truman in April, 1952, describing Point 4 in Costa Rica in the most glowing terms. See also "How Costa Rica Learned About Conservation," *Soil Conservation,* April 1952.

8. This account of F.A.O.'s work on inland fisheries in Indonesia and Thailand is based on an article in an excellent pamphlet called "Sharing Skills" published by the United Nations Department of Public Information in 1953.

9. The expert referred to is Raymond W. Miller of California and Washington, D.C. See, for example, his article, written with C. Leigh Stevens, "An Economic Program for Asia," in *Thinking Ahead for Business,* Harvard University Press, 1952.

10. For more detail, see "The Program of the Joint Com-

mission on Rural Reconstruction in China," an Economic Cooperation Administration pamphlet, published in 1951.

11. A good deal has been written about the world land reform problem. See, e.g., "Land Reform—A World Challenge," State Department Publication No. 4445; "Too Late to Save Asia?" by Wolf Ladijinsky, *The Saturday Review of Literature* (July 22, 1950); "Land Reform—Key to the Development and Stability of the Arab World," by Afif I. Tannous, *Middle East Journal* (January 1951); "Ally in Asia—Land Reform," *Fortune* (November 1950). For a bibliography on the subject, see "World Land Reform," published by the United States Department of Agriculture in September 1951.

12. The farm credit story in Paraguay is told in "Point Four Pioneers," State Department Publication 4279.

13. Senate Foreign Relations and Armed Services Committee Hearings on the Mutual Security Act of 1951, p. 327. See also pages 325-330, and 441-456.

14. A successful Point 4 program characteristically means an increase in imports from the United States and elsewhere. For example, in a favorable article on the agricultural work in El Salvador, Robert M. Hallett of the *Christian Science Monitor* wrote: "as an example that Point Four is not all a one-way street, Salvador spent more on agricultural equipment in the United States during the past two years than it did in the previous fifty years." *Christian Science Monitor* (April 30, 1953); reprinted in No. 27 of I.I.A.A.'s Building a Better Hemisphere Series.

Chapter 6—Sick People Also Eat

1. This account is drawn largely from official United Nations publications, including the pamphlet "Sharing Skills."

The Indians themselves, of course, have some of the world's foremost malariologists and have done some excellent control work of their own. Dr. Henry VanZile Hyde, Chief of the International Health Division of the Public Health Service and United States member of the W.H.O. Council, has told me of the following example: a few miles away from the W.H.O. Terai project is a sixteen thousand acre farm with one hundred tractors, modern living quarters, and a fine hospital, all occupying space which a few years ago was tiger forest. It was made possible by malaria control work carried on by the State of Uttar Pradesh, and is, says Dr. Hyde, "a splendid demonstration of the relationship of malaria control to food production."

2. The "privy plant" in San José was started originally by the Rockefeller Foundation, and later operated for a while by the Costa Rican Government. The servicio took it over in 1951 and expanded it. Like many other Point 4 operations in Latin America, the plant constitutes a shining example of good organization, efficiency and cleanliness.

3. Sanitary engineering—i.e. design and construction of safe water supply and sewage systems—has been one of the most important activities of the health servicios in Latin America. Typically, the local government and the community pay the major part of the construction expenses and the United States Government's contribution is mainly in the form of services.

4. For a vivid picture of the work of S.E.S.P., see John White's article, "Miracle on the Amazon," *Collier's* (February 3, 1951), from which the account of the *visitadora's* day was taken. See also "Program of the Rio Doce Valley," No. 4 in I.I.A.A.'s Building a Better Hemisphere Series, reprinted from *Presenca,* a Brazilian magazine (September 1952).

For other phases of the I.I.A.A. health program in Latin America, especially the remarkable, self-sustaining industrial hygiene work in Peru and the nurse-training programs, see "Dust in the Lungs," by Hazel O'Hara, *Americas Magazine,* (March 1952), No. 9 in the Building a Better Hemisphere Series; "The Point Four Program and Nursing in Panama," by Charlotte Kerr, *Revista de la Cruz Roja Panameña* (May 1952), No. 12 in the same series; "Public Health Nursing in Latin America," by Hazel O'Hara, *Public Health Nursing* (February 1950), and "Nursing Along the Amazon" by Tessie Williams, *Nursing World* (September 1951), both available as reprints from I.I.A.A.

5. The incident related in the text is anything but typical of the developmental work that has been done in Puerto Rico in the last decade. The government of Luis Muñoz Marín has made a magnificent record in its "Operation Bootstrap" and

has provided Point 4 with an inspirational example of what can be done under conditions very similar, in many respects at least, to those existing in other parts of the underdeveloped areas. Many apprentice technicians, especially from Latin America, have been sent under training grants to the University of Puerto Rico for study and observation of developmental techniques. Much has been written about Puerto Rico's recent development: a good collection of articles appears in *The Annals of the American Academy of Political and Social Science* (January 1953); an outstanding longer study is *Puerto Rico's Economic Future,* by Harvey Perloff, University of Chicago Press, 1950.

CHAPTER 7—Education for Life and Work

1. Even international agencies encounter difficulties of this kind—U.N.E.S.C.O., for example, has had a hard time with a rural education project in Syria—but the difficulties are perhaps less acute than in the case of a bilateral program. U.N.E.S.C.O. has engaged in some imaginative and successful teacher training work in what it calls "fundamental education" at centers in Mexico, Egypt, Thailand and elsewhere. See U.N.E.S.C.O. reports and the United Nations pamphlet "Sharing Skills."

2. The quotations from Dr. Mauck in the text are taken from two articles, "Pioneering the Three R's," *Pan American Magazine* (May 1950) and "More than A.B.C.'s" *Americas Magazine* (October 1949), reprinted as No. 16 in I.I.A.A.'s Building a Better Hemisphere Series. In a more scholarly vein, Dr. Mauck has written a good statement of the principles upon which a sound educational program should be based. "The Role of Education in Technical Assistance Programs," No. 8 in the Building a Better Hemisphere Series.

3. See "Industrial Education in Brazil," by Dr. J. C. Wright, *American Vocational Journal* (April 1952), reprinted as No. 6 in the Building a Better Hemisphere Series. Numbers 25 and 26 in the same series are reprints of articles on vocational education work in Paraguay and Peru, respectively.

4. The United Nations and its specialized agencies have also, of course, carried on an extensive program of making

fellowships available for students from the underdeveloped areas. By November, 1952, 2,700 fellowships had been awarded for study in some 50 different countries and in a great variety of technical fields.

CHAPTER 8—The Community Development Idea

1. The story of "Jimmy" Yen's work in China is dramatically told in *Tell the People,* by Pearl S. Buck, John Day, 1945. Dr. Yen was one of the first commissioners of the Joint Commission on Rural Reconstruction in China, and now is continuing his activity in the international development field through the International Committee of the Mass Education Movement, with headquarters in New York.

2. As of 1951, there were already two such semi-industrial communities not far from New Delhi, each built up from nothing by refugees from Pakistan territory under the inspiring leadership of an energetic young man—S. K. Dey (who later became director of the Indian Community Projects Administration) at Nilokheri, and Sudhir Ghosh at Faridabad. Mr. Ghosh has since tried, in the United States and elsewhere, to sell the idea that such communities can be built throughout the underdeveloped areas at a very low initial cost and quickly put on a self-supporting basis, but his optimism is not borne out by the experience at Nilokheri and Faridabad, both of which have had serious economic difficulties.

3. One of the best books on village life in India and the difficulties which confront those who would try to make changes is *Behind Mud Walls,* by William H. and Charlotte Wiser, published by Agricultural Missions Inc., New York, 1951. More technical, but also of great interest, are two articles by a graduate student of anthropology who lived for a time in an Uttar Pradesh village—"Social Change in an Indian Village" and "Technological Change in Overdeveloped (sic) Rural Areas," by McKim Marriott, in *Economic Development and Cultural Change,* a scholarly periodical edited and published at the University of Chicago, for June and December, 1952.

4. Whether India can in fact find the financial resources is

of course a big question, which is discussed in Chapter 12. Already in 1953, the Indian Government seemed to be watering down the plan somewhat. A National Extension Service was set up, to include the community projects program and to cover one-third of India in three years. Under the new plan, however, almost half the blocks would be little more than agricultural extension projects, with far less intensive and multi-purpose activities than the original community projects.

For a description of the total Point 4 program in India as of the fall of 1952, see an article on the subject by Chester Bowles in *The New York Times Magazine* (November 16, 1952). A detailed description of the program proposed for the fiscal year ending June 30, 1954, is contained in Senate Foreign Relations Committee Hearings on the Mutual Security Act of 1953, at pages 398-409.

CHAPTER 9—Strengthening Democratic Institutions and Industry

1. The idea that one of the principal aims of the Point 4 program was to "assist in the development of representative institutions" was a favorite of Dean Acheson's; see his January 9, 1952, speech in New York, State Department Publication 4487. See also the thoughtful report of a subcommittee of M.S.A.'s Public Advisory Board, entitled "Economic Strength for the Free World" (May 1953), pp. 8-10.

2. For a description of the Joint Commission's work, see "Brazil Builds a Future" by Mauricio Caminha deLacera, *Americas Magazine* (March 1953), reprinted as No. 23 in the Building a Better Hemisphere Series.

3. The outstanding contribution of the International Bank for Reconstruction and Development in the technical assistance field has been in the making of such surveys. Reports of these missions have been published by the Johns Hopkins Press, Baltimore. See also the Bank's recent annual reports.

4. A substantial fraction of the program in Pakistan has been devoted to assisting in the construction of a large fertilizer plant, with the objective of increasing the country's food production. In the case of Iran, nearly completed cement,

sugar-refining and textile plants have been given assistance, partly for political reasons; the sums advanced are supposed to be repaid eventually into a revolving fund to be used again for similar purposes. In both cases, the plants were nationally owned, so that no private individuals benefited from the aid.

5. There are several possible variants to the idea. For example, regional finance corporations with neighboring nations participating might prove preferable to a single, world-wide agency. Or, as suggested by August Maffry, Vice-President of the Irving Trust Company in a report prepared for T.C.A. in the fall of 1952, the powers of the Export-Import Bank might be expanded to do the same job.

6. The idea of using social workers as shirt-sleeve diplomats has often been attacked, both within and without the United States Government, largely because of a mistaken notion that such people are necessarily interested only in relief and welfare activities which have little to do with development. Admittedly, the efforts of such technicians in the past have not always been focussed on constructive projects. But if an attack is to be made on the problem of promoting community action of a self-help character in the cities and towns, there is no kind of expert better trained for the job than the modern community or social worker.

CHAPTER 10—The Role of Private Enterprise

1. An example of early Point 4 activity was the first American mission to the Hawaiian Islands, which was sent out from Boston in 1819 by the American Board of Commissioners for Foreign Missions. Besides two ministers, the party included a physician, two schoolmasters, a printer, a farmer, and their wives. One of the ministers, my great-grandfather Hiram Bingham, wrote in his account of the mission that among its purposes was "to introduce and extend the more useful arts and usages of civilized and Christianized society." The islanders readily took to the plow, the spinning wheel and loom, the scissors and needle; they learned sugar manufacture, printing, engraving and bookbinding, and otherwise began to "develop the resources of the country (which are considerable)." See *The*

Sandwich Islands, by Hiram Bingham (Hartford and New York, 1847).

The Point 4–type work of the missions, foundations and other private organizations has not been well publicized. For an idea of its scope, see the voluminous "Guide to Technical Assistance Services of United States Voluntary Agencies Abroad," Advisory Committee on Voluntary Foreign Aid, State Department, 1952. See also *The Story of the Rockefeller Foundation,* by Raymond B. Fosdick, Harpers, 1952; *Rural Reconstruction in Action: Experience in the Near and Middle East,* by H. B. Allen, Director of Education for the Near East Foundation, Cornell University Press, 1953; reports of the American International Association for Economic and Social Development, the Ford Foundation, the American Friends Service Committee, and others.

2. See, for example, the February 1950 issue of *Fortune;* "Texas Was Never Like This," an article on Aramco's operations in Saudi Arabia, *Business Week* (April 1, 1950); "Private Enterprise and Point Four," an address by Harvey S. Firestone, Jr., at the *New York Herald Tribune* Forum, October 20, 1952. The National Planning Association is doing a series of case histories to illustrate the benefits which United States private enterprise has brought to underdeveloped countries. The first study, on Sears Roebuck and Company in Mexico, was published in May, 1953.

3. For a listing of the contracts with private organizations made by T.C.A. through February 28, 1953, see "The Mutual Security Act and Overseas Private Investment," Preliminary Report of the Subcommittee on Foreign Economic Policy of the House Foreign Affairs Committee (June 3, 1953), pp. 48-50. This report and the Commerce Department's "Study of Factors Limiting American Private Foreign Investment," issued in several parts, are the most comprehensive and sophisticated documents yet to be published on the subject of private investment abroad.

4. See "American Foreign Investments in 1951 and 1952," *Survey of Current Business,* United States Department of Commerce (September 1952); also "United States Private Investment" (in Latin America), *Latin-American Business High-*

lights, published by The Chase National Bank, December, 1952.

5. See "United States Direct Investments in Foreign Countries," *Survey of Current Business* (December 1952), which is a summary of the extensive Census of American Direct Investments in Foreign Countries undertaken by the Commerce Department in 1951.

6. A possible exception is the Rockefeller brothers' International Basic Economy Corporation (I.B.E.C.), which has sought to demonstrate in Venezuela and other Latin American countries that a private concern can make money out of projects designed to contribute to local development. Its record so far is mixed. See "Nelson Rockefeller's IBEC," *Fortune* (February 1950); "Partners in Progress," S. Seegers, *Americas* (October 1951); "Rockefeller's Caribbean Rainbow," R. Hallett, *United Nations World* (October 1952).

The Eric Johnston speech referred to was reprinted in the *State Department Bulletin,* October 6, 1952.

7. A fair summary of what the various United States agencies had done and were doing as of the spring of 1953 to promote the flow of private investment overseas is contained in the House Subcommittee Report referred to in note 3.

8. For details, see the same House Subcommittee Report at page 27.

9. Annual reports of the I.B.R.D. and the Export-Import Bank and of companies such as American and Foreign Power, which has extensive power interests in Latin America, are of interest in this connection.

Early in 1953, the Export-Import Bank announced that it would make no more loans for developmental purposes.

10. In the Mutual Security Act of 1953, as passed by the House, the coverage of the guaranty program was extended to include war risks, but the provision was deleted in Conference. For details on the status of the guaranty program, see the House Subcommittee Report referred to in note 3 at pages 33-41.

11. Five-year amortization was recommended in the same House Subcommittee Report (page 70) for "new investments

overseas meeting standards to be established by the Director for Mutual Security and certified for that purpose."

The question of tax incentives for foreign investment is a peculiarly technical one and full of pitfalls for the layman. One practical obstacle to progress is that most of the real experts are in the United States Treasury, which has rather fixed notions on the subject. For a general discussion, see "The Effects of Taxation on Foreign Trade and Investment," United Nations Department of Economic Affairs, February, 1950.

12. A provocative discussion of this, and other, aspects of the overseas investment problem is contained in a report entitled "Program for Increasing Private Investment in Foreign Countries" prepared for T.C.A. in the fall of 1952 by August Maffry, Vice-President of the Irving Trust Company. A brief summary of the report appeared in *The New York Times* of December 31, 1952.

13. In the "Summary of Preliminary Findings and Recommendations" issued in July 1953 by the Department of Commerce as part of its "Study of Factors Limiting American Private Foreign Investment," the "Conclusions" begin as follows: "A greatly increased flow of private investment from this country cannot be expected in the next few years."

14. See "Measures for the Economic Development of Under-Developed Countries," United Nations Department of Economic Affairs (May 1951), pages 75-80. The United Nations experts based their figures on the assumption that 25 hundred dollars capital was "required for each person absorbed into non-agricultural employment."

Chapter 11—The Almighty Dollar Fallacy

1. See "A Proposal for a Total Peace Offensive," by Walter P. Reuther, published by the U.A.W.-C.I.O. In October, 1950, Mr. Reuther repeated his proposal in somewhat modified form at the *New York Herald Tribune* Forum. See Vital Speeches, November 15, 1950.

Probably the most extreme proposal, calling for a total of 20 billion dollars a year from all sources for fifty years, is set forth in *Peace by Investment*, by Benjamin Javits, Funk and

Wagnalls, 1950, summarized in an article by him in *United Nations World* (March 1950), called "Biggest Deal on Earth."

CHAPTER 12—The Bargain Basement Delusion

1. This course of action was unavoidable, in spite of the injunction in the Act for International Development that the local government should pay its "fair share" of the costs.

The Iran case, along with others, illustrates the weakness of this "fair share" test. For one thing, the phrase itself can be interpreted any which way—I once had to admit to the acute Senator Green of Rhode Island at a hearing that under some circumstances T.C.A. felt it could mean: "nothing." For another, serious questions can arise as to what payments by the local government are to be considered as contributions to the total program. In an effort to satisfy the Congress that the United States Point 4 expenditures were being at least matched by the recipient countries, T.C.A. on occasion stretched the concept of local contributions to include local developmental expenses over which the United States had no control whatever and which the country might well have incurred even if there were no Point 4. While the measurement of local contributions is relatively easy where there is a servicio or joint fund set-up, even in such cases there can be some figure-juggling.

This is not to question the value of having programs jointly financed to the extent possible. The whole notion of self-help is jeopardized if the local government is not expected to contribute within its means to the goal of its own development (even though programs can be operated much more easily and swiftly if the United States is putting up all the money).

But, in my judgment, the "fair share" test is unrealistic and productive of administrative finagling. It would be far more sensible if the Administrator were simply required to make a finding that the local government was making reasonable efforts to further the country's development in full cooperation with United Nations and United States agencies.

The kind of support for joint program activities which has developed in Latin America—where each United States dollar is matched by two or three or ten from local sources—cannot be forced by a statutory mandate. It will come, if at all, from a demonstration over a period of years of the value of the work, plus good across-the-table negotiating to induce ever larger contributions from the host government.

2. In its 1952 requests to the Congress for funds, the Executive Branch argued that the entire program in Iran, and also similarly "beefed up" programs in India and Pakistan, could be carried out under the Act for International Development as Point 4 programs. The rationale was that some economic aid was needed to support the work of technicians and to give the technical assistance process a chance to succeed in the short time available. The experts on Congressional relations felt that this approach would be more successful than the introduction of a new and second type of aid for the critical countries of Asia.

Their prediction proved wrong: the Congress felt that the Executive Branch was trying to put over a fast one, by unduly stretching the Point 4 concept. The House adopted a provision limiting T.C.A. expenditures for supplies and equipment in any country to three times the amount to be spent for technicians and training awards, which would have gutted the India and Pakistan programs. Although that provision was defeated in the Senate after an exciting battle and then eliminated in Conference, almost the same result was achieved by the severe cuts made in the programs at the appropriations stage.

As noted elsewhere, this result led to a decision in 1953 to divide the programs into two parts. Contrary to expectations, the special economic aid proposals went through with remarkably little difficulty.

3. The quotations from the Indian Planning Commission are taken from its Summary of the First Five-Year Plan (December 1952).

The fact that inflationary, or deficit, financing means a sacrifice on the part of consumers, much as a heavy tax program does, is not always recognized. For an interesting discussion of the factors involved, see "Some Financial Aspects of Development Programmes in Asian Countries," *Economic Bulletin for Asia and the Far East,* United Nations Economic

Commission of Asia and the Far East (E.C.A.F.E.), (November 1952). There has been one group within the United States Government, especially in the Economic Affairs Offices of the State Department, that has believed the Indian Government could safely engage in more deficit financing of its development program than it has done. The view of Finance Minister Deshmukh and others in New Delhi has been that any substantial increase in the already sizable deficit would tend to set off a violent inflationary spiral.

4. In August, 1953, India's Food Minister announced that 1953's cereal crop had been 12 per cent above the previous year's, and that only one million tons of wheat would have to be imported in 1954. *The New York Times* (August 24, 1953). If these estimates are accurate, they represent remarkable progress, at least some of which can fairly be attributed to the various developmental activities to which the United States has contributed.

5. See "Partners in Progress, A Report to the President by the International Development Advisory Board," (March 1951). The "Gray Report" was published in November, 1950, under the title "Report to the President on Foreign Economic Policies."

After Nelson Rockefeller resigned as Chairman of the I.D.A.B. in the fall of 1951, at least partly because the Board's recommendations had not been followed to any great extent, Eric Johnston was appointed Chairman. Under his leadership, the I.D.A.B. retreated from the bold position it had taken in "Partners in Progress" and urged a much more conservative approach. See "Guidelines for Point 4—Recommendations of the International Development Advisory Board" (June 5, 1952).

Chapter 13—The Role of the United Nations

1. The voluminous Fifth Report of the Technical Assistance Board to the Technical Assistance Committee of E.C.O.S.O.C., issued June 1, 1953, which contains a great deal of information about the United Nations programs in general, deals briefly with some of the organizational developments at pages 5 and

6. A summary of the discussion of these problems at the 14th Session of E.C.O.S.O.C. in mid-1952 is contained in "Plans for Economic Development and Technical Assistance," a useful, if somewhat disjointed, collection of "study material" prepared by the Committee for World Disarmament and World Reconstruction, Women's International League for Peace and Freedom, Philadelphia.

For an excellent analysis of the comparative merits of national and international agencies, see "The Institutional Framework for Technical Assistance—A Comparative Review of UN and US Experience," by Professor Walter R. Sharp, *International Organization*, Vol. VII, No. 3, 1953.

2. The scarcity of supporting funds has caused many of the United Nations experts in the field to suffer paralysis and consequent acute frustration. Although the host governments are supposed to agree in advance to provide office facilities, transportation, etc., for the visiting experts, on all too many occasions that support has not been forthcoming. Sometimes this has been traceable to lack of resources, sometimes to inefficiency, and sometimes—especially in the early days of the program—to the fact that an agency had been over-anxious for business. A traveling official of the agency might have persuaded a high official of the host government to request certain experts, but when the experts turned up a few months later, they would find no one ready to receive them; the high official would be inaccessible, and the ministries they were supposed to assist would know nothing about the request, and would be quite indifferent to the whole idea. The T.C.A. was also guilty of such over-selling on occasion, but I believe somewhat more rarely, and in any event the result was less awkward because the technicians were more self-sufficient and the program more flexible and therefore more quickly adaptable to changing circumstances.

3. See "United Nations Technical Assistance," Background Paper No. 74, United Nations Department of Public Information (January 1953).

4. The E.C.O.S.O.C. resolution referred to is No. 222 A (IX), which is reprinted as Annex II in the Background Paper mentioned in note 3.

Under the Colombo Plan, grants pledged to India and Pakistan from the Dominions of Canada, Australia and New Zealand have exceeded 75 million dollars. This is in addition to sterling balances released by the United Kingdom in much larger amounts.

Because of its non-membership in the specialized agencies, the U.S.S.R. has stated that its promised contribution is for the U.N.T.A.A. only. Because such a limitation is in conflict with Resolution 222 A, and because rubles are not very useful as a currency, the contribution may never be made.

5. These are, of course, unlikely assumptions. The British Commonwealth nations would hardly give up the Colombo Plan unless they were assured that the bulk of their contributions would go to India and Pakistan, and the United Nations specialized agencies would object strenuously to getting their program funds from an International Development Authority. Such mergers would, however, make for better integrated activities. Grant aid and technical assistance should not be administered independently, but rather as parts of a total development program.

6. On-the-spot cooperation and support has often developed in a natural and common-sense manner. In Iran, for example, where the international experts were experiencing even more than the usual amount of difficulty in getting the local officials to come through with promised transportation, the T.C.A. Director instructed his people to notify the United Nations Resident Representative whenever they were planning a field trip in one of the Point 4 jeeps or carryalls and had any seats available.

CHAPTER 14—The American Way of Life Is Not the Only Way

1. In a *New York Times Magazine* article (January 4, 1953), Chester Bowles wrote that, if he were selecting a Point 4 technician for India, he would not only test his professional competence, his patience and understanding of human beings, and his racial and religious attitudes, but would "take the specialist and his wife on a two weeks' camping trip, preferably in the

rain with a leaky tent." To pass, they would have to come through "with a smile on their faces."

Several private organizations are helping in the recruiting or training of suitable shirt-sleeve diplomats, including the International Development Placement Association (New York), the Koinonia Foundation (Baltimore), Richardson Wood and Company (New York), and Haverford College.

2. The quotation is from "Anthropologists Look at Point Four," by Dorothy Demetracopoulou Lee, *Vassar Alumnae Magazine* (June 1951). A good deal has been written about the intricacies of trying to transfer technological and cultural patterns from one society to another, especially in the technical journals. See, for example, *Cultural Patterns and Technological Change*, edited by Margaret Mead, published by U.N.E.S.C.O., 1953; and various articles in *The Progress of Underdeveloped Areas*, edited by Bert F. Hoselitz, University of Chicago Press, 1952, and *Economic Development and Cultural Change*, a periodical edited by R. Richard Wohl at the Research Center in Economic Development and Cultural Change, University of Chicago.

The danger of trying to impose American standards and cultural notions on the peoples of the underdeveloped areas is virtually the theme of the State Department Foreign Service Institute orientation course for technicians going overseas.

Chapter 15—Neither A Stick nor A Carrot

1. See, e.g., the last chapter of *Strange Lands and Friendly People,* by William O. Douglas, Harpers, 1951.

2. This is the view of Dr. Wolf I. Ladijinsky of the United States Department of Agriculture, who probably knows more about land reform in Asia and its problems than any other American. He also believes that, if we were to try to insist on land redistribution as a condition of our aid, the local government, even if it was willing, would almost certainly turn to us for the money to pay off the landlords at a reasonable rate. We would then in effect be buying the reform instead of encouraging it to proceed on a sound, indigenous basis.

3. President Truman's Materials Policy Commission, of

which Wm. S. Paley was chairman, recommended that increasing emphasis be given in the United States technical assistance programs to geological surveys, preliminary exploration, and advice on mining technology, and that as much as 4 million dollars a year be spent on this work (Chapter 13, Volume 1 of the Report, page 74). The amount actually spent for this type of work is not readily determinable, but it would probably be considerably less than 4 million dollars a year.

Recent Mutual Security Acts have wisely made separate provision for projects intended specifically to promote the production of strategic and "basic" materials. Nineteen million dollars was appropriated for this purpose in 1953. Some of these projects can contribute substantially to the overall development of the countries involved, but their real purpose should be made clear to the governments concerned, as something quite distinct from Point 4.

4. When a country gets good and mad at the United States on some political ground, it may throw out Point 4. This happened in Burma in the spring of 1953, mainly over the issue of the Chinese Nationalist guerrillas squatting in Northeastern Burma, and later that year there was talk of the same thing occurring in Jordan because of a flare-up of bitterness at the United States policy toward Israel. Such events do not prove that Point 4 cannot do the job it is supposed to do, but only that it can be a convenient target for spiteful political attack.

CHAPTER 16—The Communists Don't Worry About Malthus

1. Both Josué DeCastro (*The Geography of Hunger,* Little, Brown, 1952) and William Vogt (*Road to Survival,* Sloane, 1948) are extremists and represent minority points of view among the experts. But there can be no brushing aside Vogt's gloomy warnings about what man is doing to the soils that support him. In this connection, see also *Land for Tomorrow,* by the English geographer L. Dudley Stamp (Indiana University Press, 1952).

2. Some of the more fantastic possibilities for tapping new sources of food and power are discussed in Willard Espy's

Bold New Program, Harpers, 1950. See also "Can the Earth Feed Its Millions?" by Dr. Karl Sax, *United Nations World* (March 1951), and "Can We Make the Earth Feed Us All?," containing a good account of the Rockefeller Foundation's hybrid corn work in Mexico, by William C. Paddock, *The Saturday Evening Post* (Oct. 18, 1952).

CHAPTER 17—No Simple Answers

1. The budgetary process is without end in an operation such as Point 4. As late as July or August the agency is usually still furnishing the Congress with information in support of its requests for program funds for the fiscal year which started July 1. By that time, work on material to be submitted to the Budget Bureau in support of the agency's program requests for the *following* fiscal year will already have been started.

2. The problem of how to capitalize on the desire of thousands of private organizations to help in the Point 4 program is a major one. The Koinonia Foundation, of Baltimore, has performed a real service in compiling a "Projects Booklet" listing ways in which private individuals and organizations can help. Koinonia, the Christophers, World Neighbors, and other private groups are trying to mobilize public participation in the work of Point 4 under the slogan "AWAKE—America's War of Amazing Kindness Everywhere." See "The War of Amazing Kindness," *This Week* (May 17, 1953).

CHAPTER 18—Risking Dollars or Risking Lives

1. For a powerful exposition of this idea, see "The Requirements of an Effective Point Four Program," by Harvey Perloff, *Economic Development and Cultural Change* (October 1952).

2. Harold Stassen, Administrator of F.O.A., has suggested that he can cut down the Point 4 programs and get along with fewer people by making greater use of private agencies, particularly land-grant colleges. No one can quarrel with the idea of making maximum use of existing agencies, public or private, especially those with great experience and know-how. But the fact is that increased use of private agencies compli-

cates, rather than simplifies, the administrative task of coordination and backstopping, and hence if anything requires more personnel in toto. Moreover, unless the private agencies can find some new sources of financial support apart from the Government, any new activities on their part will have to be paid for by the taxpayers. Since their charges usually include some provision for general overhead, this method of carrying on Point 4 work, while it may be better, is not less expensive than that of using technicians employed by the Government.

Mr. Stassen's assertion that the new, centralized F.O.A. set-up will make possible great savings in personnel is also doubtful. Since there were practically no duplications of activity between M.S.A. and T.C.A., approximately the same number of people as before will be needed to do the work in the new agency.

3. A critical analysis of the changing character of the Point 4 operations, at least at the Washington end, is contained in a series of three articles by Paul Kennedy in *The New York Times*, September 24, 25, 26, 1953.

Index